Great
GERMAN
Short Stories of the
Twentieth Century

A DUAL-LANGUAGE BOOK

Große
DEUTSCHE
Kurzgeschichten
des zwanzigsten
Jahrhunderts

Edited and Translated by
M. CHARLOTTE WOLF, Ph.D.

DOVER PUBLICATIONS, INC.
Mineola, New York

ACKNOWLEDGMENTS: SEE PAGES xiii–xiv.

Copyright

Bibliographical Note

Great German Short Stories of the Twentieth Century / Große deutsche Kurzgeschichten des zwanzigsten Jahrhunderts: A Dual-Language Book, first published by Dover Publications, Inc., in 2012, is a new selection of German stories, reprinted from standard German texts, accompanied by new English translations prepared for the Dover edition by M. Charlotte Wolf, Ph.D., who also made the selection and wrote the Introduction and author biographies.

Library of Congress Cataloging-in-Publication Data

Great German short stories of the twentieth century = Große deutsche Kurzgeschichten des zwanzigsten Jahrhunderts / edited and translated by M. Charlotte Wolf.
    p. cm. — (Dual language book)
  ISBN-13: 978-0-486-47632-2 (pbk.)
  ISBN-10: 0-486-47632-4 (pbk.)
    1. Short stories, German—20th century—Translations into English. I. Wolf, M. Charlotte. II. Title: Grosse Deutsche kurzgeschichten des zwanzigsten jahrhunderts

PT1327.G745 2012
833'.010809—dc23

                  2011049436

Manufactured in the United States by LSC Communications
47632405   2018
www.doverpublications.com

CONTENTS

INTRODUCTION

The twentieth century was a time of great change in Germany. The country was transformed from a monarchy into a republic, into a dictatorship, into a divided country with two political systems—capitalist republic versus communist military occupation—and finally into a unified parliamentary democracy. It also fought in two major wars, both of which included invasions from foreign countries and ended in Germany's defeat with devastating consequences.

This caused huge political, economic, and social upheavals in the country. Among other things, Germans suffered financially from hyperinflation, had to come to terms with the consequences of a genocide they had supported and helped execute, and are still recovering from the effects of the geographic division resulting from World War II.[1]

Between 1950 and 1960, the Western sector of divided Germany managed to rebuild from the rubble of the war into a model Western industrialized nation. This period is commonly referred to as the "Wirtschaftswunder."[2] Following this, Germans have had to contend with the enormous changes occurring on the European and global scenes. The creation of the

---

[1] John Ardagh and Katharina Ardagh, *Germany and the Germans: The United Germany in the Mid-1990s* (New York: Penguin USA, 1996).

[2] West Germany's rapid economic recovery in the 1950s ("Wirtschaftswunder," or economic miracle) gave it a leading position among the world's economic powers. (*Encyclopædia Britannica Online*, s.v. "Wirtschaftswunder (German history)," accessed September 5, 2011, http://www.britannica.com/EBchecked/topic/645835/Wirtschaftswunder)

European Economic Community and subsequently the European Economic and Monetary Union (the Euro) not only blurred national geographic and cultural boundaries, but even caused national identities to fray around the edges. The rise of the Internet further blurred social and cultural boundaries that had been seen as immutable for many generations. Most recently, Germans have had to accept their involvement in military conflicts around the world, such as in Afghanistan and Iraq, something new to the generation that was born and grew up in post-World War II Germany.

Many, if not most of these events and developments resulted in involuntary changes and adaptations for which Germans were little prepared. These had a lasting impact on the geopolitical and economic landscapes of the nation. Beyond that, the upheavals involved dramatic social and cultural reversals. They greatly influenced the lives of the German people, oftentimes resulting in distress, anguish, confusion, and anger.

Literature created during these turbulent times gives insight into the attitudes and perspectives of the writers and how they were influenced by contemporary events. It provides a unique opportunity to explore the minds and lives of the people who were subject to the transformative events of those times. It is a window into the German soul.

Kurt Laßwitz and Carl Grunert wrote during a time when the German spirit was buoyed by a political system whose motto was "Deutschland, Deutschland über alles."[3]

During the late nineteenth century and up until World War I, German scientists, politicians, and above all, the German military, were venerated. Germans pointed proudly to their ac-

---

[3]"Deutschland, Deutschland über alles" (Germany, Germany above all) is the first stanza of the "Deutschlandlied" (Song of Germany), Germany's national anthem since 1922. Because of its association with World War I nationalistic and later National Socialist propaganda, the first stanza is no longer used. Today, only the third stanza is sung, beginning with the words "Einigkeit und Recht und Freiheit" (Unity and justice and freedom).

complishments in medicine,[4] economics and social history,[5] engineering,[6] and chemistry.[7]

In addition, imperial Germany was a colonial power with immense political influence. When Laßwitz's Professor Frister[8] muses about "the discovery of the vast goldfields in New Guinea and the petroleum sources in German China," his pride that Germany is a key player on the world stage is evident. And when Grunert's lovable but tyrannical archaeologist, Professor Diluvius,[9] is dead set on producing a live prehistoric creature from one-of-a-kind fossilized remains, the reader is proudly informed that such a fossil has only been found in Germany, and nowhere else!

Klabund's story "Der Bär"[10] ("The Bear"), with its matter-of-fact description of a circus animal's slow demise as a result of World War I, contrasts sharply with the patriotic tinge of the earlier stories. In particular, it no longer displays pride in the military prowess of an imperial Germany. Reflecting the disillusionment of a whole generation of artists and young people, Klabund chronicles the demise of the Kaiserreich through the lives of ordinary people, resulting in a more emotionally charged story than a collection of newspaper headlines could provide.

---

[4]German physicist Wilhelm Conrad Roentgen discovered x-rays and also produced the first x-ray picture of the body (his wife's hand) in 1895.

[5]German sociologist and political economist Max Weber was the first to categorize social authority into the distinct forms of the charismatic, traditional, and rational-legal. Weber also made various contributions to economic history as well as economic theory and methodology.

[6]The first electric elevator was built by German inventor Werner von Siemens in 1880.

[7]In 1899 German chemist Felix Hoffmann, who was working for the chemical company Bayer, rediscovered aspirin and thus introduced it to the mass market.

[8]Kurd Laßwitz, "Die Fernschule" ("The Distance Learning School"). First published in: *Nie und Nimmer: Neue Märchen* (Leipzig, 1902).

[9]Carl Grunert, "Das Ei des Archäopteryx" ("The Archaeopteryx Egg"). First published in: *Der Marsspion und andere Novellen* (Berlin and Leipzig: Buchverlag fürs Deutsche Haus, 1908).

[10]Klabund, "Der Bär" ("The Bear"). First published in: *Kriegsbuch* (Vienna: Phaidon, 1930).

Britting's story about the loss of a brother,[11] written only a few years before the Nazi takeover, is a parable that digs even deeper into the changing political allegiances of the period. He wrote during a time when Germans were becoming increasingly divided between communists and nationalists. Friends and families were being torn apart by the volatile politics churning in the wake of a lost war[12] and the tightening grip of the fascist Nazi party on a traumatized nation. A tragedy like "Fratricide in the Backwater" can be understood as a premonition to the Nazi regime with its progressive buildup of intimidation, persecution, terror, and death.

Langgässer's story, with its seemingly innocent title "Saisonbeginn"[13] ("Beginning of the Season"), captures perfectly the blind prejudice of average Germans and makes all that prejudice even more frightful, because in retrospect it seemed such an innocuous part of everyday life. The depiction of friendly townspeople in an idyllic pastoral village at the start of the story soon morphs into a painfully detailed account of reflexive and blatant anti-Semitism.

Luise Rinser's tale of the red cat ("Die rote Katze")[14] highlights a different kind of terror—that of children's daily fight for survival in an almost completely destroyed post-World War II Germany.[15] But the author's dismay over the moral turpitude of the teenage offender is overt, in sharp contrast with the unemotional modern-day news clips which report on such atrocities.

---

[11]Georg Britting, "Brudermord im Altwasser." Written in 1929 and first published in: *Die kleine Welt am Strom. Geschichten und Gedichte* (München: Nymphenburger Verlagshandlung, 1952).

[12]The 1919 Treaty of Versailles required Germany to pay large reparations to the countries they had attacked and occupied during World War I. The Nazis invented the "Dolchstosslegende" (stab-in-the-back legend) and depicted the negotiation of the penalties decided upon in the Treaty as a betrayal of German national interests, using it as a propaganda tool to stir up the German public.

[13]Elisabeth Langgässer, "Saisonbeginn" ("Beginning of the Season"). First published in: *Der Torso* (Hamburg: Claassen & Goverts, 1947).

[14]Luise Rinser, "Die rote Katze" ("The Red Cat"). First published in: *Ein Bündel weisser Narzissen, Erzählungen* (Frankfurt am Main: Fischer, 1956).

[15]Rinser's theme was later tragically illustrated in the late twentieth century when the Lord's Resistance Army child soldiers spread terror in Africa.

Peter Bichsel's story "Ein Tisch ist ein Tisch"[16] ("A Table is a Table"), about an old man whose life withers away into loneliness, is an exploration of the social deterioration resulting from modern-day consumerism. His theme is the increasing preoccupation of contemporary society with objects, which causes people to lose their ability to communicate with and reach out to each other. Bichsel suggests that the absence of meaningful communication is responsible for the grayness and bleakness in the old man's life, standing in sharp contrast to the gaudiness and noise of modern-day billboards, radio advertisements, and TV commercials.

Morgner's heroine in "Der Schöne und das Tier"[17] ("Beauty and the Beast")—a voiceless siren, half human and half bird—can be imagined as an alter ego of the author. Morgner came of age in the East German socialist regime and became a writer trying to live up to the ideals of a communist society in which, supposedly, all citizens were living in the Promised Land.[18] But soon she began to recognize the reality of a country that relied on threats and terror to keep its citizens in line. Decades of traumatic encounters with censors in the "Ministerium für Kultur" (Ministry of Culture) and "Stasi"[19] informants opened her eyes to the cruelty of a system that she had believed—at least initially—to hold the answer for a better future. Tragically, these experiences also marked the beginning of a personal fragmentation leading to Morgner's death in 1990. The immense frustra-

---

[16]Peter Bichsel, "Ein Tisch ist ein Tisch" ("A Table is a Table"). First published in: *Eine Geschichte. Gestaltet und illustriert von Angela von Roehl* (Frankfurt am Main: Suhrkamp, 1995).

[17]Irmtraud Morgner, "Der Schöne und das Tier" ("Beauty and the Beast"). First published in: *Der Schöne und das Tier. Eine Liebesgeschichte* (Frankfurt am Main: Luchterhand Literaturverlag Gmbh, 1991).

[18]In her novel *Trobadora Beatriz*, Morgner, somewhat tongue-in-cheek, equates the German Democratic Republic with the Promised Land of the Old Testament, because women supposedly enjoyed complete equality there.

[19]"Stasi," from "Ministerium für Staatsicherheit" (Ministry of State Security). The Ministry was the secret police force of East Germany's powerful "Sozialistische Einheitspartei Deutschlands" (Socialist Unity Party of Germany), which used intimidation and terror to repress East German citizens and maintain its power.

tion and pain she experienced during her frequent confrontations with the regime echoes in many of her characters.

To tell her tale "Der Bote"[20] ("The Messenger"), Iris Klockmann blends literary styles and motifs with powerful imagery, a technique now often used in postmodern narratives. Klockmann adroitly weaves fantasy[21] with the horrors of the war in Afghanistan to highlight the traumas of reality.

Henry Bienek's roots in the age of the Internet[22] and fantasy role-playing are evident in his story "Der Empfang"[23] ("The Reception"). The bloodless host of the reception bears striking resemblance to a pop culture vampire, and the setting is reminiscent of Roman Polanski's *Tanz der Vampire* (*Dance of the Vampires*),[24] which has acquired cult status among German postwar generations, particularly with followers of Dungeons and Dragons.[25] Bienek's hero, modeled after the author's

---

[20]Iris Klockmann, "Der Bote" ("The Messenger"). Published in: *Nachtfalter und andere Kreaturen der Dunkelheit* (München: Wortkuss Verlag, 2009).

[21]Fantasy literature began to emerge in Germany as a distinct class in the late eighteenth century (the Era of Romanticism). It gained a large following particularly after German translations of J.R.R. Tolkien's *The Hobbit* (1937) and *The Lord of the Rings* (1954-55) were published. These days, fantasy literature with its gods, heroes, monsters, and adventures is hugely popular. See for example: Ariane Wischnik, *Spielarten des Phantastischen - Science fiction und Fantasy im Vergleich* (Berlin: Logos, 2006).

[22]In 1985, the United States' National Science Foundation (NSF) commissioned the construction of the NSFNET, a university network backbone. The opening of the NSFNET to other networks began in 1988. (Clinton Cerf and Bernard Aboba, "How the Internet Came to Be," last modified 1993, accessed September 4, 2011, http://www.netvalley.com/archives/mirrors/cerf-how-inet.html).

[23]Henry Bienek, "Der Empfang" ("The Reception"). Published in: Martin Witzgall, ed., *Das ist unser Ernst!* (Munich: Wortkuss Verlag, 2009).

[24]*Tanz der Vampire* is the original 1967 German language version of the movie called *The Fearless Vampire Killers* in the USA. Polanski directed the original German production and later also a German musical version.

[25]Dungeons & Dragons (D&D), a popular role-playing game, was published in 1974. D&D was influenced by mythology, pulp fiction, and contemporary fantasy authors of the 1960s and 1970s. Use of mythical figures such as elves and others often draws comparisons to the work of J.R.R. Tolkien. (Rob Kuntz: "Tolkien in Dungeons & Dragons" in *Dragon* #13 & Gary Gygax: "On the Influence of J.R.R. Tolkien on the D&D and AD&D games" in *Dragon* #95.)

sometime publisher, appears a bit confused at times, rather like Professor Abronsius's bumbling sidekick, Alfred, in Polanski's movie.

Similar to Morgner, her contemporary Gabriele Wohmann focuses on the lives of ordinary people in most of her narratives. In "Glück und Unglück"[26] ("Good Luck and Bad Luck") she exposes the dysfunctional dynamics of a modern-day family primarily through the heroine's stream-of-consciousness account. As in Bichsel's story, the inability to communicate is a central motif. All of the family members seem self-absorbed and either unwilling or unable to reach out to each other. Wohmann paints this picture as being more symptomatic of modern-day German life in general than of a specific social group.

Michael Inneberger describes himself as "a storyteller from the Chiemgau" region. He draws on a variety of styles, some reminiscent of oral traditions such as nineteenth-century German folktales, and others of varying degrees of fantasy, humor, and science fiction. Two stories included in this anthology, completely dissimilar with regard to mood and style, illustrate Inneberger's talent for captivating storytelling. In "Urlaub für ewig"[27] ("Eternal Vacation"), Inneberger fleshes out the skeleton of a real-life news story with fictional details, including elements of magical realism, to tell how it just might have happened. In "Klempner Huber"[28] ("Plumber Huber"), Inneberger presents a futuristic satire, asking whether cultural homogeneity and increasing technological complexity will really make Europe a better place.

The German-speaking literature of the past century records the upheavals that the cataclysms of that era inflicted on the German people, their lives, and their "Weltanschauung" (worldview). The stories presented here are but a small part of

---

[26]Gabriele Wohmann, "Glück und Unglück" ("Good Luck and Bad Luck"). Published in: *Wann kommt die Liebe. Erzählungen* (Berlin: Aufbau Verlag, 2010).

[27]Michael Inneberger, "Urlaub für ewig" ("Eternal Vacation"). Published in: *Geschichten aus der Welt—um uns herum* (Norderstedt: Books on Demand, 2010).

[28]Michael Inneberger, "Klempner Huber" ("Plumber Huber"). Published in: *Geschichten aus der Welt—um uns herum* (Norderstedt: Books on Demand, 2010).

that record; they span the century, include well-known along with lesser-known authors, and illustrate a variety of themes, literary influences, and above all, German life experiences. I am honored to have had the privilege of translating these stories into English for the first time. I hope that you will enjoy them as much as I have.

M. Charlotte Wolf, Ph.D.
September 2011

ACKNOWLEDGMENTS

Peter Bichsel: "Ein Tisch ist ein Tisch," from: Peter Bichsel, Kindergeschichten © Suhrkamp Verlag, Frankfurt am Main, 1997. All rights reserved by Suhrkamp Verlag Berlin. Reprinted with the permission of the publisher.

Henry Bienek: "Der Empfang" by Henry Bienek from *Das ist unser Ernst!*, Martin Witzgall, editor; WortKuss Verlag, München, 2010. Reprinted with the permission of the publisher.

Georg Britting: "Brudermord im Altwasser" by George Britting from *Die Windhunde, Sämtliche Werke in 23 Bänden*, Verlag Georg-Britting-Stiftung. Reprinted with the permission of the publisher.

Michael Inneberger: "Urlaub für ewig" and "Klempner Huber" by Michael Inneberger in *Geschichten aus der Welt – um uns herum: Kurzgeschichten*, Books on Demand, Norderstedt, 2011. Reprinted with the permission of the author.

Iris Klockmann: "Der Bote" by Iris Klockmann from *Der Nachtfalter und andere Kreaturen der Dunkelheit*, WortKuss Verlag, München, 2009. Reprinted with the permission of the publisher.

Elisabeth Langgässer: "Saisonbeginn" by Elisabeth Langgässer from *Ausgewählte Erzählungen*, © 1964/1979 Claassen Verlag in der Ullstein Buchverlage GmbH, Berlin. Reprinted with the permission of the publisher.

Irmtraud Morgner: "Der Schöne und das Tier" by Irmtraud Morgner from *Luchterhand-Literaturverlag*, Verlag, Frankfurt am Main, 1991. © David Morgner.

Luise Rinser: "Die rote Katze" by Luise Rinser from *Ein Bündel weisser Narzissen, Erzählungen,* © S. Fischer Verlag GmbH, Frankfurt am Main,1956. Reprinted with the permission of the publisher.

Gabriele Wohmann: "Glück und Unglück" by Gabriele Wohmann from *Wann kommt die Liebe: Erzählungen,* Aufbau Verlag GmbH & Co., Berlin, 2010. Reprinted with the permission of the publisher.

Great German
Short Stories of the
Twentieth Century

Große deutsche
Kurzgeschichten
des zwanzigsten
Jahrhunderts

A DUAL-LANGUAGE BOOK

KURD LAßWITZ

Born in 1848 in Breslau (modern-day Wroclaw, Poland), Kurd Laßwitz was a contemporary of the psychoanalyst Sigmund Freud, the painter Gustav Klimt, and the science fiction writer H. G. Wells. As the son of a wealthy factory owner, Laßwitz had access to both money and education. In 1866 he enrolled to study mathematics and physics at the University of Breslau on the teacher education track. Seven years later in 1873, he passed the "Staatsexamen," the federal exam required for all secondary teachers. Two years later, he graduated with a doctoral degree in physics and embarked on a career as a college preparatory teacher, mostly at the Ernestinum (a college prep school) in Gotha, Thuringia. In 1884 he became a degreed professor. He wrote extensively from the end of the 1860s up to his death in 1910, often under the pseudonyms Jeremias Heiter or L. Velatus.[1]

Besides scientific and philosophical publications, Laßwitz wrote stories that would today be considered science fiction or fantasy, but were called fairy tales[2] by his contemporaries for want of a better term. The term may be justified, since narrative devices such as the interruption of dreams into the stories' "reality" are reminiscent of fairy tales written during the Romantic period such as E.T.A. Hoffmann's "The Golden Pot."

---

[1]"Projekt Gutenberg-DE: Kurd Laßwitz," SPIEGEL ONLINE, accessed July 10, 2011, http://gutenberg.spiegel.de/autor/358.

[2]Franz Rottensteiner, "Der Vater der Weltraumstation," *Wiener Zeitung*, October 15, 2010.

Laßwitz's stories often present scientific topics in a speculative, yet sophisticated manner. He earned the reputation of being the "Father of German Science Fiction" from his futuristic novel, *Auf zwei Planeten (Two Planets*, 1897). As in H.G. Wells's *War of the Worlds, Two Planets* describes an encounter between humans and aliens from the planet Mars. But unlike Wells, who portrays his aliens as anatomically different from humans and very hostile, Laßwitz gives an idealistic portrayal of humanoids that are not only ethically and socially superior, but also much more technologically advanced. Laßwitz hoped the progress of social development would parallel that of intelligence, and he felt that humans might gain much from encounters with advanced species.

Laßwitz influenced many writers of the Expressionist period[3] (such as lyricist Georg Heym), and his writings gained popularity with a larger audience starting in the late 1920s. Unfortunately, his humanistic and pacifist ideas along with his Expressionist writing style raised the hackles of the Nazi regime, so his popularity was short-lived. An upsurge of science fiction movies and writing in the late 1960s and 1970s renewed interest in Laßwitz's sci-fi stories and led to reprints of his works. Since 1980, the Kurd-Laßwitz Award, modeled after the United States' Nebula Award, has been given annually to German-speaking science fiction authors.[4]

In his short story "Die Fernschule" ("The Distance Learning School," 1902), Laßwitz depicts a futuristic school one hundred years ahead of his time. The tale is narrated in the third person and begins with a college prep teacher returning home from school. Worn out by a strenuous day, he reflects on how the daily commute is exhausting and comments on the outdated

---

[3] "Expressionism is a writing approach, process, or technique in which a writer depicts a character's feelings about a subject (or the writer's own feelings about it) rather than the objective surface reality of the subject. . . . Often, the depiction is a grotesque distortion or phantasmagoric representation of reality." (Michael J. Cummings, "Literary Terms," accessed August 22, 2011, http://www.cummingsstudyguides.net/xLitTerms.html).
[4] "Kurt Lasswitz: Leben und Werk," accessed August 9, 2011, http://www.dieter-von-reeken.de/lasswitz/frame.htm.

traditional format of teaching. He wonders if a future wherein students are responsible participants in the education process, teachers are technology wizards, and the teaching load is manageable—every teacher's dream!—is achievable. As he dozes off and dreams, his idealistic musings morph into a depiction of a future where students are still making excuses, cheating, and behaving irresponsibly. Plus, the teachers' workload continues to be overwhelming, despite the use of high-tech educational methods and gadgetry.

Laßwitz was surprisingly insightful on how technology might affect education in the future (for example, he describes teachers interacting with students via live "picture frames" on the wall). However, he couples those positive ideas with the ironic prediction that, no matter what, human nature will always remain much the same.

KURD LAßWITZ

Die Fernschule

»Es ist doch ein weiter Weg bis nach Hause – an solch heißen Tagen merkt man's. Ich glaube, ich bin müde. Aber etwas Bewegung tut freilich gut.«

So dachte der Professor Frister, als er nach vier absolvierten Unterrichtsstunden aus dem Gymnasium heimkehrte. Nun hatte er sich's in seinem Studierzimmer bequem gemacht. Er saß am Schreibtisch, stützte den Kopf in die Hände und strich das graue, vom raschen Gang noch feuchte Haar aus der Stirn. »Es ist gerade noch ein Stündchen Zeit vor Tisch. Also was tun? Arbeiten natürlich. Da liegen zwei hohe Stöße blauer Hefte, Primanerarbeiten, Korrekturen, die erledigt werden müssen. Aber das geht jetzt nicht! Es ist ja freilich sehr interessant, jedes Jahr eine neue Generation, immer neue Individuen den Weg der geistigen Entwicklung zu führen! Welch schöne Aufgabe, denselben Lehrstoff nun zum achtundzwanzigsten Mal mit immer frischen Kräften zu beleben! Schade nur, dass sich die Individuen ein wenig stark wiederholen! Was in den Heften steht, weiß ich ganz genau. Es sind immer dieselben Fehler. Höchst lehrreich für den Statistiker, wie sich bei all den Einzelnen dasselbe Gesetz des menschlichen Irrtums in seiner Entwicklung durchsetzt – höchst interessant! Aber jetzt, jetzt bin ich doch etwas zu müde.«

Frister griff nach einem Stoß Papiere, die seine eigenen Untersuchungen über den Verlauf der täglichen Temperaturkurven enthielten – äußerst wichtig für die Frage der Hitzeferien –, und vertiefte sich hinein. Da lag ein schwieriger Punkt, über

KURD LAßWITZ

The Distance Learning School

"It really is a long way home—easy to notice on such hot days. I think I'm tired. Even so, a little bit of exercise is always a good thing."

So thought Professor Frister as he returned home after teaching four classes at the high school. He had just gotten comfortable in his study. He sat down at his desk, propped his head up in his hands, and brushed his gray hair, still damp from walking so fast, off his forehead.

"There is still an hour until dinner. So, what to do? Work, of course. There are two large stacks of blue notebooks, senior student essays, and corrections that need to be done. But not just yet! It is so interesting to lead a new generation, new individuals, along the path of intellectual development! What a beautiful task to once again breathe life into the same subject matter for the twenty-eighth time! It is only a pity that the individual students resemble each other to such a large degree! I know exactly what is written in each notebook. The mistakes are always the same. It is most informative for a statistician to learn how the same law of human error asserts itself in all stages in each and every individual—most interesting! But now, now I am a bit too tired."

Frister reached for the pile of papers containing his own research on the distribution of the daily temperature curve—extremely important in terms of the debate on canceling school due to excessive heat—and immersed himself

den er noch nicht fortgekommen war. Zwar, er wusste den einzuschlagenden Weg, aber die Berechnungen, die erforderten eine Arbeit von vielen Monaten – wo sollte er die Zeit hernehmen?

Er tauchte die Feder ein, machte eine Notiz, legte die Feder wieder hin und stützte den Kopf aufs Neue zwischen die Hände.

»So ginge es schon«, dachte er. »Man müsste nur eben frisch dazu sein. Aber wann? Die vier Stunden, das viele Reden und das Aufpassen und der Ärger über dieselben Dummheiten und der Weg. – Im Ganzen sind wir doch in der Schultechnik noch sehr zurück. Sollte man da nicht etwas Besseres finden als diese alte Praxis, dass Lehrer und Schüler in eine Klasse zusammenlaufen und . . . Nun ja, natürlich, eine ideale Aufgabe ist es . . . indessen, es wird doch viel Kraft vergeudet, und – und es macht etwas müde. Ich meine, die Entwicklung der Technik könnte hier einen ökonomischeren Weg finden.«

Frister lehnte sich in den Stuhl zurück und schloss ein wenig die Augen.

»Ja«, dachte er weiter, »in hundert oder zweihundert Jahren, wie mitleidig wird man auf unsere veraltete kraftverschwenderische Methode zurückblicken! Eine Jugend, der das Verantwortlichkeitsgefühl stärker in Fleisch und Blut übergegangen ist, eine Lehrerschaft, die sich der modernsten Technik bedient; keine Entschuldigungen, keine Täuschungsversuche, keine Kindereien, keine Missgriffe, keine Überbürdung – ideale Zustände! Warum kann ich nicht bis dahin – vielleicht – Urlaub nehmen; komisch, dass mir das noch nie eingefallen ist – sehr komisch –, ich muss doch einmal fragen . . . Hat es nicht eben geklopft? – Ach, Sie sind es, Herr Kollege Voltheim – das ist ja sehr nett! Eben dachte ich an Sie. Sie sind der Mann der Erfindungen. Kennen Sie nicht eine Einrichtung, die das Unterrichten – wie soll ich sagen? – modernisiert, vereinfacht . . . hm . . .«

»Nun, ich dächte doch«, erwiderte Voltheims Stimme, »unsere Fernschule sei eine ganz vorzügliche Einrichtung.«

in it. There was a difficult problem which he had not yet been able to resolve. He knew the method he had to use, but the calculations, which would take months—where would he find the time?

He dipped his quill in the ink, made a note, put the quill down again, and propped up his head in his hands again.

"It would work," he thought. "You would just have to have the energy for it. But when? Teaching four classes, all the talking, the supervising and the constant irritation over the same foolishness, and the commute. All in all, we are still very much behind in terms of educational technology. Shouldn't we be able to find something better than this old practice of teachers and students coming together in a classroom . . . ? Well, of course, it is a supreme task . . . meanwhile, we waste a lot of energy and—and it makes one a bit tired. I mean, technology could come up with a more efficient way."

Frister leaned back in his chair and closed his eyes for a moment.

"Yes," he continued to think. "In one or two hundred years, just think how they will look back with pity on our outdated, energy-wasting method! A youth with a sense of accountability that will have become second nature, a faculty that will utilize the latest technology; no excuses, no attempts at cheating, no childish behavior, no errors or gaffes, no overload or overwork—ideal conditions! Why can't I—perhaps—take a vacation until that time; extraordinary that I never thought of this before—very bizarre—I really have got to inquire . . . Didn't I just hear a knock at the door?—Oh, there you are, my dear colleague Voltheim—that is really very nice indeed! I was just thinking about you. You are the man of inventions. Wouldn't you happen to know of an accommodation that—how should I put that—modernizes teaching or simplifies it . . . hmm . . ."

"Well, I should think so," responded Voltheim's voice. "Our Distance Learning School is an outstanding institution."

»Fernschule? Warum sehen Sie mich so – so seltsam an, Herr Kollege? Ich bin nur etwas ermüdet; bitte, nehmen Sie doch Platz.«

»Ich weiß wohl, Ihre Unterrichtsstunde wird gleich beginnen, aber ich hoffe, Sie dabei nicht zu stören.«

»Heute? Mich? Nein, natürlich nicht. Mir ist so eigen zu Mute, ich habe wohl etwas Kopfschmerz. Was haben wir denn für einen Tag?«

»Den achten Juli neunzehnhundertneunundneunzig, Herr Naturrat.«

»Soso – ganz recht. Hm! Ich dachte nur eben – Naturrat –, Sie müssen doch immer Ihre Späßchen machen.«

»Das ist nun einmal Ihr Titel als Fernlehrer der Geographie am zweihundertelften telefonischen Realgymnasium. Aber hören Sie nicht? Es klingelt. Die Schüler haben ihren Anschluss genommen. Sie können beginnen.«

Frister gab sich Mühe, seinem Kollegen ins Gesicht zu sehen, aber die Züge verschwammen vor seinem Blick. Er vernahm ein leises, melodisches Rasseln, ohne sich erklären zu können, woher es kam. Das ist gewiss so ein Witz von Voltheim, dachte er. Nun gut, ich will ihn nicht stören. Wir werden ja sehen, was er vorhat. Und lachend sprach er: »Lieber Herr Kollege, ich bin ja jetzt gar nicht vorbereitet, auch weiß ich überhaupt nicht, was Sie mit der Fernschule meinen.«

»Oh, ich bitte Sie, Herr Naturrat« – so hörte er deutlich Voltheim wieder reden –, »jetzt wollen Sie mich ein wenig aufziehen. Sie haben ja gestern schon Ihren Vortrag für heute in den Phonographen gesprochen. Und über die Fernschule haben Sie bereits im Jahre neunzehnhundertsiebenundsiebzig eine Broschüre geschrieben. Sie erinnern sich doch?«

»Bin dazu wirklich nicht im Stande.«

Voltheim lachte deutlich. »Nun, dann passen Sie auf«, sagte er. »Sie sehen doch drüben an der Wand die eigentümliche Gemäldegalerie?«

Frister blickte auf. Er war höchlichst erstaunt. In der Tat, an der Wand, wo sonst ein Bücherregal stand, befanden sich einige dreißig rechteckige Rahmen. Aber die Bilder darin waren lebendig. Junge Leute zwischen sechzehn und neunzehn Jahren

"Distance Learning School? Why are you looking at me so—so strangely, dear colleague? I am simply a bit worn out; please, sit down."

"I know very well that your lesson will start any minute, but I had hoped not to interrupt you."

"Today? Me? No, of course not. I feel so strange; I probably have a little headache. What day is today?"

"July 8, 1999, my dear Natural Sciences Professor."

"Aha—very well. Hm! I was only thinking—Natural Sciences Professor; you are always such a joker."

"But that is exactly your title as a distance learning teacher of geography at the 211ᵗʰ Telephone High School. Listen! The phone is ringing. The students have dialed your extension. You may begin."

Frister tried hard to look at his colleague's face, but the features blurred before his eyes. He noticed a quiet, melodic rattling that he couldn't explain. "This is certainly another one of Voltheim's jokes," he thought. "Very well, I won't bother him. We'll see what he's up to." And with a laugh, he said, "Dear colleague, I am not prepared at all right now, so I don't have a clue what you mean by distance learning school."

"Oh, please, my dear Natural Sciences Professor," he clearly heard Voltheim say. "Now you are just teasing me. You already recorded your lecture for today on the phonograph yesterday. And in regards to the distance learning school: you already wrote a brochure about it in 1977. You do remember that, don't you?"

"Can't really say I do."

Voltheim's laughter was clearly audible. "Well, pay attention," he said. "You do see the strange picture gallery on the wall over there, don't you?"

Frister looked up. He was extremely amazed. Indeed, on the wall where there was normally a bookcase, hung some thirty rectangular frames. However, the pictures were alive. In them, young people between sixteen and nineteen years

streckten sich da in bequemer Haltung jeder auf einem Lehnsessel. Und wahrhaftig, das waren ja seine Primaner, wenn auch in ungewohnten Anzügen. Das war sein Primus, dessen glattgeschorener Kopf kaum hinter seiner Zeitung hervorguckte. Und der Meyer rauchte sogar gemütlich seine Zigarre. Andere kauten an ihrem Frühstück.

»Ich möchte wahrhaftig glauben, dort meine Schüler zu sehen«, sagte Frister. »Sehr interessant! Wenn ich nur wüsste, was das bedeutet. Sollte ich etwa wirklich ein Jahrhundert Urlaub gehabt haben? Nehmen Sie das einmal an, Herr Kollege, und sprechen Sie zu mir, als schrieben wir heute tatsächlich das Jahr neunzehnhundertneunundneunzig, ich aber hätte momentan mein Gedächtnis verloren.«

»Sehr gern, Herr Naturrat, wenn Ihnen das Spaß macht. Diese jungen Leute bilden allerdings die Oberprima des zweihundertelften Fernlehrrealgymnasiums. Sie befinden sich nämlich in Wirklichkeit nicht etwa in einem Klassenzimmer, sondern die meisten von ihnen sitzen in ihren eigenen Wohnungen, geradeso wie Sie selbst. Nur wo die Eltern nicht die Mittel haben, den gesamten Fernlehrapparat im Hause unterzubringen, begeben sich die Schüler zu den dazu eingerichteten öffentlichen Fernlehrstellen. Die jungen Leute wohnen, wie Sie wissen, an den verschiedensten Stellen unseres Vaterlands, denn der Fernlehrverkehr lässt sich bis auf tausend Kilometer und mehr ausdehnen.«

»Ich weiß wirklich gar nichts, Herr Kollege. Sprechen Sie nur weiter. Während meines Urlaubs muss die Technik großartige Fortschritte gemacht haben.«

»Das will ich meinen! Nicht nur der Fernsprecher, sondern auch der Fernseher sind so vervollkommnet worden, dass man mit den Worten des Redenden zugleich seine Gestalt, seine Bewegungen, jede seiner Gebärden aufs Deutlichste wahrnehmen kann. Nun ist es natürlich nicht mehr nötig, dass man die weiten Schulwege zurücklegt, Lehrer und Schüler können hübsch zu Hause bleiben.«

»Sehr erfreulich«, murmelte Frister. »Aber die persönliche Anregung . . .«

old lay stretched out comfortably in easy chairs. And, if truth be told, those were his senior students, even if they were unusually attired. There was his best student, whose clean-shaven head was scarcely visible from behind his newspaper. And Meyer was even contentedly smoking a cigar. Others were munching on their breakfast.

"I would really like to believe that I am, without a doubt, seeing my students over there," Frister said. "Very interesting! If I only knew what that meant. Does this mean I really have taken a vacation one hundred years into the future? Let's assume that for the moment, my dear colleague, and please talk with me as if we really were in the year 1999, but pretend that I presently suffer from amnesia."

"Very well, my dear Natural Sciences Professor, if you find this entertaining. These young people represent the senior class of the 211th Distance Learning High School. In reality, they are not in a classroom, and most of them can be found in their own dwellings, just like you. Only in those cases where parents don't have the financial means to install the entire distance learning apparatus in their homes will the students go to the public distance learning facilities created for just such a purpose. As you know, the young people live in very different places across our country since distance learning communications can reach up to 600 miles and more."

"I don't really know anything, my dear colleague. Just continue talking. During my vacation, technology must have made great progress."

"I should think so! Not only the telephone, but television as well has been perfected in such a way that you are able to perceive a person's words as well as their body shape, movements, and every gesture in the most detailed way. So naturally it is no longer necessary to commute long distances to get to school. Teachers and students are able to stay at home."

"Very pleasant," Frister murmured. "But the personal interaction . . ."

»Fehlt nicht. So wie Sie die Schüler erblicken, so sehen diese den Lehrer, nur in einem bedeutend größeren Rahmen, sozusagen in Lebensgröße vor sich. Dagegen können die Schüler sich untereinander nicht sehen, sondern nur hören, aber was sie reden, das hören Sie dann auch alles. Sie brauchen nur auf die Taste dort vorn zu drücken, so sind Sie angeschlossen, und der Unterricht kann beginnen.«

»Ich verstehe. Wie viel Störungen sind damit ausgeschlossen! Aber ist es denn so eilig? Hören Sie, Kollege, die Einrichtung muss doch den Staat ein gutes Stück Geld gekostet haben!«

»Was tut das? Seitdem die unermesslichen Goldfelder auf Neu-Guinea und die Petroleumquellen in Deutsch-China entdeckt sind, haben wir so viel Geld, dass man es schließlich zu gar nichts Besserem als zu Bildungszwecken zu verwenden weiß.«

»Ei, ei! Was habe ich denn da jetzt für ein Gehalt?«

»Aber Sie wissen doch! Als Naturrat – fünfzigtausend Mark. Doch zur Sache. Natürlich hat die Schulhygiene nicht geringere Fortschritte gemacht. Die Überbürdungsfrage ist erledigt. Die Sessel, auf denen die Schüler ruhen, sind in sinnvollster Weise mit selbsttätigen Messapparaten versehen, die das Körpergewicht, den Pulsschlag, Druck und Menge der Ausatmung, den Verbrauch von Gehirnenergie anzeigen. Sobald die Gehirnenergie in dem statthaften Maß aufgezehrt ist, lässt der Psychograph die dadurch eingetretene Ermüdung erkennen, die Verbindung zwischen Schüler und Lehrer wird automatisch unterbrochen und der betreffende Schüler damit vom weiteren Unterricht dispensiert. Sobald ein Drittel der Klasse auf diese Weise ›abgeschnappt‹ ist, haben Sie die Stunde zu schließen.«

»Sehr gut, scheint mir. Indessen, wenn ich selbst ein wenig müde bin, wie zum Beispiel heute . . .«

»Aber bei dem Gehalt! Doch auch dafür ist gesorgt. Wenn Sie jetzt anfangen wollen, so legen Sie gefälligst erst diese gestempelte Gehirnschutzbinde an. Sie werden dadurch vor der Gefahr bewahrt, in der Schule mehr Gehirnkraft zu verschwenden, als es der Fähigkeit der Schüler und ihrer eigenen Gehaltsstufe entspricht.

". . . Is not lacking. Just as the teacher sees the students, the students see the teacher, only on a much bigger scale, life-size in front of them, as it were. However, the students are only able to hear, not see, each other; you, on the other hand, will be able to hear everything they say. You only have to push the button over there in the front so that you will be connected and the lesson is ready to begin."

"I understand. How many disruptions will be excluded that way! But is it really so urgent? Listen, my dear colleague, the implementation must have cost the government a pretty penny!"

"So what? Since the discovery of the vast goldfields in New Guinea and the petroleum sources in German China, we have had so much money that there was ultimately no better way to spend it than on education."

"Ah! So what is my salary now?"

"But you know that! As a Natural Sciences Professor—twenty-five thousand dollars. But let's get down to business. Obviously, school hygiene has made big strides. The question of overburdening has been resolved. The chairs on which the students rest have been conveniently equipped with automatic measuring devices that show body weight, pulse rate, pressure and rate of exhalation, and the consumption of intellectual energy. As soon as a student's intellectual energy is used up to a reasonable level, the psychograph will indicate the resulting exhaustion, the connection between student and teacher will be severed, and the student in question is thus excused from the rest of the lesson. As soon as a third of the class has been 'snapped off' in such a manner, you are required to conclude the lesson."

"That seems good to me. But what if I am a bit tired myself, like for example today . . ."

"At your salary! However, that is taken care of as well. If you want to start now, kindly put on this stamped brain protection wrap. You will thus be safe from the danger of wasting more brain power in school than is appropriate for your students' ability and your own salary level. And

Und nun drücken Sie. Hören Sie, es klingelt. Jetzt erscheint Ihr
Bild auch den Schülern, und Sie können mit ihnen sprechen.«
»Aber was denn? Ich bin ja nicht vorbereitet«, flüsterte Frister
leise zu Voltheim.
»Das wird sich schon finden«, erwiderte dieser ebenso. »Sie,
als erfahrener Lehrer – lassen Sie nur die Schüler reden. An jedem Rahmen steht der Name. Ihr Vortrag steckt hier im Phonographen, Sie brauchen bloß zu drücken.«

Man bemerkte sogleich, dass der Lehrer auf dem Wege der
Fernwirkung in die Klasse getreten, das heißt den Schülern sicht-
bar geworden war. Rathenberg steckte seine Zeitung fort,
Meyer brachte schleunigst seinen Zigarrenstummel beiseite,
Suppard und Neumann schluckten die letzten Bissen ihrer Früh-
stücksbrötchen hinunter.

Frist überblickte seine Bilderrahmen.

Einer der Schüler, es war Meyer, machte eine Verbeugung und
sagte: »Ich habe vorige Stunde gefehlt.«

»Warum?«

»Ich musste mir die zweite Gehirnwindung massieren lassen.«
Frister schüttelte den Kopf. Wie konnte er wissen, ob das eine
genügende Entschuldigung nach moderner Auffassung war?
»Wozu war denn das nötig?«, fragte er und gab dabei Voltheim
einen Wink, er möge ihm einhelfen.

»Ja«, sagte Meyer, »meine Eltern haben meine Träume foto-
grafieren lassen, und dabei zeigte sich, dass ich immer von Pfer-
den träumte.«

»Schwindel!«, flüsterte Voltheim. »Die Pferde sind längst ausgestorben.«

»Aber die Pferde sind ja schon lange ausgestorben«, sagte
Frister.

»Eben darum, Herr Naturrat, musste ich mich massieren
lassen.«

»Ach was, Geographie ist die beste Gehirnmassage.«

Frister merkte, dass zwei der Rahmen, die noch leer waren,
sich eben erst füllten. Er las die Namen und sagte: »Nun, Heinz,
wo kommen Sie denn erst jetzt her?«

»Entschuldigen Sie, Herr Naturrat, meine Mama hat gestern
unsere Tascheneiweißmaschine im Frauenklub auf Spitzbergen

now push the button. Listen, it's ringing. Now your students can see you and you can talk to them."

"But what am I going to say? After all, I am not prepared," Frister quietly whispered to Voltheim.

"You'll find a way," the latter replied. "You, as an experienced teacher—simply let the students talk. On every frame, you will find the name. Your lecture is right here in the phonograph. You only need to push the button."

One could see right away that the teacher had entered the class via remote action, meaning that he had become visible to the students. Rathenberg tucked his paper away, Meyer quickly put his cigar butt aside, and Suppard and Neuman swallowed the last bite of their breakfast rolls.

Frister scanned his picture frames.

One of the students, Meyer, bowed and said, "I was absent during the last lesson."

"Why?"

"I had to have my second brain convolution massaged."

Frister shook his head. How was he supposed to know if that constituted a suitable excuse according to modern opinion? "Why was that necessary?" he asked, and signaled to Voltheim that he needed help.

"Well," said Mayer, "my parents had my dreams photographed and they found out that I dream about horses."

"That's a lie!" Voltheim whispered. "Horses have been extinct for a long time."

"But horses have been extinct for a long time," said Frister.

"That's exactly why, Natural Sciences Professor, I had to have a massage."

"Fiddlesticks, geography is the best brain massage."

Frister noticed that two of the frames that had been empty were now filled. He read the names and said, "So, Heinz, where are you coming from just now?"

"I apologize, Professor, my mother forgot her pocket egg white mixer at the women's club in Spitzbergen and I had

liegen lassen, die musste ich schnell holen, und da es sehr windig war, habe ich mich etwas verspätet.«

»Und Sie, Schwarz, weshalb kommen Sie so spät?«

»Ich, ich – mein Vater ist gestern Geheimer Elektrizitätsrat geworden ...«

»Nun, da sehe ich doch keinen Kausalzusammenhang.«

»Ja, wir sind zur Feier an die Zentralsektleitung angeschlossen worden, und deshalb konnte ich nicht gleich in mein Zimmer.«

»Ausrede!« flüsterte Voltheim. »Hat gekneipt.«

»Na, na«, sagte Frister, »die Sache scheint mir nicht ganz klar. Nun sagen Sie mir einmal, Meyer, was haben wir in der vorigen Stunde durchgenommen?«

»Entschuldigen Sie, Herr Naturrat, ich habe gestern gefehlt.«

»Ach richtig. Sagen Sie mir's, Brandhaus.«

»Entschuldigen Sie, Herr Naturrat, ich konnte gestern nicht arbeiten. Hier ist die Entschuldigung von meinem Vater.«

Brandhaus drückte auf den Knopf seines Phonographen, und man hörte die Bassstimme eines ältere Mannes: »Mein Sohn Siemens konnte gestern wegen Übermüdung der Armmuskeln seine Schularbeiten nicht machen. Brandhaus.«

»Wie?«, fragte Fristen »Die Arme brauchen Sie doch nicht zum Repetieren?«

»Unser Motor ist nicht in Ordnung, und so hätte ich den Phonographen, womit ich nachgeschrieben hatte, selber drehen müssen, und das konnte ich eben nicht.«

»Wodurch haben Sie sich die Übermüdung zugezogen?«

»Bei Übungen mit dem Flugrad.«

Frister sah sich verlegen nach Voltheim um.

»Kann schon sein«, murmelte der. »Hat wahrscheinlich eine Luftpartie mit jungen Damen gemacht und zu viel Luftquadrillen getanzt.«

»Na, hören Sie, Herr Kollege, Entschuldigungen scheint's in der Fernschule nicht weniger zu geben als zu meiner Zeit.« Und er wandte sich wieder zu den Schülern.

»Nun, denn, Rathenberg, was haben wir durchgenommen?«

to go get it quickly; I am a little late because it was very windy."

"And you, Schwarz, why are you so late?"

"I, I—my father has been appointed to the secret electricity council. . ."

"Well, I don't see how those are related."

"For the celebration we were connected to the central champagne pipeline and that's why I couldn't enter my room right away."

"Excuse," Voltheim whispered. "Was out bar hopping."

"Well, I don't know," Frister said. "I'm not clear on the whole situation. Now tell me, Meyer, what did we talk about last time?"

"I'm sorry, Natural Sciences Professor, I was absent yesterday."

"Oh, right. You tell me, Brandhaus."

"I'm sorry, Natural Sciences Professor, I was unable to study yesterday. Here is the note from my father."

Brandhaus pushed the button on his phonograph and they could hear the baritone voice of an elderly man: "My son, Siemens, was unable to complete his homework because of arm muscle fatigue. Brandhaus."

"Pardon?" Frister asked. "I didn't think you needed your arms for repetition?"

"Our motor wasn't working and so I would have needed to turn the phonograph myself in order to record my notes, and I wasn't able to do that."

"How did you acquire the fatigue?"

"While exercising with the flying wheel."

Frister turned around and looked at Voltheim with embarrassment.

"Could very well be true," murmured that one. "Probably was on an air party with the some young ladies and made too many aerial maneuvers."

"Now, listen, my dear colleague, there seem to be just as many excuses in a distance learning school as they were during my time." Frister turned back to his students.

"Very well, Rathenberg, what did we learn?"

»Die Lichtfernsprechstellen mit Amerika. Aber die gibt's nicht mehr. Sie sind alle wieder eingezogen, weil man sie durch den chemischen Ferntaster ersetzt hat. Die neuentdeckten chemischen Lösungsstrahlen durchdringen nämlich das heiße Innere des Erdballs, und man ist somit in der Lage, durch die Erde hindurch auf chemischem Wege zu sprechen.«

Frister wiegte vor Verwunderung den Kopf hin und her. Der Schüler nahm dies als Zeichen eines Einwands und fuhr fort: »Herr Naturrat nannten allerdings noch die Verbindung ›Kreuzberg-Chimborasso‹, aber die ist seit heute früh auch eingezogen. Ich habe es eben im Berliner Fernanzeiger gelesen.«

»Schon gut – nun, Hornbox, fahren Sie fort.«

»Die wichtigsten Staaten Amerikas sind das Kaiserreich Kalifornien, das Königreich New York, die Anarchistenrepublik Kuba, der Kirchenstaat Mexiko und das südamerikanische Sonnenreich.«

Was man da alles hört! dachte Frister. Aber er sagte nur: »Fahren Sie fort, Schwarz.«

Schwarz begann mit einer Geläufigkeit, dass Frister den Worten kaum zu folgen vermochte: »Nachdem durch die direkte Verwendung der Sonnenstrahlung zur Arbeitskraft die Techniker der herrschende Stand geworden waren und die Arbeitsmittel der Menschheit in ihrer Hand vereinigt hatten, gründeten sie einen Staat auf Aktien, indem sie alles in Südamerika zwischen den Wendekreisen verfügbare Land ankauften. Da sie ihre Macht direkt von der Sonne ableiteten, benannten sie diesen Staat den Sonnenstaat. Über die hohen Gebirge wie über die Baumwipfel und Steppen der weiten Ebenen zogen sie ihre Strahlungssammler . . .«

»Aber, Schwarz, Sie bewegen ja gar nicht die Lippen beim Sprechen. Und warum spielen Sie denn immerfort mit den Fingern da auf Ihrem Tisch? Sie lesen wohl gar ab?«

»Bitte sehr, Herr Naturrat« – und Schwarz fingerte weiter auf seinem Platze –, »ich spiele ja auf der Sprechmaschine. Ich kann nämlich nicht selbst sprechen, weil ich mir die Zunge verbrannt habe.«

»So fahren Sie fort.«

"About the light telephone call stations in America. But they don't exist anymore. They have all been recalled because they were replaced with chemical telescanners. The newly discovered chemical dilution rays penetrate the hot interior of the globe and thus we are able to communicate by chemical means."

Frister shook his head in amazement.

The student took this as a sign of objection and continued, "You, Natural Sciences Professor, also mentioned the connection 'Kreuzberg-Chimborasso,' but that one was recalled this morning. I read it in the Berlin TeleNews."

"Okay then—now, Hornbox, continue."

"The most important nations in America are the Californian Empire, the Kingdom of New York, the Anarchist Republic of Cuba, the Papal States of Mexico, and the South American Sun Empire."

"Astonishing, the things one hears," Frister thought. But he only said, "Continue, Schwarz."

Schwarz began with such smoothness that Frister was almost unable to follow his words: "After the class of technocrats had become the ruling group because solar radiation was directly used to aid their work and all the tools of mankind had been united in their hands, they founded a nation based on stocks by buying up all the available land in South America between the Tropic of Cancer and the Tropic of Capricorn. Since they derived their power directly from the sun, they called this nation the Sun State. Across the high mountains and the canopies and the steppes of the vast plains they dragged their ray collectors . . ."

"Schwarz, you don't even move your lips when talking. And why are you constantly drumming on the desk with your fingers? You're not just lipreading along with your phonograph's text, are you?"

"Please, Natural Sciences Professor," Schwarz continued to fumble at his desk. "I am indeed playing the phonograph. I am unable to talk because I burned my tongue."

"So, continue."

»So weit waren wir gerade gekommen.«

Frister wandte sich verlegen nach Voltheim um. »Was nun?«, fragte er.

»Lassen Sie Ihren Phonographen reden.«

Frister drückte auf das Instrument, und zu seiner größten Verwunderung hörte er jetzt seine eigene Stimme: »Wir betrachten nun die Entdeckungsfahrten nach dem Südpol. Wir haben es heutzutage freilich leicht, mit unseren Flugmaschinen über die Eiswüste zu gleiten, aber bedenken Sie, welche Schwierigkeiten sich noch vor hundert Jahren boten, welcher Mut dazu gehörte, mit jenen gebrechlichen Wasserschiffen und auf dürftigen Hundeschlitten in die unzugänglichen Regionen sich zu wagen. Wenn unsere Vorfahren so bequem gewesen wären wie Sie, so wären wir niemals an den Südpol gelangt. Das waren ganz andere Leute! Nie wäre es einem Schüler des neunzehnten Jahrhunderts eingefallen, während des Unterrichts heimlich Kunstspargel zu essen, wie ich das neulich leider bemerken mußte, noch dazu ein Genussmittel, das fast an Schlemmerei grenzt. Denken Sie daran, welche Qualen des Hungers die Forschungsreisenden mitunter ausstehen mußten! Es kam vor, dass sie wochenlang nichts hatten als rohen Vogelspeck, aber auch dann verloren sie den Mut nicht, und mitten in den Qualen des Heißhungers schrieb einer jener Helden in sein Tagebuch das denkwürdige Wort ...«

»Emil, willst du heut Abend Kunstspargel essen? Sie sind nicht teuer.« Es war eine hohe Frauenstimme, die an dieser Stelle des Vortrags plötzlich zwischen den Worten des Redners sich vernehmen ließ.

Ein schallendes Gelächter sämtlicher Schüler begrüßte diese Unterbrechung. Entrüstet wandte sich Frister nach Voltheim um.

»Was war das?«, fragte er.

Voltheim lächelte ebenfalls. »Da muss«, sagte er, »gestern während Ihrer Vorbereitung zum Unterricht wohl gerade Ihre Frau Gemahlin mit dieser Frage eingetreten sein, und der Phonograph hat die Worte natürlich getreu reproduziert.«

»Aber, lieber Herr Kollege, das ist doch etwas fatal bei dieser Fernschule ...«

"That's how far we have gotten."

Frister turned around to Voltheim, embarrassed. "What now?" he asked.

"Let your phonograph do the talking."

Frister pushed the button on the instrument and to his amazement, he heard his own voice: "We are now taking a closer look at the expeditions to the South Pole. These days it's easy to glide across the frosty wilderness with our flying machines, but please bear in mind how difficult this was a hundred years ago and what kind of courage was required to venture out into the impenetrable regions on those rickety water vessels and paltry dog sleds. If our ancestors had been as lazy as you, we would have never reached the South Pole. They were people made of a different cloth. Surely it would have never occurred to a student of the nineteenth century to secretly eat artificial asparagus during instruction, which is what I noticed the other day, let alone a luxury food which almost borders on gluttony. Imagine what extreme hunger the explorers had to endure occasionally! It was not unusual for them to eat nothing but raw bird bacon, but even then they did not lose courage, and struggling with a ravenous appetite, one of those heroes wrote in his journal the noteworthy word . . ."

"Emil, would you like to eat artificial asparagus for dinner tonight? It's not expensive." At this point in the lecture, there was suddenly a high-pitched, female voice among the speaker's words.

This interruption was greeted with resounding laughter from the entire class. Indignantly, Frister turned around to face Voltheim.

"What was that?" he asked.

Voltheim was also smiling. "It seems," he said, "as if yesterday during your lesson preparation your wife interrupted with this question and, obviously, the phonograph reproduced her words accurately."

"But, my dear colleague, that is an embarrassing part of this distance learning school . . ."

»Sehen Sie, das hat auch sein Gutes. Dieser Lachkrampf hat die Schüler so angestrengt, dass acht Klappen herabgefallen sind. Diese Schüler sind übermüdet. Noch drei, und Sie müssen den Unterricht schließen.«

»Oh, das wäre mir wirklich recht, denn ich bin – wie ich Ihnen, glaub' ich, schon sagte – selbst etwas angegriffen. Nun hören Sie nur, was ist denn das wieder, diese hohe Glocke?«

»Das ist das Zeichen des Direktors, er möchte mit ihnen sprechen.«

In der Tat vernahm Frister jetzt deutlich eine fremde Stimme: »Entschuldigen Sie, lieber Herr Naturrat, dass ich Sie störe. Aber eben erfahre ich, dass der Kollege Brechberger mit seinem Luftrad gegen einen Schornstein gerannt ist und sich etwas erschreckt hat. Sie müssen so gut sein, ihn in der nächsten Stunde zu vertreten.«

»Oh, recht gern . . .«

Der Direktor klingelte ab.

»Was soll ich denn nun anfangen, bester Voltheim«, klagte Frister, »die übrigen Schüler scheinen noch ganz munter, und an den Phonographen wage ich mich nicht mehr.«

»Lassen Sie sie doch das Vorgetragene wiederholen.«

Frister wandte sich wieder zur Klasse: »Nun wiederholen Sie mir einmal, was ich gesagt habe.«

Er sah jetzt, wie alle Schüler fast gleichzeitig auf ihre Phonographen drückten, auf denen sie den Vortrag fixiert hatten. Die Apparate schnurrten ab. In ungeregeltem Zusammenklange brausten die vorgetragenen Worte von zwei Dutzend Phonographen an sein Ohr, immer schneller und schneller summte und brummte es, er fühlte, wie ihm in diesem betäubenden Gewirr schwindlig wurde, er stöhnte auf, griff nach seinem Kopf, und auf einmal war es still – ganz still.

»Ach, die Hirnbinde!« dachte er. »Gewiss bin ich zu ermüdet, da ist der Unterricht von selbst geschlossen – ich bin ausgeschaltet. Gott sei Dank!«

Da fuhr er plötzlich in die Höhe. Der Rahmen vor ihm war verschwunden. Seine alten Bücher standen wieder dort.

»Aber sagen Sie doch, was ist denn das, Kollege Voltheim?«

"Yes, but you see, some good even comes of that. The students exerted themselves so much with laughing that eight shutters have already closed. The students are overtired. Another three and you will have to conclude the lesson."

"Oh, that would be quite all right with me because I feel—as I already told you, I believe—quite a bit under the weather myself. Now listen, what is that again, this high-pitched bell?"

"That is the director's chime; he would like to talk with you."

And indeed, Frister clearly heard a voice unknown to him, "Pardon the interruption, my dear Natural Sciences Professor. However, I just heard that colleague Brechberger ran into a chimney with his air bike and suffered a slight scare. Would you please be so kind as to substitute for him for the next class?"

"Oh, I would love to . . ."

The director hung up.

"What am I supposed to do, my dearest Voltheim," Frister lamented. "The rest of the class seems to be quite alert, and I don't dare use the phonograph again."

"Just have the lecture repeated."

Frister turned back to the class, "Now, repeat what I said."

He could see how all of the students pushed down onto their phonographs, on which they had recorded the lecture, almost simultaneously. The devices began to whir away.

In uneven harmony, the recorded words of two dozen phonographs roared in his ears, faster and faster they droned and hummed, and he felt a dizziness coming on from the deafening snarl; he moaned, reached for his head, and all of a sudden it had become quiet—very quiet.

"Oh, the brain wrap!" he thought. "I am too tired, so the lesson concluded automatically of course—I am switched off. Thank God!"

He shot up from his chair abruptly. The frame before him had disappeared. His old books were there instead.

"Pray tell, what is this, my dear colleague Voltheim?"

Sein Kollege Voltheim stand neben ihm und sprach: »Entschuldigen Sie vielmals, Herr Professor – hoffentlich habe ich Sie nicht aufgeweckt. Als ich eintrat, schlummerten Sie so schön, dass ich mich ganz leise hier aufs Sofa setzte, um Sie nicht zu stören.«

»Soso, ich schlummerte? Ich hörte Sie doch noch kommen! Denken Sie, da habe ich etwas Merkwürdiges geträumt. Fünfzigtausend Mark Gehalt! Aber zuletzt sollte ich einen Kollegen vertreten . . .«

»Ja, das ist nun leider Wirklichkeit, deswegen kam ich her – der Kollege Treter . . .«

»Was Sie sagen! Wann denn?«

»Morgen früh um acht Uhr.«

»In der Klasse?«

»Wo denn sonst?«

»Ich dachte, in der Fernschule. Sie wundern sich? Ja, wenn Sie wüssten! Ich hatte nämlich hundert Jahre Urlaub! Na, nehmen Sie Platz, Kollege. Also morgen? Das ist mir lieb, denn heute bin ich wirklich etwas angegriffen.«

His colleague Voltheim stood next to him and said, "My humble apologies, Professor—I hope I didn't wake you up. When I entered the room, you were snoozing so nicely; I sat down on the sofa here quietly so as not to bother you."

"I see. I was napping? But I heard you come in! Just think, I had the strangest dream. A twenty-five thousand dollar salary! But toward the end I was supposed to substitute for a colleague . . ."

"Yes, that really is true, that's why I came here—our colleague Treter . . ."

"You don't say! When exactly?"

"Tomorrow morning at eight o'clock."

"In class?"

"Where else?"

"I thought in the Distance Learning School. You seem surprised? Hah, if you only knew! I was on a hundred-year vacation! Well, sit down, dear colleague. So, tomorrow then? I would prefer that because today I really feel a bit under the weather."

CARL GRUNERT

Carl Grunert was born in 1865 in Naumburg on Saale, at that time part of the Kingdom of Prussia. He grew up and also started his career there as a college prep teacher. He then moved to Berlin, where he held a position as municipal teacher. In the 1890s he married Erna Huth. Their son, Carl Georg Friedrich, was born in 1899. Later, his home alternated between Berlin and the picturesque Müggelsee region nearby, a situation which was not entirely voluntary; he withdrew to the soothing countryside of Müggelsee for long stretches to recover from intermittent bouts with cocaine and to escape into writing.

Before his career as a science fiction writer began, Grunert published poetry anthologies and plays under the pseudonym Carl Friedland. He later acquired a reputation for writing short utopian technological narratives which he called "futuristic novellas," or simply "novellas." His first collection of futuristic novellas, *Im irdischen Jenseits* (*In the Afterlife*) was published near the end of 1903, closely followed by *Menschen von Morgen* (*People of Tomorrow*, 1905), *Feinde im Weltall?* (*Enemies in Space*, 1907),[1] and *Der Marsspion* (*The Martian Spy*, 1908). He wrote another handful of novellas before he died of complications with pneumonia in 1918.

Sadly, most of his novellas, along with his poems and plays, have sunk into obscurity. A total of thirty-two Grunert sto-

---

[1]This story was published in 1952 under the title "Enemies in Space" in the U.S. in the anthology *Invaders of Earth*, edited by Groff Conklin. (Alpers/Fuchs/Hahn/Jeschke: *Lexikon der Science Fiction Literatur*, 1988: 504).

ries, which could be classified as "scientific romances" or
"science fiction," have been published in Germany. However,
few of his stories are still read today, mainly because in the
1970s and 1980s single stories were absorbed into larger anthologies.

Grunert was familiar with the works of Jules Verne and H.G.
Wells. His story "Pierre Maurignacs Abenteuer" ("Pierre Mau-
rignac's Adventures"), published in 1974 in the former GDR
with the title "Das Zeitfahrrad" ("The Time Traveling Bicycle"), is strongly reminiscent of H.G. Wells's *The Time Machine*.
Like Wells's time-traveling device, Grunert's machine resembles
a bicycle with dials and tubes, and Pierre, much like Wells' Time
Traveler, is a visionary who has to defend himself against the
narrow-mindedness of his Victorian-era contemporaries.

However, Grunert was influenced primarily by Kurd Laßwitz,
whose style he tried to emulate. Grunert acknowledged this fact,
but also once said that his own sketches were as far from their
inspiration (Laßwitz) as night was from day. As he grew as a
writer, he gained more self-esteem.

Like Laßwitz, Grunert includes motifs and themes in his narratives that evoke the works of Romantic writers, for example,
the use of dreams as a vehicle for the fantastic. Grunert's plots
and stories also show strong evidence of Expressionist techniques (circa 1900-1930), such as the use of altered states—
daydreams, obsessions, and symbolic and surrealistic portray-
als. Another Grunert feature is the use of strange or humorous
names for his characters. The name Professor Diluvius in "The
Archaeopteryx Egg," for example, hints at the hero's profession
as a paleontologist.

Humorous and often suspenseful, his stories provide some
remarkable examples of early twentieth-century sci-fi writing.[2] Some count Grunert among the most important writers of
the futuristic literary genre in the German language alongside

---

[2]"Carl Grunert: Leben und Werk," accessed July 25, 2011, http://www.dieter-von-ree-
ken.de/grunert/frame.htm.

Laßwitz and Oskar Hoffmann, which is remarkable considering that he only ever wrote short stories.[3]

In the story "Das Ei des Urvogels" ("The Archaeopteryx Egg," 1908), Professor Diluvius is presented with a slab of limestone that contains what he surmises to be an Archaeopteryx egg. His ambitious plan is to hatch the egg using an incubator. Although the tone of the narrative is humorous and even ironic, Grunert manages to unmask the professor's thirst for knowledge as a form of mania. While he is not an archetypal "evil scientist," his overzealous determination gets the better of him. Those around him, including his housekeeper and his cat, all eventually share in the ill effects of his obsession.

The story is emotionally charged and the pace picks up considerably as the text unfolds, mirroring the mental and emotional state of the professor. Grunert uses dashes extensively, either to mark a break in the plot or to emphasize a specific passage. The technique complements perfectly the distortion and ruptures happening in the story.[4]

---

[3]Thomas Harbach, "Carl Grunert: Von bösen Außerirdischen und wahrer Liebe," *Quarber Merkur: Franz Rottensteiners Literaturzeitschrift für Science Fiction und Phantastik* 103/104 (Passau 2006).

[4]Critic J.L. Styan writes "In its early stages expressionistic drama was a dramatization of the subconscious, a kind of scripted dream, with the consequent loss of character motivation and rational plot development of the well-made play." ("German Expressionism," accessed August 16, 2011, http://www.trashface.com/germanexpressionism. html).

CARL GRUNERT

Das Ei des Urvogels

Im Studierzimmer des alten Professors Diluvius leuchtete noch immer die elektrische Arbeitslampe. Draußen vor den enggeschlossenen Jalousien der Fenster erhellte schon der Schein des aufdämmernden Frühmorgens die Gegend. Aber der Herr Professor arbeitete noch immer. Es mußte ein seltenes und sehr interessantes Objekt sein, das den Gelehrten sich selbst und die Rücksicht auf seine leiblichen Bedürfnisse so ganz vergessen ließ.

Professor Diluvius war Vorsteher der paläontologischen Abteilung des Museums für Naturkunde. Seine Forschungen über die fossile Tierwelt, namentlich auf dem Gebiete der Dinosaurier, waren nach verschiedenen Richtungen hin epochemachend gewesen . . .

Seine eigentlichen Arbeitsräume befanden sich im ersten Stockwerke des Museums, und es mußten besondere Gründe ihn veranlassen, die Präparation eines paläontalogischen Fundes in seiner Privatwohnung vorzunehmen.

Denn ein solches fossiles Objekt lag vor ihm, und seine trotz des Alters noch immer geschickten und sicheren Hände arbeiteten emsig an seiner Enthüllung.

Es war eine Platte lithographischen Schiefers aus der Gegend von Eichstätt, unregelmäßig geformt, die der Gelehrte mit

CARL GRUNERT

The Archaeopteryx Egg

In old Professor Diluvius's study, the electric desk lamp still shone brightly.

Outside the tightly-closed venetian blinds, the light of the early morning dawn already brightened the area. And yet, the professor was still working. It had to be a rare and very interesting object that made the scholar so completely oblivious to the world around him and forget about his bodily needs.

Professor Diluvius was the chair of the Paleontology Institute of the Museum for Nature and Science. His research on fossils, specifically dinosaurs, had been epoch-making in several areas . . .

His actual workspace was located on the second floor of the museum, so it must have been special circumstances that prompted him to complete the preparation of a paleontological find in his private quarters.

For such a fossilized object was now lying before him, and his hands, still skilled and steady despite his age, were working busily to unwrap it.

It was on a slab of lithographic limestone from the area around Eichstätt,[1] irregularly formed, that the scholar was

---

[1]Archaeopteryx lithographica is the earliest bird in the fossil record. Excavations near Eichstätt, about 67 miles northeast of Munich, Germany, produced a total of 10 fossilized specimens from the Late Jurassic period. The first was found in 1861, two years after Darwin's *Origin of Species*.

seinen meißelartigen Werkzeugen bearbeitete. Vorsichtig und mit größter Schonung entfernte er, vom Rande der Platte her arbeitend, die Schichten des Kalkschiefers – bis an eine auf der Oberseite mit Bleistift umrandete, ungefähr kreisförmige Stelle. Was für ein seltsames vorsintflutliches Geschöpf lag hier versteinert in den Ablagerungen des Kalkschiefers verborgen?

Ein ganzer Berg von der Platte abgelöster Bruchstücke häufte sich schon vor ihm auf, und noch immer gönnte er den müden Fingern und den brennenden Augen keine Ruhe – immer wieder griff er die Platte an, hin und wieder die Instrumente wechselnd.

Verwundert schaute »Grauchen«, eine prachtvolle graue Katze, die sich's auf der Chaiselongue bequem gemacht hatte, dem unverständlichen nächtlichen Treiben ihres Herrn zu. Sie war noch ein Vermächtnis seiner verstorbenen Frau, die einst das hilflose junge Kätzchen fast verhungert in einer Ecke des Hausflurs gefunden. – Erst schnurrend, dann leise miauend, suchte sie die Aufmerksamkeit des Professors auf sich zu lenken, schloß aber endlich verdrießlich blinzelnd die Augen wieder, als ihre Mühe vergeblich blieb.

Eine Uhr schlug irgendwo in der Nähe. Aufhorchend zählte Professor Diluvius die Schläge.

»Vier Uhr!« sagte er. »Zwölf Stunden arbeite ich nun daran, und das Gröbste habe ich wohl herunter. Jetzt heißt es, doppelt und dreifach Vorsicht gebrauchen!«

Und wieder begann er zu sticheln und zu meißeln, und immer kleiner wurden die Kalkschüppchen, die er nun von der Platte abhob. Er arbeitete jetzt mit der kleinsten Nummer seiner stählernen Werkzeuge.

Fast zwei Stunden mochte er so in voller Emsigkeit weitergearbeitet haben. Ein etwas größeres Stück des Kalkschiefers hob sich jetzt beim Angriff des Meißels ab. –

»Da ist es!« rief Professor Diluvius.

Aus der Platte ragte die Spitze eines eiförmigen Körpers hervor. –

»Sei mir gegrüßt, du Gnadengeschenk versunkener Jahrmillionen!« frohlockte der alte Herr, in die Hände klatschend und vor Freude von einem Beine aufs andre hüpfend –

working on with his chisel-like tools. Cautiously and with the utmost care, he removed the layers of limestone, working from the edge of the slab—until he reached a circular-like area outlined in pencil on the surface.

What strange, antediluvian object was hidden there in the limestone sediments, petrified?

An entire mountain of chips that had been removed from the slab had already piled up before him, and yet he still did not allow his tired fingers and burning eyes to rest—again and again he attacked the slab, occasionally changing tools.

With astonishment, Little Gray, a magnificent gray cat that had settled down comfortably on the chaise longue, watched the incomprehensible, nightly activities of her master. She was a legacy of his deceased wife who had found the helpless, young kitten in a corner of the hallway, almost starved to death—at first by purring, then by meowing quietly, she tried to draw the Professor's attention to her; finally, blinking sullenly, she closed her eyes again when her efforts were in vain.

Somewhere nearby, a clock chimed. Attentively, Professor Diluvius counted the strikes.

"Four o'clock!" he said. "I have been working on this for twelve hours now, and I've probably finished the bulk of the work. Now I need to be extra careful!"

And again he began to scrape and chisel, and the limestone chips, which he lifted off the slab now, became smaller and smaller. By now, he was working with the smallest tools in his tool box.

He worked away with full concentration for almost two hours. Now a larger piece of limestone gave way under the chisel attack—

"There it is!" yelled Professor Diluvius.

Up from the slab rose the tip of an egg-shaped object—

"Greetings, you gift of mercy from millions of years gone by!" the old man rejoiced while clapping his hands in delight and hopping from one foot to the other—

»sei mir gegrüßt, du Spende einer rara avis! Das Ei des Kolumbus und – selbst das Ei der Leda ist gegen deinen Wert ein Schatten!«

Er hielt die Platte dicht an seine Studierlampe, den grünen Lampenschirm hochschiebend.

»Wie unscheinbar es aussieht! Wie alles, was seinen Wert im Innern trägt! – Graugrün mit schwarzen Tüpfeln! – Niemand würde vermuten, daß es gelegt wurde zu einer Zeit, da es noch keine Menschen auf unserem Planeten gab, von einem Geschöpf gelegt wurde, das eine Eidechse war und – ein Vogel werden wollte!«

Schnell griff er wieder nach seinen Werkzeugen, um es völlig aus der Hülle des Kalkschiefers freizulegen. Und so sehr ihn der erste Anblick des ersehnten Fundes begeistert hatte – mit eiserner Ruhe und Kaltblütigkeit arbeiteten seine Hände weiter, vom vorsichtig abwägenden Blick seiner scharfen grauen Augen gelenkt, bis es rund und heil und ganz vor ihm lag, das Ei des Urvogels Archäopteryx! – Und nun erst nahm er sich Zeit, das Begleitschreiben noch einmal zu studieren, das ihm sein junger Freund und ehemaliger Schüler Doktor Finder mit dem kostbaren paläontologischen Objekt gesandt hatte.

Es lautete:

Eichstätt, den 5. Juli 19..

Mein lieber, hochverehrter Herr Professor!

Anbei übersende ich Ihnen ein Objekt, das vorläufig einzig in den Sammlungen unserer Museen dastehen dürfte, ein fossiles Ei, dem Fundorte nach (es stammt aus den Schieferbrüchen hier am Blumenberg) wahrscheinlich ein Ei von Archäopteryx lithographica. Die Untersuchung der Platte durch die neue Art der Y-Strahlen zeigt nur, daß ein vollkommen gut erhaltenes Ei in der Schieferplatte steckt; ich habe die Lage des Objekts auf der Ober- und Unterseite der Platte durch eine Bleistiftlinie umrandet, so daß wenigstens ungefähr ein Anhalt für die Freilegung des Fundes gegeben ist.

"Greetings, you offering of a *rara avis*![2] The egg of Columbus and—even the egg of Leda is a mere shadow compared to your value!"

He held the slab close to his desk lamp, pushing the green lampshade up.

"How unimpressive it looks! Like everything that carries value inside!—Grayish green with black dots!—Nobody would guess that it was laid at a time when there weren't yet any humans on our planet, by a creature that was a lizard and—was to become a bird!"

Quickly, he reached for his tools again to free it completely from its limestone tomb. And, no matter how much the first glimpse of the desired find had excited him—his hands continued working with an iron calm and cold-bloodedness, directed by the carefully considerate look of his sharp gray eyes, until it lay round and whole before him, the egg of the first bird, Archaeopteryx!—And only now did he take time to carefully reread the accompanying letter that his young friend and former student, Dr. Finder, had sent along with the precious paleontological object.

It said:

Eichstätt, July 5, 19–

My dear and honorable Professor,

Enclosed you will find an object that might, at the moment, be unique in our museum collections: a fossilized egg which is, judging from its place of discovery (it comes from the limestone quarries at the Flower Mountain here), probably an *Archaeopteryx lithographica* egg. An examinination of the slab using the new y-ray method only showed that there is a perfectly well-preserved egg inside the limestone slab; I have circled the position of the objects on the top and bottom surface in pencil so that there would be at least some evidence as for how to uncover the find.

---

[2]Latin, literally meaning "rare bird." More commonly, it is used as an expression to denote an unusual, uncommon, or exceptional person or thing.

Denn diese schwerste Arbeit muß ich Ihnen leider allein überlassen, lieber, hochverehrter Herr Professor; Sie kennen ja meine
Aufgabe hier in den Kalkschieferbrüchen, die mir zu so diffizilen
Extraarbeiten keine Zeit läßt. Aber Ihre so geschickte Hand hat
schon Schwierigeres geleistet. Ich meinerseits hoffe, auch in dem
noch in der Steinhülle steckendem Geschenk wird Ihnen die Liebe und Verehrung nicht verborgen bleiben, mit der ich allezeit
sein werde

Ihr dankbarer Schüler
Dr. Finder.

P.S. Wenn man das Ei doch noch ausbrüten lassen könnte! –
Aber dazu ist es doch wohl nicht mehr »frisch« genug?

D. O.

Immer wieder kehrten die sinnenden Augen des alten Gelehrten zu diesem Postskriptum zurück. Ein ungeheuerlicher Ge-
danke drängte sich ihm auf: War es denn so ausgesprochen un-
möglich, daß die scherzhafte Wendung des »Ausbrütenlassens«
zur Wahrheit werden konnte?

Ein Geräusch an der Tür des Zimmers störte ihn in seinem
Denken. Seine alte Wirtschafterin Pauline trat ein. Vor Schreck
ließ sie Eimer und Schrubber fallen und schlug die Hände über
dem Kopfe zusammen.

»Aber, Herr Professor, Herr Professor! Wenn das die selige
Frau erlebt hätte! Sie sitzen noch über dem alten Steinklumpen?
Und sind wohl gar nicht schlafen gegangen? Ach, lieber Herr
Professor, wenn man schon über die Siebzig hinaus ist –«

»Ja, Sie haben ja recht, liebe Pauline! Aber es gibt eben Aus-
nahmen, und eine solche ist schuld, daß ich einmal eine Nacht
hindurch gearbeitet habe. Nun seien Sie hübsch vernünftig und
schelten Sie nicht mehr – sondern bringen Sie mir eine recht
große Tasse schönen Kaffee, aber so, wie nur Sie ihn zu brauen
verstehen, Pauline!«

Kopfschüttelnd zog die alte, treue Schaffnerin mit den At-
tributen des Reinemachens wieder ab.

Professor Diluvius wandte sich aufs neue dem seltsamen
Funde zu. Er nahm das Archäopteryx-Ei vorsichtig in die Hand

Unfortunately, I have to leave this most difficult task to you, honorable Professor; you are familiar with my job here in the limestone quarries which does not give me time for such complicated extra work. However, your skilled hand has managed much more difficult challenges in the past. For my part, I hope that the love and reverence I have for you will not stay hidden from you, not even in the present still concealed inside the stone package.

Your grateful student,
Dr. Finder

P.S. If one could only hatch the egg after all!—However, it might not be "fresh" enough for that anymore?!

D.O.

Again and again, the old scholar's eyes returned to this post script. An outrageous thought occurred to him: was it really so absolutely impossible that the joke of "having it hatched" might become reality?

A noise at his room door interrupted his thinking. His old housekeeper Pauline entered. Shocked, she dropped her mop and bucket and threw her hands up in horror.

"But, Professor, Professor! If your wife, may God rest her soul, had seen this! You are *still* sitting over that lump of stone? And you haven't even slept yet? Oh, my dear Professor, if one is already past seventy—"

"Yes, you are so right, dear Pauline! But there are exceptions, and that is the reason why I worked through the night, just this once. Now be reasonable and don't chide me anymore—instead, bring me a really big cup of good coffee, brewed the way only you know how, Pauline!"

Shaking her head, the old, loyal caretaker with the cleaning supplies took off again.

Professor Diluvius turned again to the strange discovery. Carefully, he took the Archaeopteryx egg into his hand and

und hielt es gegen das Licht der Studierlampe. Es erschien gleichmäßig undurchsichtig, als ob die Schale dicker sei als die unserer jetzigen Vogeleier. Das Bauernmittel fiel ihm ein: er hielt das kostbare Ei erst mit dem einen, dann mit dem andern Ende an die Lippe.

Beinahe hätte er es vor freudigem Schreck aus der Hand fallen lassen.

Das eine Ende erschien ihm wärmer als das andere! Das Blut hämmerte ihm in den Schläfen vor plötzlicher Aufregung. Ungleich warme Hälften! Aber vielleicht war es eine Sinnestäuschung – –

Er legte das Geschenk der Vorzeit mit zitternden Fingern auf die Platte seines Arbeitstisches und stand auf . . .

Der Morgen lugte durch die Spalten der Jalousien. Der Professor zog sie auf und schaltete die Lampe seines Zimmers aus. Dann ging er ein paarmal auf und ab, öffnete im Vorbeigehen ein Fenster und lehnte sich ein Weilchen hinaus, mit vollen Zügen die duftige Frühluft atmend. Er wollte sich erst völlig wieder in der Gewalt haben, erst ganz wieder Herr seiner Nerven sein, ehe er die entscheidende Untersuchung des Objekts von neuem vornahm.

Nun erschien auch Pauline wieder mit dem duftenden Frühtrunk. Ihr gutes, etwas alltägliches Gesicht und ein Schluck des braunen Trankes wirkten besänftigend auf ihn ein. Schnell entschlossen, reichte er seiner Köchin das kostbare Urvogelei.

»Hier, liebe Pauline, prüfen Sie einmal, als wenn es ein Hühnerei wäre, ob dies ein frisches Ei ist! Aber vorsichtig, vorsichtig!«

Pauline machte die Probe ähnlich, wie ein Weilchen vorher der Herr Professor Diluvius – nur hatte die einfache Köchin das Urteil der größeren Erfahrung vor ihm voraus.

»Es ist noch gut, Herr Professor! Soll ich's Ihnen kochen? Es ist wohl so'n ausländischer Leckerbissen?«

Mit beiden Händen griff der alte Herr nach dem wunderbaren Schatze.

»Nein – nein! Um Gotteswillen, Pauline! Dies Ei stammt von einem vogelartigen Geschöpf, welches vor langen, langen Zeiten auf unserer Erde gelebt hat.«

held it up against the light of his desk lamp. It appeared nontransparent throughout, as if the shell were thicker than that of modern-day bird eggs. He remembered a folk remedy: he held the precious egg to his lips, first with one end, then with the other.

He almost dropped it from his hand in shocked delight. To him, one end appeared to be warmer than the other!

His temples throbbed as blood rushed through them with his sudden excitement. *Irregularly* warm halves! But, maybe it was a hallucination—

With shaking fingers, he put the prehistoric present down on the surface of his desk and got up . . .

The morning peeked through the slats of the venetian blinds. The professor pulled them open and turned off the room lights. Then he paced back and forth a couple of times; in passing, he opened a window and leaned out for a moment, inhaling deeply to breathe in the fragrant spring air. He wanted to gain complete control over himself again, wanted to be master of his senses again, before he launched back into the crucial investigation of the object.

Now Pauline reappeared with a sweet-scented breakfast drink. Her good, somewhat average face and a sip of the brown brew had a calming effect on him. He quickly made up his mind and handed his cook the precious first bird egg.

"Here, dear Pauline, go ahead and check if this egg is fresh, as if it were a chicken egg. But please do it carefully; be careful!"

Pauline performed the test similar to the way the professor had done it just a little while ago—only the simple cook had an advantage over him from more experience.

"It is still good, Professor! You want me to cook it for you? Surely it is some sort of an exotic delicacy, isn't it?"

With both hands, the old man reached for the wonderful treasure.

"No—no! For heaven's sake, Pauline! This egg comes from a bird-like creature that lived on the earth a long, long time ago."

»Das Ei ist aber noch frisch, dafür garantiere ich Ihnen, Herr Professor! Und nun frühstücken Sie nur erst, und machen Sie ein bißchen Morgentoilette, wenn Sie doch nicht mehr schlafen gehen wollen!« Damit ging sie hinaus.

Der Professor nahm nun selbst nochmals das Ei zur Prüfung in die Hand.

Kein Zweifel! Das eine Ende war entschieden wärmer als das andere. Pauline hatte recht: es war »noch gut«. Seinem Gewicht nach war es kaum schwerer als ein mittelgroßes Hühnerei – eine Fossilisation des Inhalts erschien also merkwürdigerweise ausgeschlossen! Vielleicht hatte der feine Kalkschlamm des Jura-Meeres die Poren der Eierschale so hermetisch verschlossen, daß die Fäulniskeime der Luft keinen Zutritt fanden und der Inhalt konserviert blieb . . .

Aber dann! – Dann konnte man es ja im Brutofen ausbrüten lassen! Dann war ja das Eiweiß noch lebens- und entwicklungsfähig – trotz des undenkbar langen Zeitraumes, den das Ei im verhärteten Kalkschlamm von Eichstätt eingebettet gelegen! Die Gedanken des Professors Diluvius begannen aufs Neue zu kreisen . . .

Dann hatte er am Ende das unbeschreibliche Glück, einen lebendigen Urvogel, eine leibhaftig fliegende Archäopteryx aus dem Wunderei hervorkriechen zu sehen!

Es war ein Glück, daß die alte Pauline längst wieder das Zimmer verlassen hatte und den indianischen Freudentanz nicht sehen konnte, den ihr alter Professor zwischen den Möbeln seines Arbeitszimmers ausführte. »Grauchens« Verwunderung, die abermals in ihrem Schlummer gestört worden war, war vielleicht noch größer – aber sie blieb stumm.

Ein paar Stunden später hatte sich Professor Diluvius durch einen Diener des paläontologischen Instituts einen Brutapparat besorgen lassen, ihn in Betrieb gesetzt und das kostbare Archäopteryx-Ei sorglich darin eingebettet. – Wahrscheinlich brüteten die Urvögel der Jurazeit noch nicht selbst ihre Eier aus, sondern überließen dies Geschäft wegen ihrer noch schwachen Befiederung der Allmutter Sonne, so daß ein allzustrenges Einhalten einer genauen Brutwärme auch in der Natur wohl nicht möglich gewesen war. Die einzige Bedingung

"But the egg is still fresh, I guarantee it, Professor! Now, go have breakfast first and then wash up if you don't want to go to sleep anymore!" Having said that, she left.

The Professor took the egg in his hands again for another check.

No doubt! The one end was definitely warmer than the other. Pauline had been right: it was "still good." Judging from its weight, it was hardly heavier than a medium-sized chicken egg—fossilization of the contents appeared, for some strange reason, impossible! Maybe the fine calcareous ooze of the Jurassic ocean had sealed the pores of the egg shell so hermetically that the airborne bacteria responsible for decomposition had found it impossible to enter and thus the contents remained preserved . . .

But then!—that meant one could hatch it in an incubator! That also meant that the egg white was still alive and able to develop—notwithstanding the unimaginably long time for which the egg had been sitting in the hardened calcareous ooze of Eichstätt! The wheels in Professor Diluvius's head began to turn anew . . .

Then, in the end, he would have the unspeakable fortune of seeing a living first bird, a flying Archaeopteryx in the flesh, crawl from the miracle egg!

It was fortunate that Pauline had left the room a while ago and was unable to see the Native American-style jig the Professor was performing amidst the furniture of his study. Little Gray's amazement, after her slumber was once again disturbed, might have been even bigger—but she remained silent.

A few hours later, Professor Diluvius had managed to procure an incubator through an attendant of the paleontological institute, set it up, and carefully placed the precious Archaeopteryx egg into it.—The first birds of the Jurassic period had probably not hatched their eggs themselves, but, because of their rather sparse plumage, had left this business to our foremost mother, the sun; therefore, an all too strict observation of an exact incubation temperature had presumably not been possible, not even in nature. The only

blieb, eine gewisse obere Temperaturgrenze (etwa 60 Grad) nicht zu überschreiten, weil sonst das Eiweiß gerinnen mußte. Der Brutapparat, der durch eine Lampe erhitzt wurde, regulierte seine Temperatur selbst, nachdem er einmal auf eine maximale Wärme eingestellt worden war. Beim Erreichen dieser zulässigen Höchstgrenze ertönte entweder ein Alarmsignal für den Beobachter – oder der Apparat steuerte automatisch die Wärmezufuhr zurück auf ein geringeres Maß. Die letztere Einrichtung ist die gebräuchlichere. Da aber Professor Diluvius sich selbst mehr Vertrauen schenkte als dem besten Automaten, so hatte er den Apparat auf »Alarm« gestellt, um eventuell selbst die Überschreitung des Maximums zu regulieren. Mit Angst und Sorge dachte er aber schon an die Nachtstunden, wo er seinen unbezahlbaren Schatz schließlich doch der Selbstregulierung des Brutofens überlassen mußte. Einen Augenblick hatte er allerdings den Gedanken gehegt, sich mit seiner Wirtschafterin Pauline in die Zeit von je vierundzwanzig Stunden zu teilen, solange das Ausbrüten dauern würde – aber er wagte nicht, diesen Vorschlag der alten, treuen Seele zu machen, obwohl er für sein Teil gern alle Nächte und auch noch den halben Tag gewacht hätte.

Aber ungefähr mußte er sie doch in die Handhabung des Brutofens einweihen. – Er rief sie herein und erklärte ihr kurz die Wirkung des Apparates. Ungläubig lächelnd sah die brave Pauline auf den seltsamen Kasten – und dies Lächeln wurde sogar ein wenig spöttisch, als sie ihren alten Herrn Professor betrachtete, der ihr voller Eifer seinen geheimnisvollen Plan auseinandersetzte.

»Und das Küken soll ganz ohne Glucke aus dem Ei kommen?«

Der Herr Professor nickte.

»Wer pickt ihm denn die Schale auf, wenn es fertig ist, Herr Professor?«

Auch darüber beruhigte er sie und war froh, daß sie wenigstens die Handgriffe verstanden hatte, durch die einer Überschreitung der zulässigen Brutwärme vorgebeugt wurde.

»Und wie lange wird die blecherne Henne zu dem Küken brauchen, Herr Professor?« fragte sie beim Hinausgehen.

condition that remained was not to exceed an upper temperature limit (around 140° F) because otherwise the egg white would start to congeal. The incubator, which was heated by a lamp, regulated the temperature through an automatic regulation mechanism after it had been set to a maximum temperature. Once this acceptable maximum temperature was reached, either an alarm went off to alert a possible observer—or the device automatically adjusted the heat supply to a lower level. The latter setup is much more common. However, since Professor Diluvius trusted himself much more than he trusted the best automatic device, he switched the apparatus to "alarm" to be able to regulate the temperature manually, in case it should exceed the maximum. With fear and anguish he thought about the night hours when he finally had to leave his priceless treasure to the automatic regulation mechanism of the incubator. A moment earlier he had sported the idea of splitting the twenty-four-hour watch time with his housekeeper Pauline as long as the incubation was in progress—however, he did not dare to propose this idea to the old, loyal soul; although he, for *his* part, would have gladly watched all nights and even half of the days.

But he had to let her in on how to operate the incubator, at least to some degree.—He called her into the room and briefly explained how the device operated. With an incredulous smile, the good Pauline looked at the peculiar box—and her smile even turned a bit derisive when she regarded her old professor who explained his mysterious plan to her with great fervor.

"And the chicken is supposed to emerge from the egg, entirely without the help of a sitting hen?"

The professor nodded.

"Then who's going to peck the shell when it's done, Professor?"

He also put her mind to ease about that one and was glad that she had at least understood the maneuvers required to prevent the incubation heat from exceeding a tolerable limit.

"And how long will it take the tin hen to produce the chick, Professor?" she asked in leaving.

»Wir müssen es abwarten, Pauline. Aber hoffentlich nicht viel länger als eine mit Fleisch und Federn!«

Professor Diluvius lebte nur noch für seinen Urvogel. In dem Gedanken an das zu erwartende »freudige Ereignis« vergaß er Essen, Trinken und Schlafen.

Die alte Pauline war in heller Verzweiflung. Vergebens kochte sie ihm ihre schmackhaftesten Gerichte, vergebens ermahnte sie ihn, im Andenken an die »selige Frau Professor«, seinem alten Körper die nötige Pflege und Ruhe zu gönnen.

Drei Tage und Nächte hatte er so schon hintereinander vor der »blechernen Henne« gesessen. Neben ihm auf dem Tische lag aufgeschlagen die schöne Abbildung der Archaeopteryx litographica aus den »Paläontologischen Abhandlungen von Dames und Kayser« (Bd. 2, Heft 3, vom Jahre 1884).

»Was für ein kostbares Objekt ist schon dieser prachtvoll erhaltene Abdruck aus dem Solnhofener Schiefer!« murmelte er. »Das Deutsche Reich hat damals 26 000 Mark für die Erwerbung der Platte mit der Archäopteryx gezahlt – und ich, ich werde der Glückliche sein, der Einzige auf Erden, der ein lebendiges Exemplar sein Eigen nennt! Wie wird man mich beneiden! Wie werden sie kommen aus aller Herren Ländern, meine lieben, ungläubigen Kollegen, um den Wundervogel zu schauen! Und was werden sie mir bieten, um ihn käuflich zu erwerben! Aber nicht um die Welt soll er mir feil sein! Nicht um alles Gold dieser Erde!«

Mit dieser stolzen Wendung schloß der alte Gelehrte regelmäßig seinen Dithyrambus auf den Urvogel, den die belebende Wärme in still-schaffender Arbeit aus dem Ei hervorlocken sollte. –

Ein leises Schnurren klang durch das Zimmer, und der Herr Professor fühlte gleichzeitig, wie sich »Grauchen« an seinen Knien rieb. Liebkosend strich er ihr über den Rücken; er wollte Versäumtes ein wenig wieder nachholen. Dann aber sagte er:

»Du wirst dich vorläufig gewöhnen müssen, in der Küche zu hausen, liebes »Grauchen«! – Zwar bist du eine sehr artige Miesmies – aber ein Raubtier steckt doch in deinem weichen,

"We'll have to wait and see, Pauline. But I hope it won't take longer than one made of flesh and feathers!"

Henceforth, Professor Diluvius lived only for his Archaeopteryx. Completely absorbed in thoughts about the impending "happy event," he forgot to eat, drink, and sleep. Old Pauline was in great despair. In vain, she cooked the tastiest dishes for him, in vain she admonished him, in memoriam of the professor's wife, and may God rest her soul, to grant his aging body indispensable care and rest.

Three days and nights, one after the other, he had been sitting in front of the "metal hen." On the table beside him lay open the page with the fine-looking *Archaeopteryx lithographica* picture in the "Paleontological Treatise by Dames and Kayser" (Vol. 2, Issue 3, 1884).

"What a valuable object is even this magnificently preserved impression from the Solnhofen limestone quarries!" he murmured. "In those days, the German Empire shelled out 26,000 marks to purchase a slate of the Archaeopteryx—and I, I will be the fortunate one, the only one in the world, who is going to own a *living* exemplar! How they will envy me! How they will come from all over the world to take a look at my miracle bird; my dear, incredulous colleagues! And what will they offer me to buy it! But no money in the world will be good enough! Not for all the gold of this earth!"

With this proud statement, the old scholar concluded his dithyramb[3] about the ancient bird, which was to be lured out of the egg by the silent, invigorating heat.—

A quiet purring sounded through the room and at the same time, the professor felt Little Gray rub against his knees. Caressing her, he stroked her back; he wanted to make up a little for his neglect. Then, however, he said, "You will have to get used to staying in the kitchen for a while, my dear Little Gray!—you are a very well-behaved pussycat—but there is still a predator hidden under your

---

[3]A dithyramb is wildly enthusiastic speech or writing.

schönen Fell, und noch dazu eins, das eine besondere Vorliebe für junge Vögelchen hat!«

»Grauchen« wollte auf seine Knie springen, um wieder einmal den alten Platz einzunehmen, der ihr jahrelang eingeräumt worden war – aber der alte Herr wehrte ihr, stand auf und öffnete die Tür, um sie hinauszuweisen.

Eben wollte auch Pauline ins Zimmer treten. –

»Liebe Pauline, die Katze müssen wir vorläufig von meinem Zimmer fernhalten; sie ist ja auch in Ihrer Küche gut aufgehoben.«

»Jawohl Herr Professor – wie Sie wünschen! – Herr Professor, ich wollte nur fragen, ob Sie für die nächsten Stunden allein bleiben wollten; ich wollte gern mal meine Verwandten einen Augenblick besuchen –«

»Gehen Sie, gehen Sie, Pauline! Zum Abend sind Sie ja doch wieder hier –«

»Gewiß doch. Dann adieu, Herr Professor!«

Damit ging sie, »Grauchen« auf den Arm hebend, aus dem Zimmer . . .

Pauline, die gute, sorgende Seele, war am Ende mit ihrer Weisheit. Heute hatte sie das Unglaublichste erlebt: der Professor hatte sein Leibgericht: Frikassee vom Huhn – nicht angerührt! Das konnte nicht gut enden! Und alles wegen des unglückseligen Vogeleies!

Nicht ihre Verwandten suchte sie auf, sondern – den alten Hausarzt ihres Herrn, den Sanitätsrat Hartmann. Ihm schüttete sie ihr altes, treues Herz mit all seinen Sorgen aus: wie vor ein paar Tagen der Herr Professor eine große Steinplatte erhalten habe, wie er Tag und Nacht daran herumgemeißelt, um ein Ei herauszukriegen, das darin gesteckt habe, wie er nun seit drei Tagen und Nächten sich keine Ruhe gönne, kaum einen Bissen esse (nicht einmal sein Leibgericht!), wie er die schöne

soft, beautiful fur, and more so, one that has a special taste for young little birds!"

Little Gray wanted to jump on his knees to take up her old place once again, which had been conceded to her for years—but the old man fended her off, got up, and opened the door to send her out.

At that moment, Pauline was just about to enter the room.—

"Dear Pauline, we have to keep the cat away from my study for the time being; she is also in good hands in your kitchen."

"Quite so, Professor—as you wish!—Professor, I only wanted to ask if you could manage by yourself for the next couple of hours; I would like to visit my relatives for a while—"

"Just go, Pauline, go! You will be back in the evening, won't you—"

"Of course. Goodbye then, Professor!"

Having said that she left the room, carrying Little Gray on her arm . . .

Pauline, the kind, caring soul, was at her wits' end. She had witnessed the most incredible thing today: the professor had not touched his favorite dish: chicken fricassee! That *was not* going to end well! And simply because of that unfortunate bird egg!

She was not going to visit her relatives, but instead—her master's long-time family doctor, Dr. Hartman, Counselor of Health.[4] She poured out her old, loyal heart to him, with all its worries: how the professor had received a large slab of stone a couple of days ago; how he had chiseled away on it, day and night, to remove an egg that was hidden within; how he recently hadn't allowed himself any rest for three days and nights and hardly eaten a bite (not even his

---

[4]The German "Sanitätsrat" (Counselor of Health) is a title awarded to health professionals who have earned distinction in their field. It is an honorary title usually awarded by a country's highest authorities (e.g., president, reigning monarch, etc.).

Graukatze, die der Herr Sanitätsrat ja als ein Vermächtnis der Seligen auch kenne, aus dem Zimmer gejagt habe – – und das alles, um das verwünschte Vogelei, das er in einen geheizten Blechkasten gelegt habe, zum Ausbrüten zu bringen! – Sie schloß ihren Bericht mit heißen Tränen und mit der inständigen Bitte, der Herr Sanitätsrat möchte doch einmal ihrem Herrn ins Gewissen reden, ehe es zu spät wäre!

»Schön, Fräulein Pauline, soll geschehen! Gehen Sie immer voraus, ich werde gleich hinterherkommen. Meine Sprechstunde ist ja ohnehin vorüber, und er soll denken, es handle sich um einen gelegentlichen Besuch, den ich nicht als Hausarzt, sondern als sein alter Freund bei ihm mache!«

Als eine Stunde später Sanitätsrat Hartmann die Tür zum Zimmer seines alten Freundes öffnen wollte, vernahm er schon vorher ein in kurzen Absätzen sich wiederholendes Klingelsignal.

Er trat ein, von Pauline gefolgt, die das Zeichen auch gehört hatte. –

Und – da lag der alte Herr, fest schlummernd – und sein weißgelocktes Haupt ruhte auf dem Bilde der Archäopteryx, das oben erwähnt wurde. So fest schlief er, daß er das schrille Klingeln vom Brutapparat nicht vernommen hatte.

Der Sanitätsrat übersah mit einem Blick die Situation. »Da bin ich wohl doch zu rechter Zeit gekommen!« murmelte er. Er sah dem Schlafenden scharf ins Gesicht, prüfte seinen Puls und sagte dann:

»Seien Sie ohne Sorge, Fräulein Pauline, ich kenne seine Natur! Er wird im Schlaf alles Versäumte wieder einholen. Wir wollen ihm hier auf der Chaiselongue ein Lager zurecht machen: morgen um diese Zeit ist er wieder ganz auf dem Posten und wohl auch – vernünftiger!«

Dann trat der alte Sanitätsrat an den Brutofen heran . . . Es gab auch hier manches zu tun –

Ungefähr vierundzwanzig Stunden später erwachte Professor Diluvius.

Verwundert schaute er sich um, fand sich auf der Chaiselongue liegend, sorglich mit Kissen und Decken umgeben. –

Einen Augenblick lang irrten seine Gedanken ratlos umher. Da fiel sein Blick auf den Brutofen auf dem Arbeitstische.

favorite dish!); how he had chased the beautiful gray cat, which the Counselor knew very well was a legacy of his deceased wife, out of his study—and all to try and hatch the accursed bird egg, which he had placed in a heated tin box!—She concluded her report with warm tears and begged the Counselor to talk some sense into her master before it was too late!

"All right, Miss Pauline, it will be done! Go ahead; I'll be along shortly. My consultation hours are already over, and he needs to think that it is a casual visit I'm paying him, not as a family doctor, but as an old friend."

When Counselor of Health Dr. Hartmann opened the door to his old friend's study, he noticed a short, repeating alarm right away.

He entered, followed by Pauline, who also heard the alarm.—

And—there he laid, the old man, napping away—and his white, curly hair resting on the aforementioned image of the Archaeopteryx. He slept so deeply that he had not heard the shrill alarm of the incubator.

With a glance, the Counselor took in the situation. "It looks like I arrived at the right time after all!" he murmured. Looking closely at the face of the sleeping man, he checked his pulse and then said:

"Don't you worry, Miss Pauline, I am familiar with his physical condition! He will catch up on all his missing sleep. Let's make up a bed for him here on the chaise longue; by this time tomorrow he will have recovered completely and might even be—more reasonable!"

Then the old Counselor approached the incubator . . . there was much to do here as well—

Approximately twenty-four hours later, Professor Diluvius awoke.

Astonished, he looked around, found himself lying on the chaise longue, carefully surrounded with pillows and blankets.—

For a moment, his thoughts wandered, perplexed. Then his gaze came to rest on the incubator on top of his desk.

Mit der Gewandtheit eines Jünglings sprang er auf und eilte an den Apparat.

Da lag das Ei – unversehrt, und das Thermometer zeigte die vorschriftsmäßige Brutwärme! Der Herr Professor klingelte. Pauline mußte ganz in der Nähe gewesen sein, so schnell erschien sie.

»Guten Tag, liebe Pauline! Ich habe wohl lange geschlafen?«

»Es geht, lieber Herr Professor! Sie hatten sich wohl ein bißchen auf die Chaiselongue gelegt; ich habe Ihnen dann noch ein paar Kissen gebracht. Als ich von meinen Verwandten kam, da schliefen Sie so schön, daß ich Sie nicht stören wollte. Und da der Brutofen auch in Ordnung war –«

»Ja, richtig, Pauline – ich sehe eben, daß ich den Apparat auf »Selbstregulierung« umgestellt habe, statt auf »Alarm«. Wahrscheinlich habe ich gefühlt, daß ich müde wurde, und habe noch zu rechter Zeit die Umschaltung besorgt. Gott sei Dank, daß alles richtig funktioniert hat! Der Apparat ist doch zuverlässiger als ein Mensch. – Und nun, Paulinchen, besorgen Sie mir etwas zu essen! Haben Sie vielleicht noch Frikassee?«

»Jawohl, jawohl, lieber Herr Professor! Gleich sollen Sie es haben – sofort!«

Und strahlend vor Freude eilte sie in die Küche.

Seit ihr alter Herr Professor wieder Frikassee aß, sorgte sich die gute Pauline nicht mehr um ihn. Und auch er selber hatte den Paroxismus der ersten Tage überwunden, seit er sich überzeugt hatte, daß man sich auf die automatische Regulierung des Brutapparates sicher verlassen konnte.

Erschien er so äußerlich als derselbe kühle und bedächtige Gelehrte wie sonst, so war doch sein Inneres von der aufgehenden Sonne seiner großen Hoffnung erhellt und verklärt!

So gingen die Tage in ruhigem Gleichmaß – und aus den Tagen wurden Wochen . . .

Am Nachmittage des vierundzwanzigsten Tages saß der Professor Diluvius in seinem Arbeitszimmer. Es war ein schwüler Tag, und die Julisonne mit ihrer Glut machte schläfrig. –

Ein leichter Halbschlaf, ein Träumen mit offenen Augen hatte seine Sinne gefangen genommen. Ihm war es, als schöben sich

With the agility of a youth, he jumped up and hurried to the device.

There was the egg—intact, and the thermometer displayed the specified incubation heat! The professor rang for Pauline.

Pauline must have been close by, judging from how quickly she appeared.

"Hello, dear Pauline! I slept quite long, I assume?"

"Just a little bit, dear Professor! You were resting for a moment on the chaise longue; I brought you a few pillows. When I returned from my relatives' house you were sleeping so comfortably that I didn't have the heart to disturb you. And since the incubator seemed alright—"

"Yes, right, Pauline—I just noticed that I switched the device to 'automatic regulation,' instead of 'alarm.' I probably noticed myself getting tired and was able to switch it just in time. Thank God that everything has worked correctly! The device is more reliable than a human, after all.—And now, little Pauline, get me something to eat! Perhaps you still have some fricassee left?"

"Yes, sir, dear Professor! You shall have it—right away!"

And, beaming with pleasure, she hurried into the kitchen.

Since her old professor had started eating fricassee again, Pauline no longer worried. And as far as the professor himself was concerned, he seemed to have overcome the paroxysms of the days before, as now he was sure that the incubator's automatic regulation system was reliable.

Although outwardly he appeared to be the same deliberate and thoughtful scholar he had always been, deep down inside he felt brightened and glorified by the rising sun of his great hope!

So the days passed in a calm and steady rhythm—and the days turned into weeks . . .

On the afternoon of the twenty-fourth day, Professor Diluvius was sitting in his study. It was a muggy, stifling day, and the July sun, with its burning heat, made him sleepy.—

He dozed, half asleep, daydreaming with his eyes open. It seemed to him as if the tapestry-covered walls of his study

die tapetengeschmückten Wände seines Zimmers auseinander
– eine endlose Ferne öffnete sich, und ein Weg lag vor ihm in
ein weites grünes Tal. Seltsame Pflanzen überragten in treib-
hausartiger Fülle und in wunderlich-grotesken Formen den
Pfad. Zu seinen Füßen webte und lebte es und in dem Urwalddi-
ckicht regte und bewegte es sich von phantastischen, niegesehenen
Lebewesen.

Plötzlich fiel ein gleitender Schatten auf seinen Weg.

Ein fliegendes Geschöpf schwang sich von einem der seltsamen Baumstämme hinüber zum andern.

Metallisch grün glänzte sein Gefieder, besonders der lange,
wie ein Palmwedel geformte Schwanz. Nun flog das seltsame
Wesen dicht über dem Haupte des Wandernden hinweg und
hängte sich an einen der kandelaberartig verzweigten Stämme.

Da hing es mit zusammengeschlagenen Flügeln – an den langen, scharfen Krallen, die aus den Schwungfedern dicht am
Flügelgelenk hervorragten. Und als es jetzt den Schnabel öffnete, um eine erhaschte Beute zu verspeisen, zeigten sich deutlich darin die spitzen, weißen Zähne.

»Archäopteryx!« kam es unbewußt von den Lippen des
Gelehrten.

Und noch in die letzten Sekunden seines Halbtraumes hinein
tönte – ein scharfes Klirren, wie von plötzlich zerbrechendem
Glase!

Professor Diluvius fuhr empor. Eben huschte ein Schatten an
seinem noch halb geschlossenen Augen vorbei.

War sein Traum beglückende Wirklichkeit geworden? Er
stürzte nach dem Brutapparat – da lag die zerbrochene Eierschale, die das ausgeschlüpfte Geschöpfchen abgestreift hatte.
– Wo aber war es? – Und wie hatte es die Glasscheiben des Ap-
parats zerbrechen können?

In fieberhafter Eile durchsuchte er alle Ecken und alle Schlupf-
winkel seines Studierzimmers – umsonst!

Er kroch in den Kamin – Auch da nichts.

Er stellte einen Stuhl auf den Tisch und untersuchte die Auf-
sätze seiner Spinden und die Falten der Stoffgardinen – Alles
vergebens!

Da – unter der Chaiselongue – ein Geräusch!

were pushing apart—opening up to reveal an endless distance, and before him lay a path leading into a vast, green valley. Bizarre plants in greenhouse-like abundance and in strangely grotesque shapes were hanging over the path. It weaved and lived under his feet, and the thick jungle stirred and moved with fantastic creatures never seen before.

Suddenly, a gliding shadow dropped onto his path.

A flying creature was swinging from one of the weird and wonderful tree trunks to the next.

Its plumage shimmered metallic green, especially the long tail that was shaped like a palm leaf. Just now, the strange creature was flying closely over the wanderer to cling onto one of the tree trunks that branched out like candelabras.

From there it dangled, suspended with folded wings—on its long, sharp talons which protruded from the flight feathers close to the joints. And as it was opening its beak to eat the quarry it had snatched, the sharp, white teeth in it were unmistakably visible.

"Archaeopteryx!" the lips of the scholar unconsciously mouthed.

Suddenly, into the last moments of his doze sounded—a sharp clang, as of glass shattering!

Professor Diluvius sat bolt upright. Just then, a shadow flitted by his half-closed eyes.

Had his dream become exciting reality? He rushed to the incubator—there were the broken egg shells which the hatched little creature had shed.—But, where was it?—And how had it managed to destroy the glass panes of the incubator?

In a feverish hurry, he searched all the corners and nooks in his study—to no avail!

He squeezed into the chimney—nothing was there either!

He placed a chair on top of the table and examined the area above his lockers and the folds of the fabric curtains—all in vain!

There—under the chaise longue—a noise!

Schnell faßte er zu –

Und seine zitternden Hände fassen – fassen – »Grauchen«, die Hauskatze, die sich unbemerkt eingeschlichen hat!

Sie leckt sich noch die blutige Schnauze – –

Einen Augenblick steht Professor Diluvius starr wie eine Bildsäule. Die weißen Locken ringeln sich wie Medusenhaare um seine marmorblassen Züge. Dann aber kehrt ihm Leben und Besinnung zurück. Seine grauen Augen sprühen Blitze! In namenloser Wut packt er jetzt die Übeltäterin im Genick. Wie ein Rasender stürmt er umher.

»Pauline,« ruft er, heiser vor Aufregung, »Pauline!«

Pauline stürzt entsetzt ins Zimmer.

»Die Bestie – hat sich hier eingeschlichen – hat die Glasscheibe des Brutofens eingedrückt – und – meine – eben – ausgebrütete Archäopteryx – gefressen!«

In einzelnen Absätzen hat er die Worte hervorgestoßen.

– Und halb wahnsinnig vor Enttäuschung und Erbitterung setzte er hinzu:

»Ich werde das heimtückische Vieh töten und sezieren, um wenigstens die zermalmten Überreste meines kostbaren Urvogels zu retten!«

Und er schüttelt »Grauchen«, die sich vergebens aus den eisernen Klammern seiner Hände zu befreien sucht.

»O, du Bestie, du vermaledeite, hinterlistige Bestie! Das sollst du mir büßen! Das sollst du mir büßen!«

Pauline stand mit gefalteten Händen vor dem Wütenden.

»Herr Professor, lieber, guter Herr Professor –«

»Auch Sie haben Schuld, Pauline! Warum haben Sie nicht besser acht gegeben auf das schändliche Vieh? – Meine Archäopterix, meine Sehnsucht, mein Traum und meine Hoffnung – die Frucht aller meiner wochenlangen Mühen und Sorgen! Das Geschenk ungezählter Jahrtausende, mir beschert durch die Gunst des Geschicks – gefressen von – einer mordlustigen Katze!«

Er trat an den Apparat.

»Da liegen die Scherben meines Glückes!« Tausende hätten mich beneidet um diesen Schatz – und nun« – –

Quickly, he closed his hands around it—

And his shaking hands catch—catch—Little Gray, the house cat who had slipped in unseen!

She is still licking her bloody snout—

For a split second, Professor Diluvius stands rigid, like an ornamented column. His white locks curl around his marble white features like the hair of Medusa. But then, his consciousness and senses return. His gray eyes throw daggers! In a blind rage, he grabs the evildoer by the neck. Like a madman, he dashes back and forth.

"Pauline," he shouts, hoarse with agitation. "Pauline!"

Aghast, Pauline storms into the room.

"The beast—sneaked in here—broke the glass pane of the incubator—and—has—*eaten*—my—freshly—hatched—Archaeopteryx!"

He uttered the words in disjointed chunks.

—And, half-crazy with disappointment and exasperation, he added:

"I will kill and perform an autopsy on the treacherous brute to salvage at least the mauled remains of my precious first bird!"

And he shook Little Gray, who tried, in vain, to free himself from the iron grip of his hands.

"Oh, you monster, you accursed, deceitful monster! You'll pay for this! You'll pay for this!"

Pauline stood before the furious man with her hands folded.

"Professor, dear, good Professor—"

"It's your fault too, Pauline! Why didn't you do a better job supervising the blameworthy beast?—My Archaeopteryx, my aspiration, my dream, and my hope—the fruit of all my toils and troubles that lasted these past weeks! The present of countless millennia, bestowed upon me through the grace of fate—eaten by—a bloodthirsty cat!"

He went to the incubator.

"There they are, the broken glass shards of my luck! Thousands would have envied me for this treasure—and now"—

»Herr Professor –«

»Zu denken, daß es glücklich ausgebrütet wurde – daß es lebte! Und ich habe es nicht einmal lebend gesehen! Nicht lebend gesehen! O, mein Archäopteryx!« – –

»Herr Professor, lieber guter Herr Professor,« begann Pauline wieder, und aus den Augen der treuen Dienerin rollten die Tränen – »hören Sie mich an: Es war gar nicht das Ei von dem unaussprechlichen Vieh, das – Sie ausgebrütet haben.« –

Professor Diluvius ließ die Katze los und starrte seine Köchin mit weit aufgerissenen Augen an.

»Herr Professor,« fuhr Pauline fort – »schon vor drei Wochen, als sie einmal so sehr fest eingeschlafen waren, ist das entzweigegangen! Der Herr Sanitätsrat war gerade hier, um Sie zu besuchen. Er sagte, die Hitze in dem Blechkasten wäre zu groß geworden, weil er aber fürchtete, daß der Ärger über den Verlust Ihnen schaden könnte, hat er ein anderes Ei mit Tinte betüpfelt und in den Brutkasten gelegt. Der Vogel, der heute ausgekommen ist, war – eine Ente!«

"Professor—"

"To think that it had managed to hatch—that it lived! And I didn't even see it alive! Didn't see it alive! Oh, my Archaeopteryx!"—

"Professor, dear, good Professor," Pauline began again, and tears rolled down the cheeks of the loyal servant— "Listen to me: It wasn't the egg of the unpronounceable brute that—you hatched."—

Professor Diluvius let the cat go and stared at his cook, his eyes wide open.

"Professor," Pauline continued—"it already broke three weeks ago, that day when you had been sleeping so deeply! The Counselor of Health was here to visit you. He said the temperature in the tin box had gotten too hot, but since he was afraid that the anger over the loss would be too painful for you, he painted ink dots onto a different egg and placed it into the incubator. The bird that hatched today was—a *duck!*"

ALFRED HENSCHKE (AKA KLABUND)

German poet, dramatist, lyricist, and narrator Alfred Henschke was born in 1890 in Crossen an der Oder (modern-day Krosno Odrzańskie, Poland) as the son of a pharmacist. At sixteen he developed a lung disease, almost certainly tuberculosis. The ailment became a defining factor in his life, forcing him to frequently spend time in Swiss sanatoriums. After high school, he studied philosophy and literature in Munich and Lausanne; later, he earned a living in Munich and Berlin as a freelance writer. In May of 1928 he developed pneumonia, and because the tuberculosis had never been completely cured, the infection became life-threatening. Although he was taken to Davos, Switzerland, for treatment,[1] his condition deteriorated further, and he died with his second wife Carola Neher by his side.

Henschke's style was heavily influenced by both Impressionism[2] and Expressionism. He was also a close friend of the famous writer and poet Gottfried Benn, who delivered the eulogy at his burial. He was often entangled in moral and political scandals—once he was even accused of blasphemy, which at that time was a criminal offense.

---

[1] Its mild climate together with its altitude (at 5,118 ft., Davos is the highest city in Europe) has made Davos an ideal location for treating respiratory diseases.

[2] Impressionistic literature, often referred to as stream of consciousness literature, is characterized by an author's attempt to focus the story on the character's impressions, feelings, sensations, thoughts, and emotions through the character's own eyes.

Like many of his generation, Henschke had euphorically welcomed the war.[3] He intended to support the volunteer army with adaptations of Chinese war songs as well as his own compositions. However, his fanaticism cooled off as the war dragged on, and he ultimately became disenchanted with it. By 1916 he had become an outspoken pacifist. (In this he was influenced by Brunhilde Irene, his first wife; he preferred to use her second name, Irene, meaning "peaceful".) In 1917 Henschke published an open letter in the *Neue Zürcher Zeitung* (*New Zurich Newspaper*) to the German emperor, asking him to abdicate. Not surprisingly, Henschke was indicted with high treason and lese majeste. He was saved from execution by the 1918 Armistice, after which the German emperor fled.

Klabund is a common family name among pharmacists in the northern and northeastern parts of Germany. But Henschke chose the nom de plume Klabund in 1912 for a different reason. Klabund is a combination of the words "Klabautermann," referring to a ship's goblin, and "Vagabund," referring to a vagabond.

As Klabund, he wrote twenty-five plays and fourteen novels—most of which were published only posthumously—including narratives, numerous adaptations, and works on the history of literature. The most recent publication of his works was a complete edition in eight volumes, released between 1998 and 2003.

In "Der Bär" ("The Bear," 1924), Klabund tells of a circus family that arrives in a small German town to give performances, only to find that declaring war on Russia has completely wiped out any interest the townspeople might have had in their shows. The star attraction, Hugo the bear, is immediately affected by the townpeople's lack of enthusiasm for peaceful pastimes. Klabund's factual and unemotional description suggests

---

[3] "World War I gave new ferocity and intensity to the Expressionist movement. Initially there was belief that the upheavals would bring about a new civilisation. . . . The reality of war, however, turned many Expressionists against it." ("German Expressionism," accessed August 16, 2011, http://www.trashface.com/germanexpressionism.html).

that the bear's fate parallels the fate of the townspeople as the rah-rah patriotism of early twentieth-century imperial Germany is replaced by slow starvation.

ALFRED HENSCHKE (AKA KLABUND)

Der Bär

Diese Geschichte beginnt wie ein Märchen der Brüder Grimm. Es ist aber kein Märchen. Es ist auch keine rechte Geschichte mit dem nötigen Schlußpunkt: eine runde Geschichte etwa, rund und durchsichtig wie eine Glaskugel, mit einer schillernden Moral. Diese Geschichte ist nämlich (beinahe) wahr und hat sich zugetragen in der kleinen Stadt, in der ich kürzlich zu Besuch weilte. Sie ist nichts als eine traurige und lächerliche Arabeske zu dem erhabenen Ereignis des Krieges, das sich draußen (weit von hier, die kleine Stadt weiß nicht wo . . .) abspielt.

An dem Tage, an dem Deutschland an Rußland den Krieg erklärte, traf in der kleinen Stadt der weit- und weltberühmte Zauberer Francesco Salandrini ein, welcher dort eine Vorstellung seiner großen und geheimen Künste zu geben gedachte. Er vermochte Wasser in Wein und Wein in Wasser zu verwandeln. Er zog den Bauernburschen auf dem Lande und den verblüfften Jünglingen und den kichernden Fräuleins der kleinen Städte nur so die Taler aus Nase und Ohren und ließ sie klappernd in seinen schwarz polierten Zylinder springen, obgleich offensichtlich zutage trat, daß er selber nicht im Besitze eines einzigen dieser silbernen Dinger war. Er zerschlug in seinem bereits erwähnten Zylinder, dem man gewisse magische Kräfte nicht absprechen durfte, ein halbes Dutzend roher Eier und buk ohne Feuer und ohne Pfanne in nichts als eben diesem Zylinder einen veritablen wohlschmeckenden Eierkuchen.

ALFRED HENSCHKE (AKA KLABUND)

The Bear

This story begins like one of the Grimm Brothers' fairy tales. However, it is not a fairy tale. And neither is it a proper story with the required ending: a rounded story, for example, round and transparent like a crystal ball, with an iridescent moral. This story is (almost) true and happened in the little town which I recently visited. It is nothing but a sad and ridiculous embellishment compared to the grand event of the war that is happening out there—far away, in a place the little town does not know.

On the same day that Germany declared war on Russia, the well-known and world-famous magician Francesco Salandrini arrived in the little town; it had been his intention to give a performance of his great and secret arts in that very place. Supposedly, he had the capability of turning water into wine and wine into water. He amazed the townspeople and pulled coins from the noses and ears of the town's baffled young men and nervously laughing young ladies, and then he had the coins leap into his black top hat with a clacking sound, even though it became quite apparent that he himself was not in possession of a single one of these silvery objects. In said top hat, which certainly had magical powers that could not be discounted, he cracked half a dozen raw eggs and, without a flame or a frying pan and in nothing else but this top hat, he cooked a mouth-watering omelet, if truth be told.

Herrn Salandrinis Gefährt, das mit einigen kleinen Fenstern versehen und ziegelrot angestrichen war, rollte, von einem schwermütigen und betagten Pferde gezogen, über die Oderbrücke rumpelnd in die Stadt ein. In seiner Begleitung befanden sich noch seine Frau Bella, die Schlangendame, die schwebende Jungfrau, das überirdische Medium und eine Person, welche den prosaischen Namen Hugo führte.

Herr Salandrini, der sich mit Weltgeschichte und Politik noch nie in seinem Leben befaßt hatte (und es auch fürder nicht zu tun gedachte, da er Steuern zu zahlen weder willens noch fähig war), verwunderte sich nicht wenig, die kleine Stadt in heller Aufregung zu finden. Alle Leute liefen durcheinander, die Kinder schrien und sangen, und die Frauen sahen besorgt aus den Fenstern.

Nichtsdestoweniger lenkte Herr Salandrini seinen Wagen ruhig und besonnen nach dem Salzplatz, wo an Jahrmärkten die Würfelbuden prunken und die Karussels sich munter drehen, um dort sein »Interessantes Wundertheater« aufzuschlagen.

Er hatte mit Hilfe der schwebenden Jungfrau gerade den ersten Pflock in die Erde getrieben, einen Strick darum geschlungen und Hugo daran gebunden, als sich federnden Schrittes der dicke Polizist Neumann nahte, der ihn ebenso bestimmt wie freundlich darauf aufmerksam machte, daß er sich die weitere Mühe der Errichtung seines »Interessanten Wundertheaters« sparen könne. Der Krieg sei erklärt. Die für heute abend angesagte Vorstellung könne vom Bürgermeister in Anbetracht der ernsten Zeitumstände nicht mehr gestattet werden. Es gehe jetzt um andere Dinge als um den Eierkuchen im Zylinder oder um den gedankenlesenden Bären Hugo. Kein Mensch habe Lust, sich derlei abenteuerlichen Unsinn jetzt anzusehen. Er möge sein »Interessantes Wundertheater« bis auf günstigere Zeiten suspendieren. Damit entfernte sich der Polizist Neumann, freundlich und bestimmt, wie er gekommen war.

Herr Salandrini war wie vor den Kopf geschlagen. Die Möglichkeit eines internationalen Konfliktes, der ihn um Beruf und Brot bringen konnte, hatte er nie im entferntesten

Mr. Salandrini's circus caravan, which was equipped with several little windows and had been given a brick-red coat of paint, rolled into town traversing the Oder Bridge, drawn by a melancholy and elderly horse. In his company were also his wife Bella, the snake lady, the levitating assistant, the supernatural medium, and an individual with the mundane name of Hugo.

Mr. Salandrini, who had never before in his life concerned himself with the affairs of the world and politics—and had not planned on doing so in the future, since he was neither willing to pay taxes nor was he able to—was more than a little surprised to find the town in a state of agitation. Everybody was running around in disarray; children were crying and hollering, and women looked anxiously out of their windows.

Nevertheless, quiet and cool-headed, Mr. Salandrini led his trailer to the Salt Square, where gambling booths sit proudly and merry-go-rounds turn briskly during carnivals, in order to set up his "Interesting Magical Theater."

With the help of the levitating assistant, he had just forced the first peg into the ground, fixed a piece of rope around it, and tied Hugo up, when Neumann, the corpulent police officer, approached with a spring in his step and pointed out in a way that was equally authoritative and friendly that Mr. Salandrini could spare himself further efforts to set up his "Interesting Magical Theater." War had been declared. The performance that had been announced for tonight could no longer be permitted due to the grave circumstances of the current situation. At this time, things other than an omelet in a top hat or a mind-reading bear named Hugo were of importance. Nobody was inclined to watch a performance of such audacious nonsense. He should suspend his "Interesting Magical Theater" until a better time. Having said that, Officer Neumann strode away, as friendly and authoritative as when he had arrived.

Mr. Salandrini was taken aback. He had never taken into account the possibility of an international conflict that might cost him his occupation and rob him of his liv-

in Berechnung gezogen. Auch Hugo, der gedankenlesende und wahrsagende Bär, hatte ihn davon in Kenntnis zu setzen verabsäumt, ja, er schien selber noch nichts von dem drohenden Unheil, das sich auch über seinem Haupte in dunklen Wolken zusammenballte, zu ahnen. Er saß klein und verhungert neben dem Pflock, knabberte wie ein Kind an seinen Pfotennägeln und starrte mit jenem Ausdruck beseelten Stumpfsinns vor sich hin, der unsere Lachmuskeln eben so reizt, wie er unser Grauen erweckt.

Herr Salandrini setzte sich auf die Wagendeichsel und sann den ganzen Tag, was er nun anfangen solle, um sich und seine Familie durchzubringen. Er hieß eigentlich Schorsch Krautwickerl und war aus Bamberg. Zum Heeresdienst würde man ihn nicht mehr einziehen, dazu war er zu alt. Im übrigen war er sich sehr klar, daß er augenblicklich bei niemand auf Verständnis und Teilnahme für seine merkwürdigen Kartenkunststücke und die erstaunliche Begabung des gedankenlesenden Bären Hugo zu zählen habe.

Er sann mehrere Tage. Dann ging er auf das Bürgermeisteramt und bat um irgendeine, wenn auch die geringste, Arbeit. Die schwebende Jungfrau und der Bär blieben in banger Erwartung zurück. Sie teilte schwesterlich mit ihm eine alte Brotkruste.

Herr Salandrini kehrte mit der frohen Botschaft zurück, daß er als Koksarbeiter bei der städtischen Gasanstalt Verwendung gefunden habe. Das war wenigstens etwas, wenn auch nicht viel, denn das Gehalt, das Herr Salandrini empfing, reichte kaum für einen Magen (der Bedarf an Koksarbeitern ist schon im Frieden nicht nennenswert).

Wenn also die schwebende Jungfrau zur Not noch mit versorgt war – vielleicht fände sie in der Stadt eine Stelle als Aufwaschfrau? –, was sollte aus dem kleinen, sowieso schon halb verhungerten Bären, ihrem Liebling, Kapital und Abgott werden?

ing, not even remotely. Hugo, the mind-reading and fortune-telling bear, had also failed to let him know him this; he didn't even give the impression of having the slightest misgivings toward the doom that was forming in sinister clouds above his head. He sat next to the peg, diminutive and starving, nibbling on his claws like a child and staring into space with an expression of soulful monotony that provokes laughter as much as it arouses dread.

Mr. Salandrini sat down on the drawbar of his circus caravan and meditated the entire day on what steps he should take in order to make ends meet for himself and his family. As a matter of fact, his real name was Georg "Schorsch" Stuffedcabbage and he was originally from Bamberg.[1] He would not be drafted into military service because he was too old for it. For the rest, it was crystal clear in his mind that at the moment he would not be able to count on sympathy for or interest in his weird and wonderful card tricks and the amazing talents of the mind-reading bear Hugo, not from anybody.

He mulled this over for several days. Then he went to the town hall and asked for any, even the most menial, job. The levitating assistant and the bear stayed back in fearful anticipation. Like a sister, she shared an old bread crust with him.

Mr. Salandrini returned with the good news that he had found a job as a charcoal worker in the town's gasworks. That was at least something, though not a lot, because the salary Mr. Salandrini received was hardly enough to fill one mouth—the demand for charcoal workers is not noteworthy even in peaceful times.

Even if the levitating assistant could take care of herself—possibly she might be able to find a job in the town as a cleaning woman—what would become of the little bear who was already half starved, their beloved, asset, and idol?

---

[1]Bamberg is a city in Bavaria, Germany. It is located in Upper Franconia on the river Regnitz, close to its confluence with the river Main. Bamberg prides itself with being on seven hills, as it symbolizes a similarity to Rome.

Am nächsten Tage erschien in der Zeitung ein Inserat: »Edle Herrschaften werden um Abfälle gebeten für den wahrsagenden Bären des Zauberers Salandrini.«

So sättigte sich der Bär Hugo von nun ab an den Abfällen edler Herrschaften, die ihm nicht so reichlich zukamen, daß sie ihn völlig befriedigten. Er saß auf dem Salzplatz, an seinen Pflock gebunden, unter Aufsicht der schwebenden Jungfrau, welche Wäsche ausbesserte, und der Herbstregen wusch seinen Pelz. Es wurde Spätherbst, und der Bär fror. Sein Pelz zitterte und seine müden Augen sahen furchtsam zum bleiernen Himmel empor. Die schwebende Jungfrau weinte.

Da kam Herr Salandrini auf einen guten Gedanken. Er war ja Koksarbeiter an der Gasanstalt. Er bat den Magistrat um Erlaubnis, den Bären in einen leeren warmen Raum der Gasanstalt, neben den großen Öfen, unterbringen zu dürfen. Der Magistrat, der sich von der Harmlosigkeit des halb verhungerten und schwächlichen kleinen Bären längst überzeugt hatte, gab die Einwilligung, und der Bär hockte nun hinter einer hölzernen Gittertür und blickte mit traurigen Augen in die feurige Glut der Öfen. Hin und wieder besuchten ihn die Kinder des Gasanstaltsinspektors und brachten ihm ein Stück Kriegsbrot oder Küchenreste. Er fraß alles, was ihm zwischen die Zähne gestopft wurde.

Eines Morgens aber lag er tot hinter dem Gitter, und das rosa Licht der Öfen tanzte über sein dunkelbraunes spärliches Fell.

Herr Salandrini war erschüttert, aber als Koksarbeiter hatte er keine Zeit zu langen Meditationen. Die schwebende Jungfrau warf sich schreiend über den toten Bären und das ganze sah aus wie ein Bild von Piloty.

Ob der Bär an Gasvergiftung oder an Unterernährung zugrunde ging, war nicht festzustellen.

Herr Rechtsanwalt K. kaufte Herrn Salandrini das Bärenfell samt dem Kopfe ab. Herr K. ist im Begriff, die Stadt zu verlassen

The next day, an announcement appeared in the newspaper: "The nobility is hereby asked to donate scraps for the fortune-telling bear of the Magician Sandrini.

Henceforth, the bear fed on scraps from the nobility, but there were not enough to satisfy him completely. He sat in the Salt Square, tied to his peg and supervised by the levitating assistant who mended clothes while the fall rain cleaned his skin. Late fall arrived and the bear was cold. His skin shivered and his tired eyes looked up at the leaden sky with fear. The levitating assistant cried.

Then Mr. Salandrini had a great idea. After all, he was a charcoal worker at the gasworks. He asked the magistrate for permission to house the bear in one of the empty, warm rooms of the gasworks plant, next to the big boilers. The magistrate, who had already assured himself that the half-starved and frail little bear was harmless, gave his consent, and so the bear was now sitting behind a wooden lattice door, looking into the blazing flames of the boilers. Now and again, the children of the director of the gasworks came to visit and brought him a piece of war bread or kitchen scraps. He ate everything that was stuffed into his mouth.

One morning, however, he lay dead behind the bars, and the pink light of the boilers danced over his dark brown, thin skin.

Mr. Salandrini was distressed, but as a charcoal worker he didn't have a lot of time to dwell on it. The levitating assistant screamed and threw herself over the dead bear, and the whole scene looked like an image from Piloty.[2]

It could not be determined if the bear had died of gas poisoning or of malnutrition.

Attorney-at-law Mr. K. purchased the bear skin, including the head, from Mr. Salandrini. Mr. K. is about to leave

---

[2]Karl Theodor von Piloty (October 1, 1826 - July 21, 1886) was a German painter. He was the foremost representative of the realistic school in Germany, most notably of historical subjects. Among well-known paintings of Piloty are *The Death of Wallenstein and the The Death of Caesar*.

und in Z. eine neue Praxis aufzunehmen. Er wird sich das Fell des wahrsagenden Bären Hugo in seinem Herrenzimmer an die Wand nageln, und wenn er Freunde bei sich zu Gast hat, wird er mit einer großen Gebärde auf das Fell deuten, seine Zigarrenasche nachlässig abschlagen und zerstreut zu erzählen beginnen:

»Als ich noch in den schwarzen Bergen Bären jagte ...«

the town in order to open a new practice in Z. He will mount the skin of the fortune-telling bear Hugo on the wall of his study and when he has friends over, he will point to the skin with a dramatic gesture, knock off the ashes of his cigar, and begin to tell absent-mindedly, "When I was still hunting for bears in the Black Mountains . . ."

GEORG BRITTING

Georg Britting was born and raised in Regensburg, a Bavarian city with a long history predating the Roman conquest of Germany. Starting at age twenty in 1911, he published poems, feature pages, and book and drama reviews in the liberal daily paper *Regensburger Neuesten Nachrichten* (*Regensburg Latest News*). In 1914 he enlisted as a volunteer for World War I. After the war ended in 1918, he joined the workers and soldiers union in his hometown and reviewed drama for the left-leaning *Neue Donau Post* (*New Danube Courier*).

He became co-editor of *Die Sichel* (*The Scythe*), a magazine for poetry and graphics, which published his first story, "Marion," in 1921. Later that year, he moved to Munich and began work as a freelance writer. While less successful with plays such as "Das Storchennest" ("The Stork's Nest," 1922), his poems and prose were in high demand and even included in textbook selections for public schools.

He managed to keep publishing during the Third Reich, despite his leftist views. After the war, he married German actress Ingeborg Fröhlich and also became a founding member of the prestigious "Bayerische Akademie der Schönen Künste" (Bavarian Academy of Fine Arts). Throughout his career, he mentored younger and lesser-known fellow writers.

Britting was undoubtedly a master writer, as was indicated by the honors bestowed upon him. Among many other awards, he received the Munich Poets Award (1935), the prestigious Order of Merit of the Federal Republic of Germany - Cross of Merit, First Class (1959), and the Order of Merit of Bavaria (1961).

By the time he died in 1964, he had earned his place in the pantheon[1] of famous German writers.

Although Britting did not write in dialect, the syntax and vocabulary of his artistic compositions mirror the peculiarities of his southern German idiom. As a poet, Britting was a master of concentrated and compact expression, which rubbed off on his prose. He is able to create a disturbing, often grotesque, and sometimes horrifying plotline developed within an apparently unspoiled and harmonious setting, in which evil can replace good within the blink of an eye.

"Brudermord im Altwasser" ("Fratricide in the Backwater," 1929) illustrates this paradigm perfectly. It opens with a powerful description of a primeval landscape that reveals itself to be a mini-cosmos ruled by an unending struggle for survival, governed by the laws of hunting and being hunted. It is a world of predators and victims, wherein there is no ideal and evil always lurks just beneath the surface. One hot summer afternoon, three teenage brothers stumble onto the scene, and the struggle of life and death they set in motion changes their lives forever.

---

[1]In 2000, Georg Britting's bust was placed into the Bavarian "Ruhmeshalle" (hall of fame). The "Ruhmeshalle" honors Bavarians who have made significant contributions to the Bavarian state.

GEORG BRITTING

Brudermord im Altwasser

Das sind grünschwarze Tümpel, von Weiden überhangen, von Wasserjungfern übersurrt, das heißt: wie Tümpel und kleine Weiher, und auch große Weiher, ist es anzusehen, und ist es doch nur Donauwasser, durch Steindämme abgesondert, vom großen, grünen Strom, Altwasser, wie man es in der Gegend nennt. Fische gibt es im Altwasser, viele, Fischkönig ist der Bürstling, ein Raubtier mit zackiger, kratzender Rückenflosse, mit bösen Augen, einem gefräßigen Maul, grünschwarz schillernd wie das Wasser, darin er jagt. Und wie heiß es hier im Sommer ist! Die Weiden schlucken den Wind, der draußen über dem Strom immer geht. Und aus dem Schlamm steigt ein Geruch wie Fäulnis und Kot und Tod. Kein besserer Ort ist zu finden für Knabenspiele als dieses gründämmerige Gebiet. Und hier geschah, was ich jetzt erzähle.

Die drei Hofberger Buben, elfjährig, zwölfjährig, dreizehnjährig, waren damals im August jeden Tag auf den heißen Steindämmen, hockten unter den Weiden, waren Indianer im Dickicht und Wurzelgeflecht, pflückten Brombeeren, die schwarzfeucht, stachlig geschützt, glänzten, schlichen durch das Schilf, das in hohen Stangen wuchs, schnitten sich Weidenruten, rauften, schlugen auch wohl einmal dem Jüngsten, dem Elfjährigen, eine tiefe Schramme, dass sein Gesicht rot beschmiert war wie eine Menschenfressermaske, brachen wie Hirsche und schreiend durch Buschwerk und Graben zur breit fließenden Donau vor, wuschen den blutigen Kopf, und die Haare deckten die Wunde

GEORG BRITTING

Fratricide in the Backwater

There are these greenish black pools, overhung with willows and more than full of activity with the whirring of
dragonflies, meaning: it looks as if these were pools and
little ponds, and even big ponds and, nevertheless, it is only
the waters of the Danube separated from the large, green
river by embankments of stone; "backwater," they call it
around here. There are fish aplenty in the backwater; the
king of fish is the perch, a predator with a jagged, scratchy
dorsal fin, malevolent eyes, and a rapacious mouth, greenish black like the water in which it hunts. And how hot it is
in the summer! The willows swallow up the wind that provides a constant draft out over the river. And from the mud
rises an odor like decay and dung and death. There is no
better place for boys' games than this green and dusky site.
And what happened here is what I am going to tell you.

At that time in August, the three Hofberg boys, eleven,
twelve, and thirteen, were outside everyday on the hot embankments of stone, squatting under willows, playing Indi-
ans in the thicket and network of roots, picking blackberries
protected by thorns that glistened black and wet, creeping
through the reeds that grew in tall stakes, cutting down wil-
low withes, fighting, even cutting a deep mark into the face
of the youngest one, the eleven year old, so it was smeared
red like a cannibal's mask, bursting through the shrubs
and ditches all the way to the wide Danube, cleaning the
bloody head so that hair covered the wound, and reconcil-

dann, und waren gleich wieder versöhnt. Die Eltern durften natürlich nichts erfahren von solchen bösen Streichen, und sie lachten alle drei und vereinbarten wie immer:»Zu Hause sagen wir aber nichts davon.«

Die Altwässer ziehen sich stundenweit die Donau entlang. Bei einem Streifzug einmal waren die drei tief in die Wildnis vorgedrungen, tiefer als je zuvor, bis zu einem Weiher, größer, als sie je einen gesehen hatten, schwarz der Wasserspiegel, und am Ufer lag ein Fischerboot angekettet. Den Pfahl, an dem die Kette hing, rissen sie aus dem schlammigen Boden, warfen Kette und Pfahl ins Boot, stiegen ein, ein Ruder lag auch dabei, und ruderten in die Mitte des Weihers hinaus. Nun waren sie Seeräuber und träumten und brüteten wilde Pläne. Die Sonne schien auf ihre bloßen Köpfe, das Boot lag unbeweglich, unbeweglich stand das Schilf am jenseitigen Ufer, Staunzen fuhren leise summend durch die Luft, kleine Blutsauger, aber die abgehärteten Knaben spürten die Stiche nicht mehr. Der Dreizehnjährige begann, das Boot leicht zu schaukeln. Gleich wiegten die beiden anderen sich mit, auf und nieder, Wasserringe liefen über den Weiher, Wellen schlugen platschend ans Ufer, die Binsen schwankten und wackelten. Die Knaben schaukelten heftiger, dass der Bootsrand bis zum Wasserspiegel sich neigte, das aufgeregte Wasser ins Boot hineinschwappte. Der Kleinste, der Elfjährige, hatte einen Fuß auf den Bootsrand gesetzt und tat juchzend seine Schaukelarbeit. Da gab der Älteste dem Zwölfjährigen ein Zeichen, den Kleinen zu erschrecken, und plötzlich warfen sich beide auf die Bootsseite, wo der Kleine stand, und das Boot neigte sich tief, und dann lag der Jüngste im Wasser und schrie, und ging unter und schlug von unten gegen das Boot, und schrie nicht mehr und pochte nicht mehr und kam auch nicht mehr unter dem Boot hervor, unter dem Boot nicht mehr hervor, nie mehr. Die beiden Brüder saßen stumm und käsegelb auf den Ruderbänken in der prallen Sonne, ein Fisch schnappte, sprang über das Wasser hinaus.

Die Wasserringe hatten sich verlaufen, die Binsen standen wieder unbeweglich, die Staunzen summten bös und stachen.

ing at once. Naturally, the parents must not hear of those evil pranks, and the three of them laughed and made a deal, as always, saying, "At home, we won't even bring it up."

The backwater runs for hours alongside the Danube. On one of their excursions, the three had pressed forward deep into the wilderness, deeper than they ever had gone before, until they arrived at a pond that was the largest they had ever seen; the surface of the water was black, and a fishing boat was chained at the shore. From the muddy ground, they ripped up the pole on which the chain hung, threw the chain and pole into the boat, embarked, as it came with an oar, and rowed to the middle of the pond. They were pirates now and they dreamed of, and hatched, wild plans. The sun burnt down on their bare heads, the boat lay unmoving, unmoving stood the reeds on the opposite shore, mosquitoes trailed through the air humming silently, little bloodsuckers, but the hardy boys didn't feel the stings anymore. The thirteen year old began to rock the boat, softly. Right away the two other joined in the rocking, up and down, water rings ran over the surface of the pond, waves swashed ashore, the reeds moved back and forth and quivered. The boys rocked the boat more vehemently, so that the edge of the boat leaned down past the surface of the water, making it spill into the boat. The smallest of them, the eleven year old, had placed a foot on the edge of the boat and, shouting cheerfully, performed his task of rocking. That was when the oldest one motioned to the twelve year old, and, without prior notice, they both threw themselves onto the side of the boat where the little one stood and the boat leaned down low, and subsequently the youngest one was lying in the water, yelling, and he went under water and thumped at the boat from underneath, and then did not yell anymore and did not thump at the boat anymore, and did not emerge from underneath the boat anymore, would never again. The two brothers were sitting, unresponsive and white as sheets on the thwarts in the blazing sun; a fish snapped and jumped across the water.

The water rings had subsided, the reeds stood unmoving, the mosquitoes buzzed maliciously and stung. The brothers

Die Brüder ruderten das Boot wieder ans Ufer, trieben den Pfahl mit der Kette wieder in den Uferschlamm, stiegen aus, trabten auf dem langen Steindamm dahin, trabten stadteinwärts, wagten nicht sich anzusehen, liefen hintereinander, achteten der Weiden nicht, die ihnen ins Gesicht schlugen, nicht der Brombeersträucherstacheln, die an ihnen rissen, stolperten über Wurzelschlangen, liefen, liefen, liefen.

Die Altwässer blieben zurück, die grüne Donau kam, breit, und behäbig, rauschte der Stadt zu, die ersten Häuser sahen sie, sie sahen den Dom; sie sahen das Dach des Vaterhauses. Sie hielten, schweißüberronnen, zitterten verstört, die Knaben, die Mörder, und dann sagte der Ältere wie immer nach einem Streich: »Zu Hause sagen wir aber nichts davon!« Der andere nickte, von wilder Hoffnung überwuchert, und sie gingen, entschlossen, ewig zu schweigen, auf die Haustüre zu, die sie wie ein schwarzes Loch verschluckte.

rowed the boat back to the shore, rammed the pole with the chain into the mud on the shore, disembarked, trotted all the way down the long embankment of stone, trotted back to town, didn't dare to look at each other, ran single file, didn't pay attention to the willows that lashed against their faces or to the thorns on the brambles that tore at them, stumbled over entangled roots; they ran and ran and ran.

The backwater stayed back, the green Danube River came into sight, wide and imperturbable, rushed toward the town, they saw the first houses, they saw the cathedral, they saw the roof of their parental home. They stopped, soaked with sweat and shaking with distress, the boys, the murderers, and then the older one said, like always after a prank, "At home, we won't even bring it up." Overcome with wild hope, the other one nodded, and, determined to remain silent forever, they went to the front door that swallowed them up like a black hole.

ELISABETH LANGGÄSSER

Elisabeth Langgässer was born in 1899 in Alzey, a city located between Wiesbaden and Kaiserslautern. She was the daughter of a Catholic architectural consultant, Eduard, and his Jewish wife Eugenie, and was raised Catholic. After graduating from college prep school, she enrolled in a teacher preparation program. From 1919 until 1928 she worked as an elementary teacher in Seligenstadt, a small town outside Würzbürg, as well as Griesheim, near Darmstadt. In 1929 she gave birth out of wedlock to daughter Cordelia, fathered by Jewish constitutional law professor Hermann Heller (which was to have consequences later). Subsequently, Langgässer moved to Berlin, where she worked again as a teacher.

Her writing career started with the publication of her first poetry collection, *Der Wendekreis des Lammes* (*Tropic of the Lamb*, 1924). From 1931 on she earned her living as a freelance writer. Among other things, she created radio plays for the broadcasting station Funk-Stunde Berlin (Radio Hour Berlin). After the takeover by the National Socialists, she voted in the last free election in March of 1933, casting her ballot in favor of Adolf Hitler. That same year, she served as co-publisher of a collection of contemporary women's poems together with Nazi writer Ina Seidel.[1] In 1935 Langgässer published another collec-

---

[1] Seidel strongly identified with the ideology of National Socialism. In October 1933, she was one of 88 writers who signed a pledge of "most loyal allegiance" to Adolf Hitler. Her poem "Lichtdom" ("Cathedral of Light") is an overt glorification of Hitler, ending with the lines "Here we all stand around the One, unified, and the One is the heart of the people." (*Dem Führer: Worte deutscher Dichter*. Selected by August Friedrich Velmede. Satchel Writings of the Leading Commando of the German Army, Department of Domestic Affairs, 1941: 15.)

tion of poems, called *Tierkreisgedichte* (*Poems of the Zodiac*), and also married the journalist Wilhelm Hoffmann. Because he had married a woman considered half-Jewish according to the Nuremberg Race Laws, Hoffmann lost his job.[2] In 1936, Langgässer managed to publish her novel *Der Gang durch das Ried* (*Walking through the Marsh*), but was excluded from membership in the "Reichschrifttumskammer," the Nazi's writer union, shortly thereafter. However, she defied the publication ban and managed to publish the novel *Rettung am Rhein* (*Rescue on the Rhine*) through a publisher in Salzburg, shortly before Austria's annexation in 1938. Afterward, she secretly began work on her famous novel *Das unauslöschliche Siegel* (*The Indelible Seal*).

In 1942, during World War II, Langgässer was forced to work in an ammunition factory because of her Jewish ancestry. This was also the year her multiple sclerosis began to manifest.

Meanwhile, her daughter Cordelia, who was considered fully Jewish according to the Nuremberg Race Laws because her father had been Jewish, had gained Spanish citizenship through adoption in 1943. However, she was not allowed to emigrate there. In 1944, Cordelia was deported to the Theresienstadt concentration camp and then to Auschwitz, but was rescued by a Swedish Red Cross mission and taken to Sweden. Mother and daughter had since lost touch with each other.

In 1945 Elisabeth Langgässer was finally able to conclude the novel *The Indelible Seal*. During that year, her multiple sclerosis worsened. A year later, she was contacted out of the blue by Cordelia, who was living in Sweden, but sadly the family was never reunited.

In 1948 Langgässer published her short story collection *Der Torso* (*The Torso*). In March of 1950 she became a founding member of the Academy of Science and Literature in Mainz. By then, her multiple sclerosis had worsened considerably, and in July she died in a hospital in Karlsruhe after a ten-day coma.

Langgässer's literary efforts in the years following 1945 are illustrative of how German authors tried to make sense of the

[2]Ernst Klee, *Das Kulturlexikon zum Dritten Reich. Wer war was vor und nach 1945* (Frankfurt am Main: S. Fischer, 2007).

chaos and horrors of the Third Reich through post-war German literature. Not surprisingly for someone persecuted by the Nazi regime and with a daughter who survived the death camps, the Shoah[3] was a key motif in her narratives, even though sometimes it was more an underlying theme than an explicit focus. She did not restrain her criticism of writers of the so-called "innere Emigration" (Inner Emigration).[4] Nor did she try to defend her own beliefs and attitudes during the Third Reich, which she described later as "Trifling with flowers and florets over the horrid, wide open abyss of the mass graves that are covered with precisely these florets."[5] Her last novel, *Märkische Argonautenfahrt* (*An Argonaut's Journey through Brandenburg*, 1950) was published after her death.

Posthumously, she was awarded the Georg-Büchner-Preis, the most prestigious literary award for German-speaking writers. Since 1988, the Elisabeth-Langgässer-Literaturpreis is awarded every three years by the town of Alzey. In her memory, a college prep school in Alzey also carries her name.

Her short story "Saisonbeginn" ("Beginning of the Season," 1947) portrays a 1930s German Alpine village where three workers erect a sign forbidding the entry of Jews. The spot chosen is opposite a wooden cross with the crucified Jesus at the en-

---

[3]The Shoah (Hebrew "HaShoah", meaning catastrophe), colloquially called the Holocaust, refers to the genocide of European Jews during World War II. A systematic operation by Nazi Germany, inititated and led by Adolf Hitler throughout Nazi-occupied Europe, Russia, and northern Africa, it led to the mass murder of approximately six of the nine million Jews living in Europe before the Holocaust.

[4]After the Third Reich, the term was used to describe politicians, artists, and writers who had kept their mouths shut despite either being critical of Nazi ideology, being banned from working, accused of producing "decadent" works, or being prevented from fleeing Germany by personal or family obligations. A common criticism of those who had opted for Inner Emigration was that they had let themselves be kept on a leash and were corrupted by bribes from the Nazi regime. See also: Ralf Schnell, "Literarische Innere Emigration," in *Dichtung in finsteren Zeiten: Deutsche Literatur und Faschismus* (Hamburg: Rororo, 1998) 120-160.

[5]"Tändeln mit Blumen und Blümchen über dem scheußlichen, weit geöffneten, aber eben mit diesen Blümchen überdeckten Abgrund der Massengräber." Sonja Hilzinger, *Elisabeth Langgässer - Eine Biografie* (Berlin: Verlag für Berlin-Brandenburg, 2009), 441.

trance to the village. The hypocrisy of the workers is contrasted with the peaceful and idyllic Alpine town that advertises itself as the perfect recreation spot. Langgässer proceeds to highlight the indifference of the townspeople who happen to pass by and who show no interest in the goings-on.

Langgässer describes the events dispassionately, in stark contrast to the hideous implications of the erection of the sign. Although not obvious at first glance, this story is a passionate appeal to all of us to speak up for our fellow human beings, not to simply look past and walk away when injustice is committed.

ELISABETH LANGGÄSSER

Saisonbeginn

Die Arbeiter kamen mit ihrem Schild und einem hölzernen Pfosten, auf den es genagelt werden sollte, zu dem Eingang der Ortschaft, die hoch in den Bergen an der letzten Passkehre lag. Es war ein heißer Spätfrühlingstag, die Schneegrenze hatte sich schon hinauf zu den Gletscherwänden gezogen. Überall standen die Wiesen wieder in Saft und Kraft; die Wucherblume verschwendete sich, der Löwenzahn strotzte und blähte sein Haupt über den milchigen Stengeln; Trollblumen, welche wie eingefettet mit gelber Sahne waren, platzten vor Glück, und in strahlenden Tümpeln kleinblütiger Enziane spiegelte sich ein Himmel von unwahrscheinlichem Blau. Auch die Häuser und Gasthöfe waren wie neu: ihre Fensterläden frisch angestrichen, die Schindeldächer gut ausgebessert, die Scherenzäune ergänzt. Ein Atemzug noch: dann würden die Fremden, die Sommergäste kommen die Lehrerinnen, die mutigen Sachsen, die Kinderreichen, die Alpinisten, aber vor allem die Autobesitzer in ihren großen Wagen ... Ford und Mercedes, Fiat und Opel, blitzend von Chrom und Glas. Das Geld würde anrollen. Alles war darauf vorbereitet. Ein Schild kam zum anderen, die Haarnadelkurve zu dem Totenkopf, Kilometerschilder und Schilder für Fußgänger: Zwei Minuten zum Café Alpenrose.

An der Stelle, wo die Männer den Pfosten in die Erde einrammen wollten, stand ein Holzkreuz, über dem Kopf des Christus war auch ein Schild angebracht. Seine Inschrift war bis heute die gleiche, wie sie Pilatus entworfen hatte: J. N. R. J. , die Ent-

ELISABETH LANGGÄSSER

Beginning of the Season

The workers came with their sign and a wooden post to nail it to, that is to say they came to the entrance of the village located high in the mountains at the last hairpin bend of the pass. It was a hot day late in spring; the snowline had withdrawn all the way up to the walls of the glacier. Everywhere the meadows were full of sap and strength; the chrysanthemum flowered lavishly, the dandelion bristled, their heads bulging on top of milky stalks; the globeflowers, looking as if they had been basted with yellow cream, burst open with joy, and the glistening pools made up by the gentians, with their small flowers, reflected a sky that was incredibly blue. The houses and inns looked like new as well: their window shutters had been freshly painted, the shingle roofs mended well, and the trelliswork fences completed. One more breath, and the strangers and the summer guests would arrive—female teachers, hardy Saxons, those blessed with many children, alpinists, but first and foremost the car owners in their big vehicles . . . Röhr and Mercedes, Fiat and Opel, shiny with chrome and glass. Money would start rolling in. Everything was ready for that. One sign was added to the next, the hairpin curve to the skull, signs showing mileage and signs for pedestrians: two minutes to the Café Alpenrose.

On the site where the men were going to ram the post into the ground, there was a wooden cross and above the head of Christ was another sign. Still today its inscription is the same one that Pilate had designed: J.N.R.J.—the dis-

täuschung darüber, dass es im Grunde hätte heißen sollen: er behauptet nur, dieser König zu sein, hatte im Lauf der Jahrhunderte an Heftigkeit eingebüßt. Die beiden Männer, welche den Posten, das Schild und die große Schaufel, um den Pfosten in die Erde zu graben, auf ihren Schultern trugen, setzten alles unter dem Wegkreuz ab; der dritte stellte den Werkzeugkasten, Hammer, Zange und Nägel daneben und spuckte ermunternd aus.

Nun beratschlagten die drei Männer, an welcher Stelle die Inschrift des Schildes am besten zur Geltung käme; sie sollte für alle, welche das Dorf auf dem breiten Passweg betraten, besser: befuhren, als Blickfang dienen und nicht zu verfehlen sein. Man kam also überein, das Schild kurz vor dem Wegekreuz anzubringen, gewissermaßen als Gruß, den die Ortschaft jedem Fremden entgegenschickte. Leider stellt sich aber heraus, dass der Pfosten dann in den Pflasterbelag einer Tankstelle hätte gesetzt werden müssen, eine Sache, die sich selbst verbot, da die Wagen, besonders die größeren, dann am Wenden behindert waren. Die Männer schleppten also den Pfosten noch ein Stück weiter hinaus bis zu der Gemeindewiese und wollten schon mit der Arbeit beginnen, als ihnen auffiel, dass diese Stelle bereits zu weit von dem Ortsschild entfernt war, das den Namen angab und die Gemeinde, zu welcher der Flecken gehörte. Wenn also das Dorf den Vorzug dieses Schildes und seiner Inschrift für sich beanspruchen wollte, musste das Schild wieder näherrücken am besten gerade dem Kreuz gegenüber, so dass Wagen und Fußgänger zwischen beiden hätten passieren müssen.

Dieser Vorschlag, von dem Mann mit den Nägeln und dem Hammer gemacht, fand Beifall. Die beiden anderen luden von neuem den Pfosten auf ihre Schultern und schleppten ihn vor das Kreuz. Nun sollte also das Schild mit der Inschrift zu dem Wegekreuz senkrecht stehen; doch zeigte es sich, dass die uralte Buche, welche gerade hier ihre Äste mit riesiger Spanne nach beiden Seiten wie eine Mantelmadonna ihren Umhang entfaltete, die Inschrift im Sommer verdeckt und ihr Schattenspiel deren Bedeutung verwischt, aber mindestens abgeschwächt hätte.

appointment over the fact that it should have said "he only declared himself to be this king" had lost its intensity over the centuries. The two men who carried the post, the sign, and the big shovel on their shoulders put down everything under the Christian wayside shrine; the third one put the toolbox, hammer, pliers, and nails next to them and spit on the ground encouragingly.

Now the three men discussed which place would best showcase the inscription on the sign; it should serve as an eye-catcher for all those who entered on foot or drove into the village on the wide road, and it shouldn't be missed. So they agreed to put up the sign right in front of the Christian wayside shrine, meant as some sort of greeting toward every stranger. Unfortunately, they discovered this would mean that the post had to be put into the gas station's pavement surface—which was out of the question since the cars, particularly the bigger ones, would then have had trouble turning around. Therefore, the men dragged the post a little beyond that point to the town meadow and were about to start work when they noticed that this new site was too far away from the sign that showed the town and community names. So, if the village wanted to be able to enjoy the benefit of both the sign and its inscription, the sign had to be moved closer again—preferably just across the road from the Christian wayside shrine, so that cars and pedestrians would be required to pass between them.

This suggestion, conveyed by the man with the nails and the hammer, was greeted with approval. Once more, the other two loaded the post on their shoulders and dragged it before the cross. Now the sign with the inscription was meant to stand perpendicular to the inscription on the Christian wayside shrine. However, it turned out that an ancient beech tree, which unfolded her branches so that they spanned across both sides of the trunk like a Madonna opening her cloak, would cover the inscription during the summer, and the moving shadows cast on the inscription would have erased or at least weakened its meaning.

Es blieb daher nur noch die andere Seite neben dem Herrenkreuz, und da die erste, die in das Pflaster der Tankstelle überging, gewissermaßen den Platz des Schächers zur Linken bezeichnet hätte, wurde jetzt der Platz zur Rechten gewählt und endgültig beibehalten. Zwei Männer hoben die Erde aus, der dritte nagelte rasch das Schild mit wuchtigen Schlägen auf; dann stellten sie den Pfosten gemeinsam in die Grube und rammten ihn rings von allen Seiten mit größeren Feldsteinen an. Ihre Tätigkeit blieb nicht unbeobachtet. Schulkinder machten sich gegenseitig die Ehre streitig, dabei zu helfen, den Hammer, die Nägel hinzureichen und passende Steine zu suchen; auch einige Frauen blieben stehen, um die Inschrift genau zu studieren. Zwei Nonnen, welche die Blumenvase zu Fuße des Kreuzes aufs neue füllten, blickten einander unsicher an, bevor sie weitergingen. Bei den Männern, die von der Holzarbeit oder vom Acker kamen, war die Wirkung verschieden: einige lachten, andere schüttelten nur den Kopf, ohne etwas zu sagen; die Mehrzahl blieb davon unberührt und gab weder Beifall noch Ablehnung kund, sondern war gleichgültig, wie sich die Sache auch immer entwickeln würde. Im Ganzen genommen konnten die Männer mit der Wirkung zufrieden sein. Der Pfosten, kerzengerade, trug das Schild mit der weithin sichtbaren Inschrift, die Nachmittagssonne glitt wie ein Finger über die zollgroßen Buchstaben hin und fuhr jeden einzelnen langsam nach wie den Richtspruch an einer Tafel . . .

Auch der sterbende Christus, dessen blasses, blutüberronnenes Haupt im Tod nach der rechten Seite geneigt war, schien sich mit letzter Kraft zu bemühen, die Inschrift aufzunehmen: man merkte, sie ging ihn gleichfalls an, welcher bisher von den Leuten als einer der ihren betrachtet und wohl gelitten war. Unerbittlich und dauerhaft wie sein Leiden, würde sie ihm nun für lange Zeit schwarz auf weiß gegenüberstehen.

Als die Männer den Kreuzigungsort verließen und ihr Handwerkszeug wieder zusammenpackten, blickten alle drei noch einmal befriedigt zu dem Schild mit der Inschrift auf. Sie lautete: «In diesem Kurort sind Juden unerwünscht.”

Therefore, the only option left was next to the crucified Christ, and since the first option, which led into the gas station, would have marked the place of the thief to the left, they decided to choose the place to the right and that was that. Two men dug out the dirt, the third one quickly nailed the sign down with powerful blows, and then together they positioned the post into the pit and secured it with big stones all around.

Their activity did not go unnoticed. Young students competed with each other to help the men by handing them the hammer and nails and finding compatible stones; several women also stopped to examine the inscription more closely. Two nuns, who had been refilling the flower vase at the feet of the cross, looked doubtfully at each other before they went away. The effect on the men who returned home from working in the forest or fields was different: some laughed, others simply shook their heads without saying anything, and most remained unmoved, showing neither approval nor rejection and uninterested in however the matter would proceed. All in all, the men could be satisfied with their work. The post, sitting bolt upright, carried the sign with the inscription that was easy to read from a distance; the afternoon sun glided like a finger across the inch-sized letters und slowly traced each of them like a verdict on a board . . .

Even the dying Christ, whose pale and blood-covered head leaned to the right in death, seemed to strain to take in the inscription in a last effort: one could see that it concerned him as well, a man who, up to this point, had been regarded by the people as one of them and also been welcomed. Relentless and long-lasting like his suffering, it would now sit across him for a long time, in black and white.

When the men left the site of the crucifixion and packed up their tools, all three of them looked back at the sign, satisfied with the inscription. It read, "In this mountain resort Jews are unwanted."

LUISE RINSER

Luise Rinser was born April 30, 1911, in Pitzling, a suburb of Landsberg am Lech in Upper Bavaria. She attended school in Munich and, after graduating from college, worked as a teacher's aide and later as a teacher in various schools in the region. During that time, she began publishing short stories in the journal *Herdfeuer* (*Fire in the Hearth*), which continued until 1941. Following the "Machtergreifung" (Nazi Seizure of Power) in 1933, she managed to evade membership in the Nazi Party, which everyone who worked as a public employee was required to join. In 1936, however, she reluctantly joined the Nazi women's organization and, to keep her job until her resignation from teaching in 1939, also belonged to the Nazi teachers association. But in 1944, Rinser was imprisoned for undermining military morale. The end of the war terminated the legal proceedings and provided a narrow escape from an almost inevitable death sentence.

She detailed her experience in the women's prison[1] in her *Gefängnistagebuch* (*Prison Journals*, 1946), noting that it helped free her of upper middle-class illusions. "I have never seen life as I'm getting to see it here: naked, ugly, tough, but unfaked and real," she wrote. "If ever I return to normal life I shall be transformed."[2]

---

[1] Ernst Klee, *Das Kulturlexikon zum Dritten Reich. Wer war was vor und nach 1945* (Frankfurt am Main: S. Fischer, 2007), 487 ff.

[2] Wolfgang Saxon, "Luise Rinser Is Dead at 90; Wrote on Horrors of Nazism," *New York Times – Obituaries*, last modified March 24 2002, accessed August 10, 2011, http://www.nytimes.com/2002/03/24/nyregion/luise-rinser-is-dead-at-90-wrote-on-horrors-of-nazism.html?src=pm

From 1945 to 1953, she was a freelance writer for the *Neue Zeitung München* (*New Daily News Munich*). In 1959 she moved to Italy and settled there for almost three decades. In 1986 she returned to Munich, where she lived until her death. All her life, Rinser was an active and critical participant in political and social discussions in Germany as a feminist, environmentalist, pacifist, and protester against atomic weapons. During the 1971–1972 election campaign for German chancellor, she was a strong supporter of Willy Brandt.[3] In the 1970s and early 1980s, she joined her fellow writers, among them Heinrich Böll and Günter Grass, in their outspoken public protest against the nuclear stockpiling and arms build-up on German soil. A staunch Catholic, she sharply criticized the Catholic Church for its misogynist stance, among other things. She also criticized the prosecution of the leaders of the Red Army Faction.[4]

During those years she traveled extensively, visiting the Soviet Union, the USA, Spain, India, Indonesia, South Korea, North Korea, Iran, Japan, Colombia, and other countries. She became a leading voice for social reforms and the rights of the disenfranchised—including women, as she saw it—and campaigned for abolition of the German anti-abortion law (which had been reinstated by the Nazis). She was nominated to be president of Germany in 1984 by the newly-emerging Green Party.

Rinser sold more than 5 million copies of her books during her lifetime, both in the original German and in translations of 20 languages, and is considered one of the great twentieth-century German authors of novels and short stories. Those books include *Die gläsernen Ringe* (*The Glass Rings*, 1941), *Erste Liebe* (*First Love*, 1946), *Mitte des Lebens* (*The Middle of Life*, 1950), *Daniela* (1952), *Mirjam* (1983), *Abelard's Liebe* (*Abelard's Love*, 1991) and *Saturn auf der Sonne* (*Saturn on the Sun*, 1994).

---

[3]Willy Brandt, born December 1913 and died October 1992, was the mayor of West Berlin from 1957-1966, chancellor of West Germany from 1969-1974, and, from 1964-1987, leader of the Social Democratic Party of Germany (SPD).

[4]Butz Peters, *Tödlicher Irrtum: Die Geschichte der RAF* (Berlin: Argon, 2004), 135.

Rinser was awarded a number of prestigious awards for her literary work, both national and international. These include the Order of Merit of the Federal Republic of Germany - Cross of Merit, First Class (1977), the Roswitha-Gedenkmedaille (Roswitha Prize, 1979) of the City of Gandersheim, the Elisabeth Langgässer Prize for Literature (1987), and the Kunst-und Kultur-Preis (Art and Culture Prize, 1991) from her city of birth, Landsberg am Lech. She died March 17, 2002.

A concern and deep love for her fellow humans inform all of her novels and short stories as well as her political rhetoric. She said it had always been her desire to help her readers to love and live more fulfilling lives. In 2002, German president Johannes Rau remarked on her "lifetime commitment to freedom and democracy," and praised "her ability to address the basic, important questions of life in her literature."[5]

"Die rote Katze" ("The Red Cat," 1948), first published in the collection *Ein Bündel weißer Narzissen (A Bundle of White Narcissus*, 1956), exemplifies her conviction that all creatures are created equal and that humans and animals share a deep connection.[6] The story is set in a devastated post-World War II Germany and illustrates how poverty and hunger have the power to make even children callous and cruel. While the author does not judge the main character, a nameless 13-year-old boy, she describes in detail how living conditions turn a child into a murderer—even if only as the killer of a cat. The act dehumanizes the boy, as every murder does to its perpetrator. However, Rinser also makes it clear that the burden of his circumstances—taking care of his mother and two younger siblings—overwhelms the adolescent, as it forces him to act like an adult and a surrogate for his father who seems to have perished in the war.

The story is told from the perspective of the teenage protagonist. By jumping between the present and past tenses, Rinser

---

[5]Paul A. Schons, "One of the Great Story-tellers: Luise Rinser." Originally published by the Germanic-American Institute in November 2002, accessed August 14, 2011.

[6]"It will be a long time before humanity will understand that it is not only the peoples of the earth who are one people, but that people, plants and animals together are the 'Kingdom of God' and that the fate of one is the fate of all." Ibid.

disrupts the otherwise even flow of the narrative; she uses the present tense to underscore the sense of urgency and volatility reflected in key events. The young teenager's dialect-hampered speech emphasizes the discrepancy between his age and his adult responsibilities, highlighting his vulnerability and helplessness as he fights in the ruthless struggle for survival.

LUISE RINSER

Die rote Katze

Ich muss immer an diesen roten Teufel von einer Katze denken, und ich weiß nicht, ob das richtig war, was ich getan hab. Es hat damit angefangen, dass ich auf dem Steinhaufen neben dem Bombentrichter in unserm Garten saß. Der Steinhaufen ist die größere Hälfte von unserm Haus. Die kleinere steht noch, und da wohnen wir, ich und die Mutter und Peter und Leni, das sind meine kleinen Geschwister.

Also, ich sitz da auf den Steinen, da wächst überall schon Gras und Brennnesseln und anderes Grünes. Ich halt ein Stück Brot in der Hand, das ist schon hart, aber meine Mutter sagt, altes Brot ist gesünder als frisches. In Wirklichkeit ist es deswegen, weil sie meint, am alten Brot muss man länger kauen und dann wird man von weniger satt. Bei mir stimmt das nicht. Plötzlich fällt mir ein Brocken herunter. Ich bück mich, aber im nämlichen Augenblick fährt eine rote Pfote aus den Brennnesseln und angelt sich das Brot. Ich hab nur dumm schauen können, so schnell ist es gegangen. Und da seh ich, dass in den Brennnesseln eine Katze hockt, rot wie ein Fuchs und ganz mager. »Verdammtes Biest«, sag ich und werf einen Stein nach ihr. Ich hab sie gar nicht treffen wollen, nur verscheuchen. Aber ich muss sie doch getroffen haben, denn sie hat geschrien, nur ein einziges Mal, aber so wie ein Kind.

Fortgelaufen ist sie nicht. Da hat es mir leid getan, dass ich nach ihr geworfen hab, und ich hab sie gelockt. Aber sie ist nicht aus den Nesseln rausgegangen. Sie hat ganz schnell geatmet. Ich hab gesehen, wie ihr rotes Fell über dem Bauch auf und ab gegangen ist. Sie hat mich immerfort angeschaut mit ihren grünen

94

LUISE RINSER

The Red Cat

I always think about this red devil of a cat, and I don't know whether it was right what I did. It started with me sitting on a pile of rubble next to the bomb crater in our front yard. The pile of rubble is the bigger half of our house. The smaller one is still standing, and that is where we live, I and Mother and Peter and Leni, which are my smaller siblings.

So, as I am sitting on the rubble there is already grass and stinging nettles and other green stuff growing. I am holding a piece of bread in my hand which is already hard, but Mother says that old bread is healthier than fresh. In reality it's because she thinks you have to chew old bread longer and so you will be full with less. That's not the case with me. Suddenly, a piece breaks off. I bend down, but in the same instant, a red paw darts from the stinging nettles and snags the bread. It happened so fast that all I could do was look stupid. And there I see a cat sitting in the stinging nettles, red as a fox and quite scrawny. "Damned beast," I say and throw a rock after her. I did not mean to hit her, only scare her away. But I must have still hit her because she cried, only once, but in the manner of a child.

She did not run away. So I regretted throwing something at her and I beckoned to her. However, she did not emerge from the stinging nettles. She was breathing quickly. I saw her red fur rise and fall over her belly. She kept looking at me with her green eyes. That's when I asked her, "What

95

Augen. Da hab ich sie gefragt: »Was willst du eigentlich?« Das war verrückt, denn sie ist doch kein Mensch, mit dem man reden kann. Dann bin ich ärgerlich geworden über sie und auch über mich, und ich hab einfach nicht mehr hingeschaut und hab ganz schnell mein Brot hinuntergewürgt. Den letzten Bissen, das war noch ein großes Stück, den hab ich ihr hingeworfen und bin ganz zornig fortgegangen.

Im Vorgarten, da waren Peter und Leni und haben Bohnen geschnitten. Sie haben sich die grünen Bohnen in den Mund gestopft, dass es nur so geknirscht hat, und Leni hat ganz leise gefragt, ob ich nicht noch ein Stückchen Brot hab. »Na«, hab ich gesagt, »du hast doch genau so ein großes Stück bekommen wie ich und du bist erst neun, und ich bin dreizehn. Größere brauchen mehr.« - »Ja«, hat sie gesagt, sonst nichts. Da hat Peter gesagt: »Weil sie ihr Brot doch der Katze gegeben hat.« - »Was für einer Katze?« hab ich gefragt. »Ach«, sagt Leni, »da ist so eine Katze gekommen, eine rote, wie so ein kleiner Fuchs und so schrecklich mager. Die hat mich immer angeschaut, wie ich mein Brot hab essen wollen.« - »Dummkopf«, hab ich ärgerlich gesagt, »wo wir doch selber nichts zu essen haben.« Aber sie hat nur mit den Achseln gezuckt und ganz schnell zu Peter hingeschaut, der hat einen roten Kopf gehabt, und ich bin sicher, er hat sein Brot auch der Katze gegeben. Da bin ich wirklich ärgerlich gewesen und hab ganz schnell weggehen müssen.

Wie ich auf die Hauptstraße komm, steht da ein amerikanisches Auto, so ein großer langer Wagen, ein Buick, glaub ich, und da fragt mich der Fahrer nach dem Rathaus. Auf Englisch hat er gefragt, und ich kann doch ein bisschen Englisch. »The next street«, hab ich gesagt, »and then left and then« - geradeaus hab ich nicht gewusst auf englisch, das hab ich mit dem Arm gezeigt, und er hat mich schon verstanden. - »And behind the Church is the marketplace with the Rathaus.« Ich glaub, das war ein ganz gutes Amerikanisch, und die Frau im Auto hat mir ein paar Schnitten Weißbrot gegeben, ganz weißes, und wie ich's aufklapp, ist Wurst dazwischen, ganz dick. Da bin ich gleich heimgerannt mit dem Brot. Wie ich in die Küche komm, da verstecken die zwei Kleinen schnell was unterm Sofa, aber ich hab es doch gesehen. Es ist die rote Katze gewesen. Und auf dem Boden war ein biss-

is it that you want, actually?" That was crazy since she really isn't a human being with whom you can talk. Then I became annoyed with her and also with me, and I simply stopped looking at her and quickly stuffed down my bread. I threw her the last bite, which was still a large piece and walked away pretty angrily.

In the front yard, Peter and Leni were cutting beans. They stuffed the green beans into their mouths with loud crunching sounds and Leni asked quietly if I didn't have a little piece of bread. "Well," I said, "your piece was just as big as mine and you are only nine and I am thirteen. When you are bigger you need more."—"Yes," she said, and nothing else. Then Peter said, "Because she gave her bread to the cat."—"What cat?" I asked. "Oh," Leni said, "there was a cat, a red one, like a little fox and so terribly skinny. She kept looking at me, as I was going to eat my bread."—"You fool," I said angrily. "Why, we don't have enough to eat ourselves." But she only shrugged her shoulders and quickly looked at Peter whose face was all red, so I'm sure that he also gave the cat his bread. That's when I got really angry and had to walk away very quickly.

When I come to the main street, there is an American car, a big and long car, a Buick, I think, and the driver is asking me for directions to the city hall. He asked in English and I can really speak a little bit of English. "The next street," I said, "and then left and then"— I didn't know how to say "straight ahead" so I motioned with my arm instead, and he understood.—"And behind the church is the marketplace with the city hall." I think that was pretty good American English and the woman in the car gave me a couple of slices of white bread, really white, and as I open them up I see a piece of sausage between the slices, really thick. So I ran home quickly with the bread. As I enter the kitchen I see the two little ones quickly hide something under the sofa, but I saw it anyway. It was the red cat. On the floor was a little bit of spilled milk, and I knew everything. "You must be

chen Milch verschüttet, und da hab ich alles gewusst.»Ihr seid wohl verrückt«, hab ich geschrien,»wo wir doch nur einen halben Liter Magermilch haben im Tag, für vier Personen.« Und ich hab die Katze unterm Sofa herausgezogen und hab sie zum Fenster hinausgeworfen. Die beiden Kleinen haben kein Wort gesagt. Dann hab ich das amerikanische Weißbrot in vier Teile geschnitten und den Teil für die Mutter im Küchenschrank versteckt. »Woher hast du das?« haben sie gefragt und ganz ängstlich geschaut.»Gestohlen«, hab ich gesagt und bin hinausgegangen. Ich hab nur schnell nachsehn wollen, ob auf der Straße keine Kohlen liegen, weil nämlich ein Kohlenauto vorbeigefahren war, und die verlieren manchmal was. Da sitzt im Vorgarten die rote Katze und schaut so an mir rauf.»Geh weg«, hab ich gesagt und mit dem Fuß nach ihr gestoßen. Aber sie ist nicht weggegangen. Sie hat bloß ihr kleines Maul aufgemacht und gesagt:»Miau.« Sie hat nicht geschrien wie andere Katzen, sie hat es einfach so gesagt, ich kann das nicht erklären. Dabei hat sie mich ganz starr angeschaut mit den grünen Augen. Da hab ich ihr voll Zorn einen Brocken von dem amerikanischen Weißbrot hingeworfen. Nachher hat's mich gereut.

Wie ich auf die Straße komm, da sind schon zwei andere da, Größere, die haben die Kohlen aufgehoben. Da bin ich einfach vorbeigegangen. Sie haben einen ganzen Eimer voll gehabt. Ich hab schnell hineingespuckt. Wär das mit der Katze nicht gewesen, hätte ich sie alle allein gekriegt. Und wir hätten ein ganzes Abendessen damit kochen können. Es waren so schöne glänzende Dinger. Nachher hab ich dafür einen Wagen mit Frühkartoffeln getroffen, da bin ich ein bisschen drangestoßen, und da sind ein paar runtergekollert und noch ein paar. Ich hab sie in die Taschen gesteckt und in die Mütze. Wie der Fuhrmann umgeschaut hat, hab ich gesagt:»Sie verlieren Ihre Kartoffeln.« Dann bin ich schnell heimgegangen. Die Mutter war allein daheim, und auf ihrem Schoß, da war die rote Katze.»Himmeldonnerwetter«, hab ich gesagt,»ist das Biest schon wieder da?« - »Red doch nicht so grob«, hat die Mutter gesagt,»das ist eine herrenlose Katze, und wer weiß, wie lange sie nichts mehr gefressen hat. Schau nur, wie mager sie ist.« - »Wir sind auch mager«, hab ich gesagt.»Ich hab ihr ein bisschen was von meinem Brot gegeben«, hat sie gesagt

crazy," I shouted, "we only have a half a liter of skim milk per day, for four people." And I pulled the cat out from under the sofa and threw her out of the window. The two little ones did not say a word. Then I cut the American white bread into four pieces und put the piece for Mother in the fridge.

"Where did you get that?" they asked, looking anxious. "I stole it," I said, and went outside. I just wanted to see if there were any coals lying around in the street since a coal truck had passed and sometimes they lose some. There I see the cat sitting in the front yard looking up to me. "Go away," I said, and kicked after her. But she did not go away. She simply opened her little mouth and said, "Meow." She did not cry like other cats, she simply said it, I do not know how to explain it. With that, she fixed me with a stare from her green eyes. So, full of anger, I threw a lump of the American white bread at her. Afterwards, I regretted it.

When I get to the street, two other people are there already, bigger ones, who had picked up the coals. So I kept walking. They had filled a whole bucket. I quickly spat into it. If that incident with the cat hadn't happened, they would have all been mine. And we would have been able to cook a complete dinner with them. They were pretty, shiny ones. Afterwards I found a cart with new potatoes instead, so I pushed against it and a few rolled off, and then a few more. I put them into my pockets and into my hat. When the driver turned around I said, "You are losing your potatoes." Then I quickly went home. Mother was home alone and on her lap there was the red cat. "Well, I'll be damned," I said. "Is the beast here again?"—"Don't talk so rudely," said Mother. "This is an abandoned cat and who knows how long it is since she has eaten. Look how scrawny she is."—"We're scrawny too," I said. "I gave her some of my bread," she said

und mich schief angeschaut. Ich hab an unsere Brote gedacht und
an die Milch und an das Weißbrot, aber gesagt hab ich nichts.
Dann haben wir die Kartoffeln gekocht, und die Mutter war froh.
Aber woher ich sie hab, hat sie nicht gefragt.
Meinetwegen hätte sie schon fragen können. Nachher hat
die Mutter ihren Kaffee schwarz getrunken, und sie haben alle
zugeschaut, wie das rote Biest die Milch ausgesoffen hat. Dann
ist sie endlich durchs Fenster hinausgesprungen. Ich hab schnell
zugemacht und richtig aufgeatmet. Am Morgen, um sechs, hab
ich mich für Gemüse angestellt. Wie ich um acht Uhr heim-
komm, sitzen die Kleinen beim Frühstück, und auf dem Stuhl
dazwischen hockt das Vieh und frisst eingeweichtes Brot aus
Lenis Untertasse. Nach ein paar Minuten kommt die Mutter
zurück, die ist seit halb sechs beim Metzger angestanden. Die
Katze springt gleich zu ihr hin, und wie die Mutter denkt, ich
geb nicht acht, lässt sie ein Stück Wurst fallen. Es war zwar
markenfreie Wurst, so graues Zeug, aber wir hätten sie uns auch
gern aufs Brot gestrichen, das hätte Mutter doch wissen müssen. Ich verschluck meinen Zorn, nehm die Mütze und geh. Ich
hab das alte Rad aus dem Keller geholt und bin vor die Stadt
gefahren. Da ist ein Teich, in dem gibts Fische. Ich hab keine
Angel, nur so einen Stecken mit zwei spitzen Nägeln drin, mit
dem stech ich nach den Fischen. Ich hab schon oft Glück gehabt
und diesmal auch. Es ist noch nicht zehn Uhr, da hab ich zwei
ganz nette Dinger, genug für ein Mittagessen. Ich fahr heim, so
schnell ich kann, und daheim leg ich die Fische auf den Küchentisch. Ich geh nur rasch in den Keller und sags der Mutter, die
hat Waschtag. Sie kommt auch gleich mit herauf. Aber da ist nur
mehr ein Fisch da und ausgerechnet der kleinere. Und auf dem
Fensterbrett, da sitzt der rote Teufel und frisst den letzten Bissen. Da krieg ich aber die Wut und werf ein Stück Holz nach ihr,
und ich treff sie auch. Sie kollert vom Fensterbrett, und ich hör
sie wie einen Sack im Garten aufplumpsen. »So«, sag ich, »die
hat genug.« Aber da krieg ich von der Mutter eine Ohrfeige,
dass es nur so klatscht. Ich bin dreizehn und hab sicher seit fünf
Jahren keine mehr gekriegt. »Tierquäler«, schreit die Mutter
und ist ganz blass vor Zorn über mich. Ich hab nichts anderes
tun können als fortgehen. Mittags hat es dann doch Fischsalat

and looked at me with her head tilted. I thought about our bread and the milk and the white bread, but I didn't say anything. Then we cooked the potatoes and Mother was glad. But she didn't ask where I had gotten them. I wouldn't have minded her asking. After that Mother drank her coffee black and they all watched the red beast drink up the milk. Then she finally jumped out through the window. I quickly closed it and breathed a deep sigh of relief. The next morning at six, I lined up to get vegetables. When I arrive home at eight, the little ones sit with their breakfast and on a chair between them sits the critter and eats soaked bread from Leni's saucer. A few minutes later Mother returns; she was in line at the butcher's since half past five. Quickly, the cat jumps toward her and when Mother thinks that I'm not looking she drops a piece of meat. Although this meat is not a rationed item, some gray stuff, we would have liked to spread it on our bread, Mother should have known that. I swallow my anger, take my hat, and leave. I got the old bike from the basement and rode outside of town. There is a pond with fish. I don't have a pole, only a stick with two sharp nails in it and I try to lance fish with it. I have been lucky quite a few times before and I was lucky this time too. It is not even ten o'clock and I have two pretty nice fish, enough for lunch. I ride home as fast as I can and put the fish on the kitchen table. I only go quickly into the basement to tell Mother; it's her laundry day. She comes up with me right away. But there is only one fish left and just the smaller one. And on the window sill there sits the red devil finishing the last bite. So I fly into a rage and throw a piece of wood at her and I manage to hit her. She falls off the window sill and I hear her hit the ground in the yard like a sack of potatoes. "There," I say. "She's had enough." But then I get a slap in the face, with a really loud smack, from Mother. I am thirteen and for sure haven't gotten one for five years. "Animal torturer," Mother yells and is really pale with rage at me. I couldn't do anything else but leave. For lunch we did have fish

gegeben mit mehr Kartoffeln als Fisch. Jedenfalls sind wir das rote Biest los gewesen. Aber glaub ja keiner, dass das besser gewesen ist. Die Kleinen sind durch die Gärten gelaufen und haben immer nach der Katze gerufen, und die Mutter hat jeden Abend ein Schälchen mit Milch vor die Tür gestellt, und sie hat mich vorwurfsvoll angeschaut. Und da hab ich selber angefangen, in allen Winkeln nach dem Vieh zu suchen, es hätte ja irgendwo krank oder tot liegen können. Aber nach drei Tagen war die Katze wieder da. Sie hat gehinkt und hat eine Wunde am Bein gehabt, am rechten Vorderbein, das war von meinem Scheit. Die Mutter hat sie verbunden, und sie hat ihr auch was zu fressen gegeben. Von da an ist sie jeden Tag gekommen. Es hat keine Mahlzeit gegeben ohne das rote Vieh, und keiner von uns hat irgendwas vor ihm verheimlichen können. Kaum hat man was gegessen, so ist sie schon dagesessen und hat einen angestarrt. Und alle haben wir ihr gegeben, was sie hat haben wollen, ich auch. Obwohl ich wütend war. Sie ist immer fetter geworden, und eigentlich war es eine schöne Katze, glaub ich. Und dann ist der Winter sechsundvierzig auf siebenundvierzig gekommen. Da haben wir wirklich kaum mehr was zu essen gehabt. Es hat ein paar Wochen lang kein Gramm Fleisch gegeben und nur gefrorene Kartoffeln, und die Kleider haben nur so geschlottert an uns. Und einmal hat Leni ein Stück Brot gestohlen beim Bäcker vor Hunger. Aber das weiß nur ich. Und Anfang Februar, da hab ich zur Mutter gesagt: »Jetzt schlachten wir das Vieh.« – »Was für ein Vieh?« hat sie gefragt und hat mich scharf angeschaut. »Die Katze halt«, hab ich gesagt und hab gleichgültig getan, aber ich hab schon gewusst, was kommt. Sie sind alle über mich hergefallen. »Was? Unsere Katze? Schämst du dich nicht?« - »Nein«, hab ich gesagt, »ich schäm mich nicht. Wir haben sie von unserm Essen gemästet, und sie ist fett wie ein Spanferkel, jung ist sie auch noch, also?« Aber Leni hat angefangen zu heulen, und Peter hat mir unterm Tisch einen Fußtritt gegeben, und Mutter hat traurig gesagt: »dass du so ein böses Herz hast, hab ich nicht geglaubt.« Die Katze ist auf dem Herd gesessen und hat geschlafen. Sie war wirklich ganz rund und sie war so faul, dass sie kaum mehr aus dem Haus zu jagen war. Wie es dann im April keine Kartoffeln

salad with more potatoes than fish. In any case, we got rid
of the beast. But don't believe for a minute that this made
things better. The little ones ran through the yards calling
the cat and every evening. Mother set a little saucer with
milk outside the door, looking at me with reproach. And
so I too began to look for the critter in all corners; it might
have been lying somewhere sick or dead. But three days
later, the cat was back. She limped and had a wound on
her leg, the right front leg, which was caused by the piece
of wood I had thrown. Mother put bandages on her and
also gave her something to eat. From that time on, she
came every day. There was no single meal without the red
critter, and nobody was able to keep anything secret from
it. As soon as someone started eating something, she was
there, sitting and staring. And all of us gave her what she
wanted, even me. But I was enraged. She became fatter
and fatter and, as a matter of fact, she was a pretty cat, I
think. And then the winter of '46 to '47 arrived. We hardly had anything left to eat. For a couple of weeks there
was not a gram of meat and only frozen potatoes, and
the clothes were hanging off us like nothing. And once,
Leni stole a piece of bread at the baker's because she was
so hungry. But only I know that. And at the beginning of
February, I told Mother, "Now we are going to butcher
the critter."—"What critter?" she asked and looked at me
closely. "Well, the cat," I said with feigned casualness, but
I knew what was coming. They all attacked me. "What?
Our cat? Aren't you ashamed of yourself?"—"No," I said,
"I am not ashamed. Why, we fattened her up with our
food, and she is fat like a suckling pig, she's still young."
But Leni started to sob and Peter kicked me under the
table, and Mother said with sadness in her voice, "I didn't
believe that you had such an evil heart." The cat sat on the
hearth, sleeping. She really was pretty plump and she was
so lazy that we hardly ever managed to chase her out of
the house. When April came and we ran out of potatoes,

mehr gegeben hat, da haben wir nicht mehr gewusst, was wir essen sollen. Eines Tages, ich war schon ganz verrückt, da hab ich sie mir vorgenommen und hab gesagt: »Also hör mal, wir haben nichts mehr, siehst du das nicht ein?« Und ich hab ihr die leere Kartoffelkiste gezeigt und den leeren Brotkasten. »Geh fort«, hab ich ihr gesagt, »du siehst ja, wie's bei uns ist.« Aber sie hat nur geblinzelt und sich auf dem Herd herumgedreht. Da hab ich vor Zorn geheult und auf den Küchentisch geschlagen. Aber sie hat sich nicht darum gekümmert. Da hab ich sie gepackt und untern Arm genommen. Es war schon ein bisschen dunkel draußen, und die Kleinen waren mit der Mutter fort, Kohlen am Bahndamm zusammensuchen. Das rote Vieh war so faul, dass es sich einfach forttragen hat lassen. Ich bin an den Fluss gegangen. Auf einmal ist mir ein Mann begegnet, der hat gefragt, ob ich die Katze verkauf. »Ja«, hab ich gesagt und hab mich schon gefreut. Aber er hat nur gelacht und ist weitergegangen. Und dann war ich auf einmal am Fluss. Da war Treibeis und Nebel und kalt war es. Da hat sich die Katze ganz nah an mich gekuschelt, und dann hab ich sie gestreichelt und mit ihr geredet. »Ich kann das nicht mehr sehen«, hab ich ihr gesagt, »es geht nicht, dass meine Geschwister hungern, und du bist fett, ich kann das einfach nicht mehr mit ansehen.« Und auf einmal hab ich ganz laut geschrien, und dann hab ich das rote Vieh an den Hinterläufen genommen und habs an einen Baumstamm geschlagen. Aber sie hat bloß geschrien. Tot war sie noch lange nicht. Da hab ich sie an eine Eisscholle gehaut, aber davon hat sie nur ein Loch im Kopf bekommen, und da ist das Blut herausgeflossen, und überall im Schnee waren dunkle Flecken. Sie hat geschrien wie ein Kind. Ich hätt gern aufgehört, aber jetzt hab ich's schon fertig tun müssen. Ich hab sie immer wieder an die Eisscholle geschlagen, es hat gekracht, ich weiß nicht, ob es ihre Knochen waren oder das Eis, und sie war immer noch nicht tot. Eine Katze hat sieben Leben, sagen die Leute, aber die hat mehr gehabt. Bei jedem Schlag hat sie laut geschrien, und auf einmal hab ich auch geschrien, und ich war ganz nass vor Schweiß bei aller Kälte. Aber einmal war sie dann doch tot. Da hab ich sie in den Fluss geworfen und hab mir meine Hände im Schnee gewaschen, und wie ich noch einmal nach dem Vieh schau, da

we really didn't know anymore what to eat. One day, I was feeling really crazy. I had a go at her and said, "Now listen, we don't have anything to eat anymore, can't you understand?" And I showed her the empty potato crate and the empty bread box. "Go away," I told her. "You see how it is with us." But she only blinked and turned around on the hearth. So I howled with rage and pounded the kitchen table. But she didn't pay any attention. So I picked her up and tucked her under my arm. It had already turned a bit dark outside and the little ones were out and about with Mother, to gather coals at the railway embankment. The red critter was so lazy that it simply allowed me to carry it away. I went along the river. All of a sudden, I passed a young man who asked if I was going to sell the cat. "Yes," I said and began to feel joy. But he only laughed and continued walking. And then, all of a sudden, there was the river. There was drift ice and fog, and it was cold. So the cat snuggled up close to me, and then I stroked her and talked to her. "I cannot watch this any longer," I said to her. "I cannot let my siblings go hungry and you are so fat, I simply cannot watch this any longer." And suddenly, I shouted really loud and then I took the critter by its hind legs and slammed it against the trunk of a tree. But she only cried. She wasn't dead by a long shot. So I slammed her against a block of ice, but that only got her a hole in the head from which blood flowed, and there were dark stains in the snow everywhere. She cried like a child. I would have liked to stop, but now I really had to finish it. Again and again, I slammed her into the block of ice; there was a cracking and I don't know if that was from her bones or the ice, and still she wasn't dead. A cat has nine lives, that's what people say, but she had more than that. Every time I slammed her, she cried out loud and all of a sudden I cried too and I was pretty wet with sweat, the cold notwithstanding. But finally she was really dead. So I threw her into the river and washed my hands in the snow and as

schwimmt es schon weit draußen mitten unter den Eisschollen, dann war es im Nebel verschwunden. Dann hat mich gefroren, aber ich hab noch nicht heimgehen mögen. Ich bin noch in der Stadt herumgelaufen, aber dann bin ich doch heimgegangen. »Was hast du denn?« hat die Mutter gefragt, »du bist ja käseweiß. Und was ist das für Blut an deiner Jacke?« - »Ich hab Nasenbluten gehabt«, hab ich gesagt. Sie hat mich nicht angeschaut und ist an den Herd gegangen und hat mir Pfefferminztee gemacht. Auf einmal ist mir schlecht geworden, da hab ich schnell hinausgehen müssen, dann bin ich gleich ins Bett gegangen. Später ist die Mutter gekommen und hat ganz ruhig gesagt: »Ich versteh dich schon. Denk nimmer dran.« Aber nachher hab ich Peter und Leni die halbe Nacht unterm Kissen heulen hören. Und jetzt weiß ich nicht, ob es richtig war, dass ich das rote Biest umgebracht hab. Eigentlich frisst so ein Tier doch gar nicht viel.

I look for the critter, I see it floating far out there amidst the drifting ice, then it disappeared in the fog.

By then I was freezing, but I didn't want to go home. I ran around in town, but finally I went home. "What's wrong with you," Mother asked. "You are pasty white. And what about the blood on your jacket?"—"I had a nosebleed," I said. She looked at me and went to the stove and made peppermint tea for me. Suddenly, I became nauseated and had to quickly go outside, after that I went to bed right away. Later Mother came and said to me quietly, "I understand, believe me. Don't think of it anymore." However, later I heard Peter and Leni cry half the night under the pillow. And now I don't know anymore whether it was right to kill the red beast or not. After all, an animal like her doesn't really eat that much.

PETER BICHSEL

Peter Bichsel was born March 24, 1935, in Lucerne, Switzerland, to working-class parents. After finishing school, he was an elementary school teacher for a little over a decade. Since 1968, Bichsel has worked as a freelance writer; in the early 1970s and 1980s, he worked primarily as a journalist. Currently, Bichsel lives near Solothurn, Switzerland, and continues to be a popular Swiss-German author and journalist.

Bichsel made his writing debut with the collection *Eigentlich möchte Frau Blum den Milchmann kennenlernen (And Really Frau Blum Would Very Much Like to Meet the Milkman,* 1968). Consisting of twenty-one prose miniatures about a series of missed opportunities, unfulfilled desires, and unspoken words, it won him immediate recognition. His later children's stories, predominantly speaking to the tendency of children to interpret words literally, thereby causing mayhem, were similarly successful. The story collection *Der Busant. Von Trinkern, Polizisten und der schönen Magelone (The Busant: Of Drunkards, Policemen, and the Beautiful Magelone,* 1985), expands on his theme of literature as a vehicle for the fundamental human need for communication.

Between 1974 and 1981 Bichsel was the personal advisor of a member of the Swiss Federal Council. From 1972 to 1997, he distinguished himself as a writer-in-residence (including 1981/82 City of Bergen; 1996 City of Mainz, Germany) and also traveled to the United States, appearing as a visiting lecturer at several universities. In 1981, he was a member of the jury at the 31st Berlin International Film Festival. Many of his magazine and newspaper columns illustrating his harsh criti-

cisms of the Swiss government were gathered in *Geschichten zur falschen Zeit* (*Stories at the Wrong Time*, 1979), *Irgendwo anderswo* (*Somewhere Elsewhere*, 1986), and *Im Gegenteil* (*On the Contrary*, 1990).[1]

Bichsel has received a number of prominent prizes and awards, including the Literature Prize of the Group 47[2] (1965), the German Youth Book Award (1970), and the European Essay Prize (2000). In 2004, he was awarded an Honorary Doctorate in Theology by the University of Basel, Switzerland.

The story "Ein Tisch ist ein Tisch" ("A Table is a Table," 1969) continues the theme of communication as an essential human need, but this time turning it on its head and juxtaposing it with the message that the toils and troubles of life are self-inflicted. The responsibility for ending boredom and misery in one's personal life rests more upon the individual than upon society.[3] The main character, an elderly man, leads a lonely and boring existence, living by himself on the top floor of an apartment building. Dissatisfied with the names of everyday objects, he wonders what would happen if he changed them. So, he starts referring to a table as a carpet, a bed as a picture, a chair as a clock, a wardrobe as a newspaper, and a photo album as a mirror, among others. At first he is excited about having breathed new life into his gray and colorless world, but soon he realizes that rather than making his life more exciting and colorful, his actions have robbed him of his ability to communicate—with unexpected consequences.

---

[1] "Peter Bichsel". *Encyclopaedia Britannica. Encyclopaedia Britannica Online.* Encyclopaedia Britannica, 2011. Web. 28 Aug. 2011. <http://www.britannica.com/EBchecked/topic/64661/Peter-Bichsel>

[2] The Literature Prize of the Gruppe 47 was awarded to up-and-coming writers starting in 1950. The original Gruppe 47 included famous writers such as Nobel Prize winner Günter Grass (1958) and lyricist Ingeborg Bachmann (1953); later it counted among its members dramatists Peter Weiss, poet Paul Celan, and writers Gabriele Wohmann, Hans Magnus Enzensberger, Martin Walser, and Gisela Elsner. The organization disbanded in 1977.

[3] Peter Bichsel. *Encyclopaedia Britannica. Encyclopaedia Britannica Online.* Encyclopaedia Britannica, 2011. Web. 13 Aug. 2011. <http://www.britannica.com/EBchecked/topic/64661/Peter-Bichsel>

Besides being a moving account of the decline of the old man, the story teaches that humans are able to relate to and understand each other because of our collective agreement about naming. Not only is it pointless to change language unilaterally, but it also may impact an individual's ability to communicate and stay in touch with the world.[4] The syntax and language of the story are plain and unadorned, complementing the portrayal of the main character.[5] From the setting to the language to the character, everything is gray, drab, and nondescript, and the old man's actions, described with a minimalist's eye, are the focus of attention. "A Table Is a Table" definitely is more than a simplistic children's story, even though it is written at the level of an elementary student's language proficiency, and adult readers will find that it contains much to reflect upon.

[4]Tempithak, Jessica. A Table Is A Table. Web. 12 Aug. 2011. <http://www.noojkz.edublogs.org/2009/08/29/a-table-is-a-table/>
[5]"Textanalyse: Ein Tisch ist ein Tisch: Forum Deutsch." Web. 13 Aug. 2011. <http://www.ehausaufgaben.de/Thema-114520-Textanalyse-Ein-Tisch-ist-ein-Tisch.php>

PETER BICHSEL

Ein Tisch ist ein Tisch

Ich will von einem alten Mann erzählen, von einem Mann, der kein Wort mehr sagt, ein müdes Gesicht hat, zu müd zum Lächeln und zu müd, um böse zu sein. Er wohnt in einer kleinen Stadt, am Ende der Straße oder nahe der Kreuzung. Es lohnt sich fast nicht, ihn zu beschreiben, kaum etwas unterscheidet ihn von anderen. Er trägt einen grauen Hut, graue Hosen, einen grauen Rock und im Winter den langen grauen Mantel, und er hat einen dünnen Hals, dessen Haut trocken und runzelig ist, die weißen Hemdkragen sind ihm viel zu weit. Im obersten Stock des Hauses hat er sein Zimmer, vielleicht war er verheiratet und hatte Kinder, vielleicht wohnte er früher in einer andern Stadt. Bestimmt war er einmal ein Kind, aber das war zu einer Zeit, wo die Kinder wie Erwachsene angezogen waren. Man sieht sie so im Fotoalbum der Großmutter. In seinem Zimmer sind zwei Stühle, ein Tisch, ein Teppich, ein Bett und ein Schrank. Auf einem kleinen Tisch steht ein Wecker, daneben liegen alte Zeitungen und das Fotoalbum, an der Wand hängen ein Spiegel und ein Bild.

Der alte Mann machte morgens einen Spaziergang und nachmittags einen Spaziergang, sprach ein paar Worte mit seinem Nachbarn, und abends saß er an seinem Tisch.

Das änderte sich nie, auch sonntags war das so. Und wenn der Mann am Tisch saß, hörte er den Wecker ticken, immer den Wecker ticken.

Dann gab es einmal einen besonderen Tag, einen Tag mit Sonne, nicht zu heiß, nicht zu kalt, mit Vogelgezwitscher, mit

PETER BICHSEL

A Table Is a Table

I want to tell you about an old man, about a man who no longer speaks a word, has a tired face; too tired to smile and too tired to be angry. He lives in a small town, at the end of a street or close to an intersection. It is hardly worth the trouble describing him; he is hardly distinguishable from other people. He wears a gray hat, gray pants, a gray jacket, and in the winter that long, gray coat, and he has a spindly neck whose skin is dry and wrinkly; the white shirt collars are much too large on him. You can find he has a room on the top floor of the house; maybe he was married and had children; maybe at an earlier time he lived in another town. He must have been a child once, but that was at a time when children were dressed like adults. You can see them dressed like that in grandmother's photo album. In his room there are two chairs, a table, a rug, a bed, and a wardrobe. On a little table there is an alarm clock; next to it there are old newspapers and the photo album; on the wall there are a mirror and a picture.

The old man went for a walk in the morning and for a walk in the afternoon, spoke a few words with his neighbors, and in the evening he sat at his table.

That never changed; even on Sundays it was like that. And when the man sat at the table he heard the alarm clock tick, always the alarm clock ticking.

Then there was a special day once, a day with sunshine, not too hot, not too cold, with birds chirping, with friendly

113

freundlichen Leuten, mit Kindern, die spielten – und das besondere war, daß das alles dem Mann plötzlich gefiel.
Er lächelte.
«Jetzt wird sich alles ändern», dachte er. Er öffnete den obersten Hemdknopf, nahm den Hut in die Hand, beschleunigte seinen Gang, wippte sogar beim Gehen in den Knien und freute sich. Er kam in seine Straße, nickte den Kindern zu, ging vor sein Haus, stieg die Treppe hoch, nahm die Schlüssel aus der Tasche und schloß sein Zimmer auf.
Aber im Zimmer war alles gleich, ein Tisch, zwei Stühle, ein Bett. Und wie er sicht hinsetzte, hörte er wieder das Ticken, und alle Freude war vorbei, denn nichts hatte sich geändert. Und den Mann überkam eine große Wut. Er sah im Spiegel sein Gesicht rot anlaufen, sah, wie er die Augen zukniff; dann verkrampfte er seine Hände zu Fäusten, hob sie und schlug mit ihnen auf die Tischplatte, erst nur einen Schlag, dann noch einen, und dann begann er auf den Tisch zu trommeln und schrie dazu immer wieder:
«Es muß sich etwas ändern.» Und er hörte den Wecker nicht mehr. Dann begannen seine Hände zu schmerzen, seine Stimme versagte, dann hörte er den Wecker wieder, und nichts änderte sich.
«Immer derselbe Tisch», sagte der Mann, «dieselben Stühle, das Bett, das Bild. Und dem Tisch sage ich Tisch, dem Bild sage ich Bild, das Bett heißt Bett, und den Stuhl nennt man Stuhl. Warum denn eigentlich?» Die Franzosen sagen dem Bett ‹li›, dem Tisch ‹tabl›, nennen das Bild ‹tablo› und den Stuhl ‹schäs›, und sie verstehen sich. Und die Chinesen verstehen sich auch.
«Warum heißt das Bett nicht Bild», dachte der Mann und lächelte, dann lachte er, lachte, bis die Nachbarn an die Wand klopften und ‹Ruhe› riefen.
«Jetzt ändert es sich», rief er, und er sagte von nun an dem Bett ‹Bild›.
«Ich bin müde, ich will ins Bild», sagte er, und morgens blieb er oft lange im Bild liegen und überlegte, wie er nun dem Stuhl sagen wolle, und er nannte den Stuhl ‹Wecker›. Hie und da träumte er schon in der neuen Sprache, und dann übersetzte er die Lieder aus seiner Schulzeit in seine Sprache, und er sang sie leise vor sich hin.

people, with children who played—and the special thing was that all of a sudden the man liked all of this.

He smiled.

"Now everything is going to change," he thought to himself. He opened the top button on his shirt, took the hat in his hand, increased the pace of his walk, even bobbed at the knees while walking, and began to enjoy himself. He arrived in his street, nodded to the children, went to the front of the house, climbed the stairs, took the keys out of his pocket, and unlocked his room.

But in the room everything was the same, a table, two chairs, a bed. And when he sat down, he heard the ticking again, and all his joy was gone because nothing had changed. And the man began to feel great anger. In the mirror, he saw his face turn red, saw how he squinted his eyes; then he clenched his hands into fists, raised them and pounded the table with them, at first only one blow, then another one, and then he began to drum the table and, shouting at each blow, "Something has got to change." And he did not hear the alarm clock any more. Then his hands began to hurt, his voice failed, he heard the alarm clock again, and nothing changed.

"Always the same table," said the man, "the same chairs, bed, picture. And the table I call table, the picture I call picture, the bed is called a bed, and the chair is called a chair. Actually, why?" The French call the bed "li," the table "tabl," they call the picture "tablo" and the chair "chais," and they understand each other. And the Chinese understand each other too. "Why isn't the bed called picture," thought the man, and smiled; then he laughed; he laughed until the neighbors knocked on the wall and shouted, "quiet."

"Now it is going to change," he shouted, and from now on he said "picture" to the bed.

"I am tired, I want to go to picture," he said, and in the morning he often stayed for a long time in the picture and began to think about what he was going to call the chair, and he called the chair "alarm clock."

Er stand also auf, zog sich an, setzte sich auf den Wecker und stützte die Arme auf den Tisch. Aber der Tisch hieß jetzt nicht mehr Tisch, er hieß jetzt Teppich. Am Morgen verließ also der Mann das Bild, zog sich an setzte sich an den Teppich auf den Wecker und überlegte, wem er wie sagen könnte.

Dem Bett sagte er Bild.
Dem Tisch sagte er Teppich.
Dem Stuhl sagte er Wecker.
Der Zeitung sagte er Bett.
Dem Spiegel sagte er Stuhl.
Dem Wecker sagte er Fotoalbum.
Dem Schrank sagte er Zeitung.
Dem Teppich sagte er Schrank.
Dem Bild sagte er Tisch.
Und dem Fotoalbum sagte er Spiegel.
Also:
Am Morgen blieb der alte Mann lange im Bild liegen, um neun läutete das Fotoalbum, der Mann stand auf und stellte sich auf den Schrank, damit er nicht an den Füßen fror, dann nahm er seine Kleider aus der Zeitung, zog sich an, schaute in den Stuhl an der Wand, setzte sich dann auf den Wecker an den Teppich, und blätterte den Spiegel durch, bis er den Tisch seiner Mutter fand.

Der Mann fand das lustig, und er übte den ganzen Tag und prägte sich die neuen Wörter ein. Jetzt wurde alles umbenannt: Er war jetzt kein Mann mehr, sondern ein Fuß, und der Fuß war ein Morgen und der Morgen ein Mann.

Jetzt könnt ihr die Geschichte selbst weiterschreiben. Und dann könnt ihr, so wie es der Mann machte, auch die andern Wörter austauschen:

läuten heißt stellen,
frieren heißt schauen,
liegen heißt läuten,

Now and then he even dreamed in the new language, and then he translated the songs from his schooldays into his language, and he quietly sang them to himself.

Consequently he got up, got dressed, sat down on the alarm clock and propped his arms up on the table. But the table was now no longer called table, it was called rug. Therefore, in the morning the man left the picture, got dressed, sat down at rug on the alarm clock and thought about which things he could label and how.

The bed he called picture.
The table he called rug.
The chair he called alarm clock.
The newspaper he called bed.
The mirror he called chair.
The alarm clock he called photo album.
The wardrobe he called newspaper.
The rug he called wardrobe.
The picture he called table.
And the photo album he called mirror.
Thus:

In the morning, the old man stayed for a long time in the picture, and at nine o' clock the photo album chimed; the man got up and stood on the wardrobe so that his feet would not get chilly and after that he removed his garments from the newspaper, dressed in them, and regarded himself in the chair at the wall; afterward he sat down on the alarm clock at the rug and he paged through the mirror until he found his mother's table.

The man found this funny and he practiced all day long and tried to remember the new words. Now everything was redefined: he was now no longer a man, but a foot, and the foot was a morning and the morning a man.

Now you can continue writing the story yourself. And then you can, like the man did, also replace the other words:

To ring is called to put,
To freeze is called to look,
To lie is called to ring,

stehen heißt frieren,
stellen heißt blättern.

So daß es dann heißt: Am Mann blieb der alte Fuß lange im Bild läuten, um neun stellte das Fotoalbum, der Fuß fror auf und blätterte sich aus dem Schrank, damit er nicht an die Morgen schaute. Der alte Mann kaufte sich blaue Schulhefte und schrieb sie mit den neuen Wörtern voll, und er hatte viel zu tun damit, und man sah ihn nur noch selten auf der Straße. Dann lernte er für alle Dinge die neuen Bezeichnungen und vergaß dabei mehr und mehr die richtigen. Er hatte jetzt eine neue Sprache, die ihm ganz allein gehörte. Aber bald fiel ihm auch das Übersetzen schwer, er hatte seine alte Sprache fast vergessen, und er mußte die richtigen Wörter in seinen blauen Heften suchen. Und es machte ihm Angst, mit den Leuten zu sprechen. Er mußte lange nachdenken, wie die Leute zu den Dingen sagen.

Seinem Bild sagen die Leute Bett.
Seinem Teppich sagen die Leute Tisch.
Seinem Wecker sagen die Leute Stuhl.
Seinem Bett sagen die Leute Zeitung.
Seinem Stuhl sagen die Leute Spiegel.
Seinem Fotoalbum sagen die Leute Wecker.
Seiner Zeitung sagen die Leute Schrank.
Seinem Schrank sagen die Leute Teppich.
Seinem Spiegel sagen die Leute Fotoalbum.
Seinem Tisch sagen die Leute Bild.

Und es kam soweit, daß der Mann lachen mußte, wenn er die Leute reden hörte.

Er mußte lachen, wenn er hörte, wie jemand sagte: «Gehen Sie morgen auch zum Fußballspiel?» Oder wenn jemand sagte: «Jetzt regnet es schon zwei Monate lang.» Oder wenn jemand sagte. «Ich habe einen Onkel in Amerika.»

Er mußte lachen, weil er all das nicht verstand.

Aber eine lustige Geschichte ist das nicht. Sie hat traurig angefangen und hört traurig auf. Der alte Mann im grauen Mantel konnte die Leute nicht mehr verstehen, das war nicht so schlimm.

To stand is called to freeze,
To put is called to page.

Consequently, it will translate like this: In the man, the old foot stayed for a long time in the picture, at nine the photo album put, the foot froze up and paged himself out of the wardrobe so that he didn't look at the mornings. The old man bought blue school notebooks and filled them with the new words, and he was very busy doing this, and he was rarely seen about. Then he learned the new concepts for all items and began to forget the real ones more and more. He now had a new language that belonged solely to him. But soon, it was also difficult for him to translate, he had almost forgotten his old language, and he had to look up the correct words in his blue notebooks. And he was afraid to talk to people. He had to think a long time to remember how people called things.

His picture, people called bed.

His rug, people called table.

His alarm clock, people called chair.

His bed, people called newspaper.

His chair, people called mirror.

His photo album, people called clock.

His newspaper, people called wardrobe.

His wardrobe, people called rug.

His mirror, people called photo alum.

His table, people called picture.

And it went so far as the old man having to laugh when he heard people talking. He had to laugh when he heard someone say, "Are you also going to the soccer game tomorrow?" Or when someone said, "It has been raining for two months now." Or when someone said," I have an uncle in America."

He had to laugh because he did not understand any of this.

However, this is not a funny story. It began sad and it ends sad. It wasn't so bad that the old man in the gray coat was no longer able to understand people.

Viel schlimmer war, sie konnten ihn nicht mehr verstehen. Und deshalb sagte er nichts mehr.

Er schwieg, sprach nur noch mit sich selbst, grüßte nicht einmal mehr.

What was much worse was that they were unable to understand him any longer. And that is why he did not talk anymore.

He was silent, talked only to himself, did not even say hello anymore.

IRMTRAUD MORGNER

Irmtraud Morgner was born August 22, 1933, in Chemnitz, known as Karl-Marx-Stadt while it was ruled by the East German communist regime. The daughter of a train engineer, her childhood dream was to become a train engineer herself.[1] From 1952 to 1956, she studied literature and philosophy in Leipzig, taking classes with famous philosopher Ernst Bloch[2] and German scholar Hans Mayer, among others. After graduating from college, she moved to Berlin and began working as an editorial assistant for the state-run publication *Neue deutsche Literatur* (*New German Literature*). From 1958 on, she worked as a freelance writer.

Until 1965, Morgner's work supported literary patterns that mirrored the government-imposed "socialist cultural revolution." The story "Das Signal steht auf Fahrt ("The Signal Says Go," 1959), the novel *Ein Haus am Rande der Stadt* (*A House at the Edge of the City*, 1964), and the narrative *Notturno* (*Nocturne*, 1964) are examples of this genre. But in 1965, the state

---

[1]Reflecting on this, Morgner wrote, "Perhaps this strong desire indicated the presence of a granule of natural resistance which a conventionally raised female human being needs as some sort of seed capital in order to take the opportunity to swim to freedom against the strong currents of tradition." Author's translation. Marlis Gerhardt, ed., *Irmtraud Morgner: Texte, Daten, Bilder* (Frankfurt: Suhrkamp Publishers, 1990), 20.

[2]On Bloch's influence on her thinking and writing, Morgner wrote, "Bloch's personality inspired. Ignited . . .The enormous knowledge Bloch spread out before us, thrown down, strewn about like flowers—our little brains were able to absorb only a tiny portion of the wealth. Actually only a notion of it . . . it helped me . . . to stay immune against the plague of cynicism, which devours all creative powers." Author's translation. Irmtraud Morgner, *Das Heroische Testament: Ein Roman in Fragmenten*, (Darmstadt: Luchterhand, 1998), 218.

censors denied permission to print her novel *Rumba auf einen Herbst* (*Rumba for an Autumn*), accusing Morgner of using it to disseminate subversive ideas.[3] The rationale was that her portrayal of the matrimonial and equality conflicts facing a woman in a socialist society contradicted the officially proclaimed progress of emancipation (of women) in a socialist society.[4]

Morgner's encounters with censorship left a lasting impression on her, and she learned to be more circumspect. A year after the birth of her son David, she published her novel *Hochzeit in Konstantinopel* (*Wedding in Constantinople*, 1968), which marked her breakthrough as a popular writer. Cloaking her criticism of the East German regime in linguistic robes, so to speak, and embedding dissenting thoughts in cheerful lightness, grotesque humor, and magically encrypted writing, Morgner presented a theme that would be central to her literary work from this time on—women entering history. The narratives *Gauklerlegende: Eine Spielfraungeschichte* (*A Juggler's Legend: Chronicled by a Woman Minstrel*, 1970), *Die wundersamen Reisen Gustav des Weltfahrers: Lügenhafter Roman mit Kommentaren* (*The Wondrous Journeys of Gustav the Globetrotter: A Tall Tale Complete with Comments*, 1972), and the unfinished *Salman Trilogy*[5] all

---

[3]The novel depicts the disillusionment of young people in the face of the attempted deployment of Soviet nuclear missiles in Cuba. The young Morgner's quest for a meaningful life in a socialist society is palpable in the female character Karla, who suffers a variety of setbacks while trying to become emancipated under socialist conditions. See also, Annemarie Auer, "Trobadora unterwegs oder Schulung in Realismus," *Sinn und Form* 5 (1976): 1067-1107.

[4]There is reason to believe that the Rumba debacle, the first of many traumatic and painful encounters with editors, censors, cultural department officials, and Stasi informants (who, incredibly, included her own husband), opened Morgner's eyes. The immense frustration and pain she experienced during her confrontations with the regime echoes in the depictions of her characters, particularly in her unfinished Salman trilogy.

[5]The Salman Trilogy consists of the novels *Leben und Abenteuer der Trobadora Beatrix nach Zeugnissen ihrer Spielfrau Laura* (*Life and Adventures of Trobadora Beatriz As Chronicled By Her Minstrel Laura*, 1974), *Amanda. Ein Hexenroman* (*Amanda: A Witches Novel*, 1983), and the posthumously published *Das heroische Testament. Ein Roman in Fragmenten* (*The Heroic Testament: A Novel in Fragments*, 1998), which interweaves the lives and adventures of the central characters Beatriz de Dia and Amanda/Laura Salman.

garnered a huge readership along with critical acclaim in both East and West Germany.

Starting in the mid-1970s, Morgner received much recognition for her work, including the coveted Heinrich-Mann Prize of the East German Academy of Arts (1975) and the DDR-Nationalpreis für Literatur (GDR National Prize for Literature, 1977)—the latter prompted her election to the Board of the East German Writers Union in the same year. In West Germany, she won the Roswitha von Gandersheim Literaturpreis (Roswitha von Gandersheim Literature Prize, 1985), and the Prize for Grotesque Humor from the City of Kassel (1989).

Because of her enthusiasm—on the surface—as an orthodox socialist writer,[6] the communist regime granted Morgner permission to travel. In 1971, she was approved for a visit to Paris, then to the Soviet Union in 1974, and from 1974 on she was allowed to travel repeatedly to West Germany, the U.S., and Switzerland.

Morgner became a major influence on an entire generation of writers who struggled with similar problems in her own country as well as within the western European and Anglo-American feminist movements, as the continuing popularity of her writings indicated.

But the frustration, pain, and fragmentation in her life took its toll. In 1987, during an appointment as a visiting lecturer in the German Department at the University of Zurich, Switzerland, Morgner became seriously ill. The following spring, she was diagnosed with colon cancer. After four operations, she died in East Berlin on May 6, 1990, less than six months after the fall of the Berlin Wall.

Der Schöne und das Tier: Eine Liebesgeschichte (*Beauty and the Beast: A Love Story*, 1991) is a mock fairy tale that reintro-

---

[6]The censors never caught on that, while paying lip service to the "promised land" of the German Democratic Republic, she dished out harsh criticism on the miserable conditions in her socialist home country. It was cleverly delivered via treatises, transcripts, letters, myths, intermezzos, and narratives within narratives, all patched together to create a narrative form that she termed the "montage novel" that both entertained her readers and made the censors' heads spin.

duces one of the heroines from the Salman Trilogy. But Morgner subverts traditional gender expectations by injecting a male Beauty into the story. This time, the culture shock of the former female troubadour Beatriz results not from awakening after an 810-year slumber in modern-day France, but from having been reborn as a siren, half human and half bird. To all appearances, she is, as the title of the story suggests, a Beast.

At the outset of the story, Beatriz is in the drunk tank of a police station, journaling the adventures that led to her arrest. The reader learns that she narrowly escaped detection by the people of Berlin by hiding in the metals struts of the roof of the central train station. When she is assaulted by a mob outside the train station, a young and handsome man comes to her rescue, the proverbial Beauty from the title of the story. Beatriz falls in love with him instantly because, besides saving her life, he also reminds her of a lover from a previous life. Beatriz and her beau break into the basement of an empty office building and spend many nights and days there making love, until they are picked up by the police.

Written in sentence fragments and narrated not strictly in chronological order, but interspersed with frequent flashbacks and ruminations, the form and structure of the story mirror the fragmentation of the traumatized siren. In fact, fragmentation is the main theme of the story (as it was of her life) and, according to Morgner, the only way to overcome it is through one thing: love.

IRMTRAUD MORGNER

Der Schöne und das Tier

Natürlich sind weibliche Trobadore aus der Mode.
Bevor sie je in ihr waren. Guten Morgen, Du Schöner, für den ich nun schreibe. In der Ausnüchterungszelle. Wo die Tagesordnung hängt, zu der übergegangen werden soll. Die neue: der alte Hut. Mir ist so kalt ums Hirn. Schmerzensschreie gehören heute zum guten Ton oder zu einem, an den man sich gewöhnt hat. Freudenschreie erwecken mitunter selbst von den Toten. Ihnen fühlte ich mich zugehörig, obgleich der gegenwärtige Weltzustand mich ausgetrieben hatte. Ich konnte unter der Erde keine Ruhe finden. Über ihr war ich noch unbehauster. Ich, Beatriz de Dia, gestorbene Comtesse und Trobadora, auferstandene Sirene ohne Stimme, nicht tot also und nicht lebendig: Wer oder was ist weniger? Guten Tag, und ich kann Dir meine Empfindung nicht erklären, es ist eine gewisse Leere – die mir halt wehe tut, ein gewisses Sehnen, das nie befriedigt wird, folglich nie aufhört, immer fordauert, ja von Tag zu Tag wächst, es ist leicht, das Leben zur Hölle zu machen, wenn man es mit Gewalt zum Paradies machen will.

IRMTRAUD MORGNER

Beauty and the Beast

Naturally, female troubadours are out of style.

Before they were ever in.

Good morning, beautiful, for whom I am writing. In the drunk tank.

Where the agenda for the day is posted on the wall, supposedly to be ignored.

The new one: an old hat.

It feels so cold around my brain.

Cries of agony strike the right note these days, or one we have gotten used to.

Cries of joy have the power to raise the dead, now and then.

I associated with the latter, although the current global situation had driven me out. I had been unable to find peace six feet under.

Above ground, I felt even more homeless.

I, Beatrice de Dia, deceased countess and female troubadour, risen siren without voice, not dead and not alive: Who or what is less?

Good day, and I cannot explain my sentiments to you, there is a kind of emptiness—which just hurts me, a kind of longing which is never stilled and thus never ends, forever continuing, even growing from day to day, and it is easy to make life hell when you want to turn it into paradise by force.

In Paris muß sich eine Frau gesagt haben: Wenn schon zu dieser uralten Tagesordnung übergehen, dann gründlich. Und schnitt sich einen Mann aus den Rippen. Aber Paris war weit und eine solche Frau unvorstellbar, und die Provence lag hinter sieben Bergen. Guten Abend, dachte ich, was suchst du in diesem häßlichen Viertel dieser häßlichen Stadt, gute Nacht, Du Schöner, und dumme Frage hier, dumme sowie zweideutige Frage bei eindeutigen Angeboten ringsum, guten Abend, gute Nacht, mit Rosen bedacht, was hat Raimbaut hier zu suchen?

Ich suchte ein Dach, um meine Federn zu trocknen.

Bekanntlich tragen Sirenen Federn. Und der Frühlingshimmel 1988 war naß und kalt und für Federvieh eine Zumutung. Für weißes Federvieh insonderheit. In Dreckwolken war mein Federkleid schnell ergraut. Andere standen zum Durchfliegen nicht zur Verfügung. Ratlosigkeit hatte mich in die Luft geworfen. Über mir Abgashimmel. Unter mir sterbende Wälder. Verzweiflung trieb mich nach Süden. Wo ich gebürtig bin. Von dero Lieblichkeit Provence erhoffte ich die verlorene Hoffnung: Meine Stimme.

Und »ich dachte« ist natürlich gelogen. Die Erscheinung traf mich wie ein Messerstich. Mit einem Messer im Kopf oder sonst kann man nicht denken. Erst als ich es weggeworfen hatte, ausgezogen wie einen Dorn und weit von mir geworfen, unters Blech des Autoverkehrs, meldete sich mein Verstand zurück und sagte mir, Raimbaut d'Aurenga war rothaarig.

Ich nahm meinen Blick aus den Locken. Von rechts Beschimpfungen.

Aber meine Ohren griffen nicht. Wenn sie taub gewesen wären: Wohltat. Erlösung, die ich außerhalb des Bahnhofs gesucht hatte. Außerhalb seines Dachs, das riesig hoch und weit war: ideal, um unter seinem Gestänge sirenische Federn zu trocknen. Schwungfedern trocknen schlecht ungespreizt. Und bei einer Flügelspannweite von zwei Metern bleibt man unter Menschen nur unbemerkt, wenn deren Sinne abgestumpft sind.

In Paris, a woman must have said to herself: If I have to adopt this ancient order of the day, then I will do it thoroughly. And so she cut a man from her ribs.

But Paris was a long way off and such a woman unimaginable, and the Provence was located over the hills and far away. Good evening, I thought, what are you doing in the ugly part of this ugly city, good night, beautiful, and what a silly question, a silly and also ambiguous question with indecent proposals all around, good evening, good night, adorned with roses, what did Raimbaut need to search for here?

I was looking for a rooftop to dry out my feathers.

As is well-known, sirens have feathers. And the 1988 spring sky was wet and cold and an imposition for poultry. For white poultry in particular. In the dirty clouds, my plumage had quickly turned gray. There were no other ones available to fly through. Helplessness had thrown me into the air. Above me, the skies were thick with exhaust fumes. Beneath me lay dying forests. Despair drove me south. Where I was born. From her loveliness, the Provence, I had hoped to receive lost hope: my voice.

And "I thought" is a lie, naturally.

The apparition hit me like a stab with a knife. One is unable to think with a knife in the head or otherwise. Only when I had thrown it away, pulled it out like a thorn and thrown it far away into the metal of road traffic, did my wits return and tell me that Raimbaut d'Aurenga had been a redhead.

I took my gaze away from his locks of hair.

From the right, profanities.

But my ears did not register them. If I had been deaf: delight, release, which I had been looking for outside of the railroad station. Outside of its roof, which was tremendously high and large: ideal for drying a siren's feathers, perching among its struts.

Flight feathers don't dry well when not spread apart. And with a wingspan of six feet, one will only go unnoticed by humans when their senses are dulled. Those who are scared shitless use perfume, I thought and counted on

Wer die Hosen voll hat, parfümiert, dachte ich und rechnete mit der abtötenden Wirkung von aufreizenden Farben, Formen, Tönen, Gerüchen, Geräuschen, Bewegungen auf die Reisenden unter mir. Rechenfehler: ich. Die Reizschwelle meiner Sinne lag weit unter der hier üblichen. Ich war untrainiert. Ich war seßhaft in einem Land, das anderes trainiert.

Als ich merkte, daß die Reizüberflutung mir sogar die Angst nahm, die mich im Grabe umgedreht hatte und schließlich ausgetrieben, floh ich den Ort. Wo Fleisch, genauer als dem natürlichen Auge natürlich wahrnehmbar, in perfekt erklügelten Stellungen bunt und nackt oder angezogen ausgezogener als nackt von allen Wänden schrie. In allen Größen. Neben dem Gestänge, auf dem ich saß, zum Beispiel so hundert Quadratmeter Fotoreklame mit weiblichem Fleisch. Porendrall und mit Wassertropfen behangen wie ein bißlüstern servierter Apfel.

Erschöpft floh ich den Bahnhof. Und gelangte ins Bahnhofsviertel, wo Menschenfleisch live zum Verkauf stand.

Ein durchschnittlich angezogener Mann ist vor einer Schminkfassade, die aus Straßenstrich und den Auslagen pornographischer Etablissements gebildet wird, bestenfalls schattenhaft wahrnehmbar. Selbst wenn er mit Jeans auf seinen hübschen Hintern aufmerksam macht.

Erst als die Beschimpfungen so unflätig wurden, daß sie meine versehrten Ohren erreichten, und ich merkte, daß die Empörung mir galt, nahm ich die bewegten Steppereien an den Jeans vor mir wieder wahr. Ich in Gestalt meines Selbsterhaltungstriebs. Er suchte nach Hilfe und vermutete: Strichkunde. Später auch: Strichjunge. Zuhälter nicht. Zuhälter haben keine Anmut.

Die Beschimpfungen wurden aus weiblichen und männlichen Mündern gespien. Große Empörung wegen Geschäftsschädigung, noch größere über die Mittel. In einer Sprache, die von der trobadorischen entfernter ist als Trapezunt von

the deadening effect of tantalizing colors, shapes, sounds, odors, noises, and movements of the travelers beneath me. I had miscalculated. My own senses' stimulus threshold was far beneath what was customary here. I was untrained. I was a resident from a nation that trained other skills. When I noticed that the sensory overload even killed off the fear that had made me spin in my grave and eventually driven me out, I made my escape from this place. Where, from all the walls around me, flesh screamed, arranged into perfect, sophisticated poses with more precision than the natural eye is able to notice naturally, multicolored and naked, or appearing even more naked than naked when in fact dressed. In all sizes. Next to the struts on which I perched were, for example, about nine hundred square feet of photo ads full of female flesh. The pores pleasingly plump and decorated with water drops like an apple, served up to sink your teeth into.

Exhausted, I fled the railroad station. And ended up in the neighborhood around the railroad station, where human flesh was offered live for sale.

A commonly clad man is at best discernible as a shadow standing in front of a dressed and painted backdrop, made up of street prostitution and the window displays of pornographic establishments, even though he accentuates his handsome behind with a pair of jeans.

Only when the name-calling became so foul-mouthed that it reached my injured ears and I realized that the outrage was directed at me, I began to notice the swirling stitch work on the jeans right before me. I, in the disguise of my self-preservation. He, looking for help and assuming: prostitute's customer. Later even: male prostitute. Not a pimp. Pimps have no style.

The obscenities spewed forth from female and male mouths. Much indignation over injuries to their business interest; much more over the manner. In a language which is more distant from that of a troubadour than Trebizond[1]

---

[1] Trebizond; modern-day Trabzon, Turkey.

Ostern, wurde mir mitgeteilt, daß ständig irgendwelchen neuen Modesauereien hinterhergehetzt werden müßte, die immer neue Ausstattungen verlangten und immer mehr Kapital fräßen, von der Inflation ganz zu schweigen, die neue Sado-Maso-Welle wäre schon teuer genug zu stehen gekommen, wer jetzt eine Sodomie-Welle langsieren wolle, würde umgelegt. Ich stand begriffsstutzig. Fußtritte. Faustschläge auf den Kopf, die mein Denkvermögen auch nicht anregten. Schließlich wurde ich, um mich ans Umgelegtwerden zu gewöhnen, geschmissen. Kurze ohnmachtähnliche Erleichterung, die der Aufprall verschaffte. Dann schwarze Mülltüten rechts, Motorradblech links, über mir Neonrosa, unter mir Asphalt.

Ich rappelte mich aus dem Straßendreck, langte nach einer Hand, um mich hochzurichten. In solcher Lage langt man nach allen Händen, die sich einem bieten. Mir bot sich eine einzige: Ich mußte nicht wählen.

Da Sirenen nur Fänge und Flügel haben, langte ich mit den Flügeln. Mit beiden. Der Herr mit den orangegesteppten Jeans ergriff den rechten Daumenfittich. Als er meine schmutztriefenden Federn mit seinem Taschentuch abputzen wollte, zog er die Wut auf sich. Handgemenge. Beschimpfungen, die alle an mich gerichteten übertrafen, weil sie zusätzlich versuchten, die Ehre abzuschneiden. Was hatte Ehre an eimen Ort zu schaffen, dessen Geschäft auf der Lust seiner Perversion gründete?

Ich muß ein ziemlich dummes Gesicht gezeigt haben – Sirenen besitzen bekanntlich Menschengesichter –, aber mein Verteidiger schien auch nicht durchzusehen. Schreckrund aufgesperrte Lider, wimpernackt in diesem Licht, das aus buntzuckenden Leuchtreklamen zusammengeflickt war. Der Mund öffnete sich mit einem an das Aufschlagen eines Wassertropfens auf Wasser erinnernden Geräusch – nichts Neues für Dich. Wozu also den sinnlichen Ausdruck beschreiben, den das Geräusch verstärkte, und den Kontrast der Nase dazu, deren schmaler, gekrümmter Grat auf Entschiedenheit oder Scharfsinn scharf machte? Genaue Kenntnisse über unsere Vorzüge nützen wenig, ja deprimieren, solange wir sie nicht geliebt wissen.

from Easter, I was informed that one constantly had to chase after new and bloody fashion trends, which required more and more new outfits and ate up more and more capital, not to mention inflation; the new sadomasochistic trend had already cost them dearly; if someone was thinking of launching a sodomy trend, they would finish them off.

I stood there, slow-witted. Kicks. Punches to the head, which also did not help to speed up my intellectual power. Finally, I was pushed down, to get me used to being finished off.

The impact caused a short, faint-like relief. Then black trash bags to the right, motorcycle metal to the left, neon pink above, asphalt beneath me.

I struggled from the dirt in the street, reached for a hand to pull me to my feet. In such a situation, one reaches for any hands that are offered. I was offered only one: I did not have to choose.

Since sirens only have fangs and wings, I reached with my wings. With both. The gentleman with the orange-stitched jeans clasped my right thumb wing. When he tried to clean my feathers, which were dripping with dirt, with his handkerchief, he incurred the wrath of the mob. Scuffles. Obscenities which surpassed the ones aimed only at me because these also tried to rob him off his dignity. What has honor got to do in a place where business is based on the lust over its perversion?

I must have displayed a rather silly facial expression—sirens, as is commonly known, have human faces—but my defender didn't seem to see through it either.

The eyelids round and opened wide with dread, lashes naked in this light stitched together with luminous advertising, twitching in many colors.

The mouth opened with a noise reminiscent of a water drop hitting water—nothing new for you. Why describe the sensual expression, which the noise amplified, and along with it the contrast of the nose, whose small, curved ridge suggested determination or discrimination? Exact knowledge of our virtues does little good, even makes one feel depressed, until we see that someone else loves them.

Als uns die Flucht gelang, wurde »Leda« hinterhergeschrien. Das Worf traf.

Ich fühlte begehrliche Blicke auf meinen Flügeln, in mir Solidarität. Sie erinnerte mich an den wirklichen Raimbaut d'Aurenga, der nicht der Wirklichkeit entsprach. Ich hatte einst auf ihn etliche Kanzonen gedichtet, die nicht überliefert sind. Nur die, in denen theoretische Liebestränen fließen, sind überliefert. Echte lassen sich nicht so handlich zu Versketten auffädeln. Denn der wirkliche Trobador Raimbaut, der nicht der Wirklichkeit entsprach, war überallemaßen schön. Ein friedliches Wesen, das Geduld aufbringen konnte, über sich lachen, verlieren, mit Kindern spielen, zuhören, lieben: nicht nur Männer oder sich, nicht nur sich im andern; sondern den andern; oder sogar den andern in sich. Selbst seine eigenen Kinder, neun an der Zahl, behandelte er konsequent als kleine Menschen, nicht als Besitz, Beweisstücke von Potenz oder Schmusgeräte auf Abruf. Er brachte ihnen nicht Wallungen, sondern stete, unerschöpfbare Zuneigung entgegen. Einmal sprach er im Rittersaal mit ähnlichen Worten beiseite: »Unsereiner wundert sich jetzt schon mal. Aber wir werden uns noch viel mehr wundern. Und noch ganz anders, hoff ich, denn es ist noch kein Ende abzusehen. Uns steht kein langweiliges Leben bevor, wenn die Damen erst tun wollen, was sie tun wollen, nicht, was sie tun sollen. Was werden sie als Menschen sagen über die Männer; nicht als Bilder, die sich die Männer von ihnen gemacht haben? Was wird geschehen, wenn sie äußern, was sie fühlen, nicht was zu fühlen wir von ihnen erwarten? Neulich sagte die Gattin eines Dichters, von Frauen wären keine Liebesgedichte zu lesen. Die Gattin hat Recht, nur wenige Damen möchten ihren Ruf dem Geruch der Abnormität preisgeben. Frauen ohne unterdrücktes Liebesleben gelten als krank (nymphoman).«

»Männer solcher Art gelten als gesund (kerngesund). Kann sein, wir werden eines Wintertags nicht mehr in die Influenza flüchten müssen, um mal schwach sein zu dürfen, kann sein, wir

When we finally escaped, they called "Leda" after us.
The word hit like a punch.
I felt my wings being watched covetously; inwardly, I felt
solidarity.
It reminded me of the real Raimbaut D'Aurenga, who
did not match reality. A long time ago, I had written quite
a few canzones about him, but they did not survive. Only
those, in which imaginary tears of love flow, survived.
Real ones cannot be assembled so neatly into strings of
poems. Because the real troubadour Raimbaut, who did
not match reality, was inordinately handsome. A peaceful
creature, capable of being patient, of laughing at himself,
of being defeated, of playing with children, of listening
and loving: not only men or himself, not only himself in
the other, but also the other, or even the other in him.
Consistently, he even treated his own children, nine in
number, as little people, not as property or proof of po-
tency or objects for cuddling at his beck and call. He did
not treat them to emotional ups and downs, but with
steady and inexhaustible affection. In the great hall, at
one occasion, he spoke similar words in an aside: "Our
sort, we are surprised, occasionally. However, we will be
a lot more surprised from now on. And in many different ways, I hope, because there is no end in sight. We
are not faced with the prospects of a boring life, once
the ladies are going to do what they wish to do and not
what they ought to do. What will they say about men as
human beings and not as images created by men? What
will happen when they express what they feel, not what
we expect them to feel? Recently, a poet's wife said that
there were no love poems written by women. The wife
was right because only few women would not mind taint-
ing their reputation with an insinuation of abnormality.
Women without a suppressed love life are considered sick
(nymphomaniac)."
"Men of such kind are considered healthy (as sound
as a bell). It may well be that one wintery day, we won't
have to use influenza as an excuse to be weak, it may well

gestatten uns eines Tages nicht nur beim Meerrettichessen eine
Träne, ach, einmal den Hof gemacht kriegen, öffentlich . . .«
Ich hatte diese Worte Raimbauts in meinem ersten Leben laut
wiederholt, auf daß alle Höflinge sie hören konnten. Da erklärte
mein Gemahl Guilhelm von Poitiers meinen Geist für krank,
führte mich aus dem Saal und hielt mich fortan in der Kemenate
gefangen. Vorm Verdacht der Ketzerei bewahrte mich damals
mein Stand.

Heute bin ich vogelfrei. Und der Traum vom wirklichen
Raimbaut, der nicht der Wirklichkeit entsprach, ist passé, bevor
er gelebt werden konnte. Nicht nur die weiblichen Trobadore,
sondern auch deren besingenswerte Phänomene sind aus der
Mode.

Sobald aufkommende Ahnungen Konturen von Weisheit ver-
raten, die sich nicht modisch bagatellisieren läßt, wird direkt
zugeschlagen. Mit Gewohnheit.

Die meisten Schläger halten eine Trobadora gottlob für ein
ständig in sie verliebtes, also schön hysterisches, nicht ernst zu
nehmendes Frauenzimmer.

Das hätte mir zu denken geben müssen, als ich meine zweite
Stimme suchte. Meine sirenische Stimme, die mir unter Zeit-
druck aberwartet wurde, unter ungeheurer Verantwortungslast,
gejagt von Rettungspflicht und Heilserwartung wegen dieser
drei Tonnen Sprengstoff, die pro Erdenbewohner bevorratet
sind. Wenn die Zeit krank ist, wird Heilung in gigantischen
Operationen gesucht. Operationsfeld nicht unter »orbis«, das
lateinische Wort rief bei mir die Begriffe Erdkugel, bewohnte
Erde, Himmelssphäre ab.

Meine Muttersprache ist der lateinischen verwandt. Ich hatte
ihre Botschaft überhört, die das Wort bringt.

Unsere Blicke mieden sich nach der ersten flüchtigen Berüh-
rung. Im Bahnhofsviertel werden andere Berührungen gesucht.

Ich fühlte einen Arm auf meinem gefiederten Rücken. Ich
hörte: »Wo wohnst du, Tier?«

be that we will allow ourselves to shed a tear, not only when eating horseradish, alas, to be courted once only, in public . . . "

In my first life, I had repeated these words of Raimbaut's in a loud voice, so that all courtiers were able to hear them. Whereupon my lord and husband, Guilhelm de Poitiers, declared my wits to be unsound, then led me out of the hall and kept me henceforth imprisoned in the bower. Only my social standing saved me from the suspicion of heresy.

Today I am an outlaw, fair game. And, dreams of the real Raimbaut, the one who does not match reality, are a thing of the past, before they became reality. Not only are female troubadours out of fashion, but so are the phenomena they chose to celebrate in their songs.

As soon as emerging premonitions show even a trace of wisdom, which cannot be trivialized into fashion, they will be squarely attacked. With confirmed habit.

Thank goodness most of these attackers take a female troubadour for a dame that is permanently in love with them, thus really hysterical and not to be taken seriously.

I should have realized that when I went to look for my second voice. My siren's voice, which faded away under the extreme burden of responsibility, hounded by an obligation to save and the anticipation to bring about salvation from the three tons of explosives which are, on average, stockpiled for each resident on planet Earth. When the times are ailing, salvation is sought through gigantic operations. The field of operations is not listed under "orbis," the Latin word called to mind for the concepts of globe, inhabited earth, heavenly sphere.

My mother tongue is related to Latin. I overheard its message, which is delivered by words.

We avoided looking at each other after the first fleeting touch. In the railroad station quarter, other kinds of touches are desired.

I felt an arm on my plumed back. I heard, "Where do you live, beast?"

Da ich die Frage nicht beantworten konnte, weil mir auch eine
neue Zunge keine Stimme hatte geben können, starrte ich. Auf
eine Gestalt, die im Eingang zu einem Travestie-Lokal lehnte.
Hochhackige Holzsandalen. Jeans. T-Shirt, dessen Ausschnitte
von weißem Trikotstoff knapp umrahmt wurden. Spitzenfächer
lachsrosa mit Pailletten, Zinnobermund, schwarzsilberne Rahmen vergrößerten die Augen zu unwiderstehlichen Blickfängen,
mittelblonde kurze Herrenfrisur. Ich blieb stehen. Heftige Bewegung des Fächers, bevor er
das Gesicht verbarg. Die Enthüllung langsam, wie man einen
Vorhang zieht. Im Gegensatz zu Theatervorhängen entblößte
der die Inszenierung, indem er sich senkte. Glitzernde Blicke,
gefallsuchtabhängig. Als ich merkte, daß sie von mir auf
meinen Begleiter wechselten und sich dort festbissen, ging ich.
»Gefällt dir das, Tier«, hörte ich fragen.
Die Anrede verstörte mich endlich.
»Möchtest du mich geschminkt, Tier?«
Der selbstverständliche Ton der Anrede »Tier« ging über
meinen Verstand. Ich versuchte, die Verwirrung mit dem
linken Flügel aus meinem Gesicht zu wischen. Sirenen haben
bekanntlich Frauengesichter. Sonst erinnerte meine Körper-
form an die der Schnee-Eule. Im Gegensatz zu dieser Tierart
war ich jedoch knapp menschengroß und wie der Uhu mit
zwei Kopfbüscheln versehen. Die Federohren wuchsen aber
nicht wie beim bubo bubo über den Augen und auch nicht
zwischen Schläfen und Hinterkopf, wo die Menschenohren
sitzen, sondern am Haaransatz. Dort, wo Männer die Geheim-
ratsecken erleiden.
»Gehörst du etwa auch zu den weiblichen Wesen, Tier, bei
denen Schweigen oder ›nein‹ ›ja‹ bedeutet«, hörte ich und sah,
wie der Mann Spiegel und Stifte aus seinen Hosentaschen fingerte. Mit Mühe, die Hosen waren so eng, daß er das Stand-
bein wechseln mußte. Die Spielbeinhaltung entspannte die
Taschenöffnungen ein wenig. Für die Daumen war kein Platz.
Kleine, hübsche Hände. Ich musterte sie, um mich aus der Be-
soffenheit zu reißen. Oder war er besoffen? Nur ein Besoffener

Since I was unable to answer the question because even a new tongue had not had the power to give me a voice, I stared. At a figure reposing at the entrance to a travesty bar. Wooden sandals with high heels. Jeans. T-shirt, the neckline and openings scantily lined with white, stretchable fabric. A lacey fan, salmon pink with sequins, the mouth in Chinese red, black, and silver frames enlarged the eyes into irresistible attention stoppers, the hair honey blond and short, in a gentleman's cut.

I stopped. He fiercely moved the fan before hiding his face. Slow uncovering, like pulling away a curtain. Contrary to theater curtains, the production was exposed by lowering them. Sparkling glances, addicted to the craving for admiration. When I noticed that they switched from me to my companion and latched onto him, I left.

"Do you like that, beast?" I heard the question.

The title unsettled me, at last.

"Would you like me with makeup, beast?"

The matter-of-fact tone of the title "beast" was beyond my grasp. I tried to wipe the confusion off my face with my left wing. As is commonly known, sirens have female faces. Otherwise, my body resembled that of a snow owl. In contrast to this species, however, I was almost as tall as the average human and, like an eagle owl, sported two tufts on my head. The feathery ears, on the other hand, did not sit above the eyes as is the case with the bubo bubo or between the temples and the back of the head, where human ears sit, but on the hairline. Precisely where men suffer their receding hairlines.

"Are you also one of those female creatures, beast, whose silence or 'no' means 'yes'?" I heard and saw the man pull mirror, pencils, and sticks from his pant pockets. With difficulty, as the pants were so tight that he had to switch his standing leg. The free leg position relaxed the opening of the pocket a little. There was no room for the thumb. Little, pretty hands. I eyed them in order to snap out of the drunkenness. Or, maybe he was drunk. Only a

konnte in einer normalen Großstadt der normalen Bundesrepublik Deutschland mit einem frauengesichtigen Tier normale Gespräche führen.

Ich beobachtete, wie er sich bemalte und dabei Fratzen in den Spiegel schnitt. Er malte mit ruhiger Hand. Also nicht besoffen, dachte ich. Also verrückt, dachte ich. Nur einem Verrückten konnte eine Sirene in einer alltäglichen Stadt alltäglich erscheinen. Also doch Leda, dachte ich ernüchtert, heißt das, ich soll den Schwan spielen? Eine Sirene mit trobadorischer Vergangenheit in der Rolle dieses Patriarchen Zeus? Scheißspiel! Und natürlich ohne mich, dachte ich.

»Nicht ungeduldig werden, Tier«, sagte der Herr in einem Sound, der griff, Schminken sei eine Kunst, und Kunst brauche Zeit, und er wisse, was Frauen mögen. Schließlich hätte ihn eine Frau gemacht.

Wer sonst, fragt sich da jeder gesunde Kopf und hat den Beweis, daß Krankheit spricht. Wahnsinn, dachte ich. Ohne das Interesse zu verlieren. Gespannt auf den Test, der drei Varianten zuläßt. Ein geschminkter Mann sieht entweder aus wie eine Frau – Ergebnis-Variante eins und zu weiblich für mich, nicht sonderlich erregend, da ich selber eine bin. Oder er sieht aus wie seine eigene Großmuter – Variante zwei und zu männlich für meinen Geschmack. Oder er sieht wie ein Mann aus, nur besser. Menschlich vollständig: Variante drei.

Ich erhoffte und fürchtete natürlich die dritte.

Und noch heute erschüttert mich die Trauer über die Augen des derzeitigen Menschengeschlechts, die erstorben in Gewohnheit über die rufenden Farben der Frauen hinsehen und ungeschminkte weibliche Wesen als nicht ordentlich angezogen empfinden.

Was, wenn statt Helden auf den Schlachtfeldern der Kriege, der Ehre, des Geistes und der platten Muskelkraft der wirkliche Raimbaut von Orange, der nicht der Wirklichkeit entsprach, Schule gemacht hätte. Die Helden türmten Taten auf, um zu imponieren, immer neu meßbare Taten und Untaten, bis zum Abgrund hin, vor dem wir jetzt stehen. Raimbaut schminkte sich gelegentlich, um mich zu erfreuen. Betörender Anblick.

lush was able to lead a normal conversation with a beast
with a female face, in a normal city in the normal Federal
Republic of Germany.

I studied how he painted himself, making faces in the
mirror while doing so. He painted with a steady hand. So,
not drunk, I thought. Maybe foolish, I thought. Only a
fool could think of a siren in a normal city as normal. Leda
it is after all, I thought, sobering, does this mean that I am
supposed to play the swan? A siren with the past of a troubadour in the role of the patriarch Zeus? What a crappy
game! And of course without me.

"Don't get impatient, beast," said the gentleman in a
tone that took effect, to paint one's face was an art and art
took time, and he knew what women wanted. After all, he
was created by a woman.

Who else, every sane head is thus asking themselves, and
has proof that illness is telling. Lunacy, I thought. Without
losing interest. Interested in the test which allows for three
options. A man with makeup either looks like a woman—
the result is option one and too feminine for me, not particularly exciting because I am a woman myself. Or, he
looks like his own grandmother—option two and too mas-
culine for my taste. Or, he looks like a man, only better. A
complete human: option three. Naturally, I hoped for and
feared the third one.

And even to this day, I am shaken with grief over the
eyes of the current human race which, grown numb with
habit, ignore the beckoning colors of women and perceive female human beings without makeup as insuffi-
ciently dressed.

What if, instead of the heroes on the battlefields of war,
of honor, of intellectual pursuit and of plain brawniness,
the real Raimbaut of Orange had become the rule. The
heroes towered deed upon deed in order to make an impression, more and more new, measurable actions and
transgressions, right up to the abyss before which we now
stand. Occasionally, Raimbaut put on makeup to please
me. A bewitching sight.

War der vor mir agierende Herr auch imaginiert und passé? Weißes Afghanhemd mit Seidenstrickereien. Auf der Schulter jeweils nur mit einem Knopf geschlossen, wodurch ein schmaler Spalt Einblick gewährte. Auf brünette Haut.

Die derzeitige Kultur dressiert auf Konsum von betörenden *Gegenständen*, für deren Herstellung und Erwerb der Mensch sein Leben hingibt. Nicht sich, Geschenk der Natur, nicht sich selber im anderen oder in Götterbildern – seine Werkstücke betet er an. Was sind diese vergleichsweise armseligen berechenbaren Werkstücke gegen die unberechenbaren Wesenheiten ihrer menschlichen Schöpfer?

Die unberechenbare Wesenheit vor mir, Stifte in der rechten Hand, Spiegel in der linken, fragte: »Bin ich dir so ein Gefallen, Tier, daß du mir ein Gefallen sein willst?«

Messer des Entzückens, ausgezogen schon mal wie einen Dorn und weit von mir geworfen, auf die Straße, unters Blech des Autoverkehrs, zum zweiten Mal nun und scharf geschliffen jetzt mit den Farben rot und schwarz gegen seine abgestumpften Sinne gezielt: Ich wollte.

Ich – schon im Vorfeld von Vergessenem, längst erstorben Geglaubtem, ich oder nicht ich und bereits unfähig mich zu wundern über das Wortzeremoniell, das einem Angehörigen der Generation, die den Mai 1968 jugendlich in Paris oder dergleichen verlebt haben mußte, geradezu verquer im Munde lag. Ich konnte auch nicht mehr unterscheiden, ob der Blicksog Schminkeffekt war oder Dämonie oder Tier. Nackte Gier auf meine Flügel.

Der Herr befingerte zitternd meine Fittiche, riß dran, umhüllte sich mit ihnen, versuchte sie zu entfalten, idem er ihnen seine Arme hingab, als ob er sich ans Kreuz nageln lassen wollte, klammerte dann meinen Leib und befahl: »Flieg, Tier!«

Obgleich der Herr leichtgewichtig war, hatte ich Startschwierigkeiten. Denn ich war ungeübt in der Beförderung menschlicher Lasten.

Schließlich hob ich aber doch ab. In einer ruhigen Nebenstraße. Und ich flog im Smog über der Stadt sieben Runden. Der Mann wälzte im Flugwind den Kopf wie im Kissen. Ich konnte beide

Was that guy who was acting right before my eyes also imagined and thus out of date? White tunic with silk stitching. Held together with one button, on each shoulder, through which a small gap allowed a close look. Onto bronzed skin. Current culture trains us to consume bewitching *objects* for whose production and acquisition a human being readily gives his life. Not himself, nature's gift, not himself in the other or in idols—he rather worships his works. What are these comparatively poor and prosaic works compared to the immeasurable essence of their human creators?

The immeasurable essence before me, pencils in the right hand, mirror in the left, asked me, "Am I indeed so pleasing to you that you are going to please me?"

The knife of delight, already pulled out like a thorn and thrown far away from me, into the street and into the metal of road traffic for a second time now and keenly sharpened, this time in red and black, aimed at his dulled senses: I was willing.

I—already in the preliminary stages of things forgotten, believed to have been dead for a long time, I or not I, and already incapable of wondering about the verbal ceremony, which tasted downright awkward to someone from the generation who had lived, as a youth, through the events of May of '68, in Paris or somewhere along the lines. I was equally incapable of noticing if the piercing glance was a result of the makeup or demonical possession, or lust. Naked lust for my wings.

With shaking fingers, the gentleman felt for my wings, pulled on them, covered himself in them, tried to fan them out by holding them up with his arms as if intending to be crucified, then embraced my body and ordered, " Fly, beast!"

Although the gentleman was a lightweight, I had trouble taking off. For I was not trained in transporting human cargo.

However, I was finally able to take off. In a quiet side street. And I completed seven rounds in the smog above the city. In the high-speed wind of the flight, the lad rolled his

Ohren, in Lockennestern versteckt, abwechselnd besehen und bebeißen. Geschlossene Lider jetzt, was verhinderte, daß ich gegen diese gläsernen Bank- und Verwaltungssilos prallte, mit denen die Stadtwüste gespickt war. Mitunter streifte ich freilich schon mal eine Wand von diesen Schauderbauten, denn die Lippen waren gepolstert, und die Trinität ihrer Bögen warf sich zyklamrot, und als diese Provokation auch noch aufbrach und Zähne blitzen ließ und Gestammel hören, ging ich im Sturzflug nieder und Schluß.

Der Herr fiel rücklings in einen Vorgarten. Die Straßenbeleuchtung zeigte sein Gesicht blaß und zufrieden. Als er sich erholt hatte, sagte er:»Danke, Tier.«

Ich scharrte mit den Fängen im Vorgartenkies. Der Herr lehnte sich an den Stamm eines Gingobaums und nestelte an seiner Halskrause. Außer Römerlatschen und Jeans und dem Afghanhemd trug er nämlich auch noch eine weiße plissierte Halskrause.

Befremdlich dies und das, milde benannt. Aber nach einer Weile schien ihm tatsächlich einzufallen, daß Fliegen nicht nur als Konsum des Geflogenwerdens lebbar ist.

Er brach jendenfalls in die Büro-Villa ein, zu der der Vorgarten gehörte, und wir liebten uns im Keller eine Nacht oder eine Woche.

Als ich aus der Raserei erwachte, war ich nackt.

Unter mir Papiere, Aktenordner. Rundum Federn. Guten Abend, gute Nacht, mit Rosen bedacht – aber mein Schöner lag nicht in Rosen, sondern in Federn. Schlief noch. In diesen Federn, die über Verwaltungspapieren verstreut lagen und den ganzen Kellerraum weißten, wälzte er sich schlafend, schnarchte sogar, in den Fetzen meines sirenischen Federkleids wälzte und räkelte er sich hemmungslos schnarchend und warf die über seine Blößen wie Omas Plumeau.

»Potzmord«, schrie ich.

Er blinzelte. Weg alle Schminke aus seinem Gesicht, weggeliebt wahrscheinlich und runtergeküßt oder wer weiß. Und wie weit runter war ich? Runtergekommen auf den Vogel Federlos? Auf die Frau Mundlos?

head as if lying on a pillow. I was able to take turns looking at and nibbling both of his ears, which were tucked away in curly layers.

His eyelids were closed now, which prevented me from hitting these banking and administrative glass buildings the deserted city was peppered with. Occasionally, I did, however, graze the wall of one of these horrible buildings, because his lips were full and the trinity of their arches was cast in the red of cyclamens, and when this provocation broke open and had its teeth blink and stammer appear, I went down in a swoop and that was the end of it.

The gentleman landed on his back in a front yard. The street lamps showed his face, pale and satisfied. When he had recovered, he said, "Thank you, beast."

With my wings, I pawed in the gravel of the front yard. The gentleman leaned against the trunk of a Gingko tree and fiddled with his neck ruffles. For besides gladiator sandals, jeans, and the tunic, he also wore white, pleated neck ruffles.

To put it mildly, some of this seemed strange. After a while, however, he appeared to remember that flying was not simply viable as a consummation of being flown.

In any case, we broke into the office building that the front yard belonged to and for a night, or for a week, we made love in the basement.

When I awoke from ecstasy, I was naked.

Beneath me, documents and folders. All around me, feathers. Good evening, good night, adorned with roses— yet my beautiful was not lying on roses, but feathers.

Still sleeping. In these feathers, which were strewn across and on top of business papers, he rolled, sleeping, even snoring, in the shreds of my siren's plumage he rolled and lolled, snoring unscrupulously, having them tossed over his bareness like grandma's featherbed.

"Well, I'll be darned," I shouted.

He blinked. All of the makeup gone from his face, probably loved or kissed away, or who knows what. And how down-and-out was I? Hit rock bottom as a featherless bird? As a voiceless woman?

»Wer schreit denn da so auf nüchternen Magen«, hörte ich klagen.

»Ich nicht«, schrie ich, »ich bestimmt nicht, auch wenn ich wollte, ich leider ganz bestimmt nicht, find meine Stimme nie und nimmer, has du schon mal eine Stumme gesehen, die schreien kann?«

»Dich«, murmelte der Langschläfer. Dann rieb er sich die Augen. Mit den Handballen. Später mit den Fäusten. »Dich«, wiederholte er gähnend, aber schon deutlich intoniert und wach. Dann hellwach plözlich. »Dich«, schrie der Nackte entsetzt zurück, »aber du bist ja nackt!«

Ich konnte es nicht leugnen, besah mich, fand meinen Wuchs nicht übel and erkundigte mich, ob die Perversität des Herrn derart spezialisiert wäre, daß ihr der Anblick einer nackten Frau als Greuel erschiene.

Der Herr bestritt nachdrücklich, pervers zu sein, räumte allerdings ein, daß er, vor die Wahl gestellt, eine nackte Frau lieben zu dürfen oder eine bekleidete mit Flügeln, sich natürlich für diese bekleidete entschiede.

Natürlich? Immer was Gescheites macht Kopfweh! Wer hatte mich denn derart entblößt oder abgehäutet oder wer weiß was wie? Ich grübelte, konnte aber keine Schmerzen oder Brutalitäten erinnern. Nur allerlei Kämpfe, Kampflüste, Lustkämpfe . . . Ich raffte eine Schwungfeder und zielte, Kiel voran, auf das Pelzmedaillon, mit dem die Haut überm Brustbein in Herzhöhe geschmückt war. Volltreffer!

Der wahrscheinlich überwach machte, weshalb der Herr beide Hände in seinen braunen Locken vergrub und kratzte und schabte – das Geräusch erinnerte an das Scheuern von Holzdielen, ich fürchtete, die Bürobesatzung der Villa könnte davon alarmiert werden, und bettelte um Ruhe und Vernunft.

»Vernunft«, höhnte der Herr und kratzte fort, »Vernunft macht meschugge, wenn man mit einem kleinen Tier ins Bett geht und mit einer großen Frau erwacht. Frauen gibts wie Sand am Meer, aber schöne weiße wilde Tiere . . .«

Ich biß sofort zu und warf mich so lange auf dem knochigen Leibe herum, bis die Reklamation ein für allemal als ungeheuerliche Verleumdung erwiesen war.

"Who is shouting like that on an empty stomach?" I heard him complain.

"Not me," I yelled. "Definitely not me, even if I wanted to, I regret to say, definitely not me, will never ever find my voice again, have you ever seen a mute who can shout?"

"You," the late riser murmured. Then he rubbed his eyes. With the palms of his hands. After that, with his fists. "You," he replied, yawning, but now markedly intoned, and awake. Then, suddenly, wide awake.

"You," the naked one yelled back, aghast, "but why, you are naked!"

I could not disagree with that and, looking at myself, found my shape not bad and inquired whether the gentleman's perversity was so specialized that it perceived the sight of a naked woman as horrific.

Emphatically, the gentleman denied to be a pervert, yet admitted that, when faced with the choice of being permitted to love a naked woman or one dressed in wings, he would of course choose the dressed one.

Of course? Always something clever causes headaches! Who was it that had denuded me in such a manner or skinned, who knows what? I pondered this, but was unable to remember any pain or brutality. Only all kinds of struggles, struggling delights, delightful struggles . . . I gathered one of the flight feathers and aimed it, pinfeather first, at the furry medallion that adorned the skin above his sternum, right about at the seat of his heart. Bull's eye!

Which probably made him hyper awake and the gentleman dug both hands into his brown locks and scratched and scraped—the sound reminded me of the scraping of timber floor boards and I feared that the office building staff might be alarmed by it and I begged for silence and sensibleness.

"Sensibleness," he scoffed and kept scraping, "sensibleness drives one crazy when you lie down with a small beast and wake up with a big woman. Women are plentiful, but beautiful, white, wild beasts . . ."

In an instant, I bit and threw myself around on the bony body until the claim proved a monstrous defamation, once and for all.

Oh wenn ich bedenke, wie lustig und kindisch wir waren und
wie ich nun lebe in der Ausnüchterungszelle mit dieser neuen
Tagesordnung, dem uralten Hut, freut mich selbst meine Arbeit
nicht: Das Buch, das ich für Dich schreibe. Und nehme ich eine
Laute nach trobadorischer Gewohnheit und singe was aus einer
alten Kanzone, muß ich gleich aufhören – es macht mir zuviel
Empfindung – basta! Wer sagt, die Liebe ist eine Produktivkraft,
ist krank. Denn sie ist natürlich eine Krankheit. Die verrückt
macht. Vor Freude verrückt und vor Sehnsucht sowieso. Nach-
machen, Leute! Vor Angst krank oder verrückt werden kann
heute jeder Rotzlöffel.

Vor Freude verrückt erinnerte ich eine gewisse Meditations-
technik, die das Mittelalter von der Antike ererbt hatte. Von
Sokrates her wohl, der den Prozeß der Selbsterkenntnis noch
geradewegs aus einer Selbstbeschauung in der Pupille eines Ge-
genauges hergeleitet haben soll. Pupilla heißt Püppchen. Das
kleine Spiegelbild des Augenpüppchens wurde als das Selbst des
Menschen angesehen, als seine Seele, sein Mittelpunkt, der als
Mikrokosmos mit dem Weltauge des Makrokosmos in strah-
lungsfähiger Verbindung stünde.

Ich öffnete also meine Augen weit, damit die anderen in meinen Mikrokosmos eingehen konnten.

Und die anderen stürzten sich auch tatsächlich sofort rein,
nachdem sie sich zum gleichen Zweck geöffnet hatten.

Augenzauber.

Der Sinne Untergang ist der Wahrheit Aufgang.

Augenzauber verlangt Starren. Selbst– und weltvergessenes
Hinstarren, denn vermag ein Mensch eine Sache – sein Selbst
oder die Welt – nicht zu begreifen, so begreift ihn die Sache.

Ein Mensch . . . Ein Mensch vermag oder vermag nicht . . .
War eine gerupfte Sirene ein Mensch?

Ich hatte die Weisheiten meiner Muttersprache, die der lateinischen verwandt ist, vergessen. Ich hatte deren Botschaft überhört, die das Wort bringt. Rettungspflicht und Heilserwartung
hatten mein Denken in die gigantischen Größenordnungen getrieben, die politische Weltenlenker gewöhnt sind, weshalb von
dem lateinischen Wort »orbis« bei mir nur die Begriffe Erdkugel, bewohnte Erde, Himmelssphäre abgerufen worden waren.

Oh, when I think about how funny and goofy we were, and how I now live in the drunk tank with this new agenda, the ancient hat, then I don't even enjoy my work: the book which I am writing for you. And when I pick up a lute, in troubadour fashion, and sing something from an old canzone, I have to quit right away—it makes me sentimental—end of story! They who say that love is a productive force are sick. For it is a malady. Which makes one crazy. With joy and with longing, in any case. Copy that, folks! These days, any little snot can be sick or crazy with fear.

Crazy with joy, I remembered a certain meditation technique which had been handed down through the Middle Ages from antiquity. Arguably from Socrates, who supposedly deduced the process of self-realization directly by observing himself in the pupil of the eye of a person opposite to him. Pupilla translates as "little doll." The mirror image of the eye's little doll was regarded as the true self of a person, as his soul, his center, which, as a microcosm, was said to be connected to the world's eye of the macrocosm via rays.

Thus, I opened my eyes wide so that the other ones were capable of entering my microcosm.

And indeed, the other ones rushed in immediately after they had opened for the same purpose.

Eye magic.

The downfall of the senses is the rise of truth.

Eye magic requires staring. Staring while forgetting oneself and the world, for if a human being does not comprehend a concept—of self or of the world—then the concept will comprehend her or him.

A human being . . . a human being is capable or incapable . . . Was a plucked siren a human being?

I had forgotten the wisdom of my mother tongue, which is related to Latin. I had ignored its messages, transmitted in words. The duty to rescue and the hope of salvation had forced my thinking into gigantic proportions that are commonly assumed by political and global leaders. That is why the Latin word "orbis" made me think of the concepts

Das Wort heißt aber auch Auge. Ertrinkend in Menschenaugen begriff mich die Botschaft, daß der menschliche Schlüssel zur Welt der Mensch ist. Billiger ist sie nicht zu haben oder zu bewahren oder zu retten. Die ganze Menschheit lieben oder glücklich machen, Millionen umschlingen wollen, ist leicht, weil nicht nachprüfbar. Aber einen einzigen Menschen glücklich machen . . . Nur wer das kann, ist legitimiert und mitunter sogar befähigt, Völkern Ratschläge zu erteilen oder mehr. Meine zweite Stimme, die meiner ersten glich und längst im Keller verhallt war, erreichte endlich mein Ohr.

Kleine Stimme, auferstanden, winzige trobadorische Stimme, wirklich und wahrhaftig auferstanden von den toten Toten und geworfen unter die lebendig verplanten Toten für den dritten Weltkrieg. Ganz leicht überhörbare Menschenstimme in seinem infernalischen Vorfeldlärm – und doch noch lebendig: Wer oder was ist jetzt mehr?

»Ich bin ein Mensch«, schrie ich und tanzte in den Federn, »ich bin wieder ein Mensch«, schrie ich, »wirklich und wahrhaftig ein Mensch, und wer bist du?«

»Die Frau, die mich aus ihren Rippen geschnitten hat, nannte mich Leander. Oder auch Désiré, was soviel heißt wie ›der Verlangende‹, ›der Sehnende‹ oder auch ›der Erwünschte‹«, hörte ich antworten. Keine Spur von französischem Akzent in der Stimme, sondern geschnurrtes »R«. Sehen konnte ich nur Federn. Meine Füße wirbelten sie durch den Kellerraum, das beste Schneegestöber hätte sich fad ausgenommen dagegen.

»Und was macht mein Erwünschter, wenn er sich keine Federn aus den Locken klaubt?«

»Désiré möchte ein Harlekin werden«, sagte er. Hohe Stimme. Er sagte »Désirrré.« Das Geschnurr dröhnte mir durch die Rippen wie Baßresonanzen von Rockmusik. Auch erkundigte er sich nach meinem Beruf.

»Trobador passé«, antwortete ich. »Werden Moden beflissen zu Grabe getragen, riecht die schöne Leiche nach Mord. Höchste Zeit, das Beerdigungszeremoniell zu verlassen.«

globe, inhabited earth, and heavenly sphere. The word can also mean "eye." Drowning in human eyes, the message that the human key to the world is the human being, comprehended me. There is no cheaper way to obtain or preserve, or rescue it.

To love or make happy all of mankind or to want to hug millions is easy because it cannot be verified. However, to make a single human being happy . . . Only those who are capable of doing that are authorized or occasionally even able to give advice to nations, or more.

My second voice, which was similar to my first one and had echoed away in the basement long ago, finally reached my ear.

Little voice, resurrected, tiny, troubadour voice, really and truly resurrected from the dead, and pushed amongst the living dead scheduled for the Third World War. This human voice, easily ignored in its infernal pre-battlefield uproar—yet still alive: who or what is now more?

"I am human," I shouted and danced in feathers. "I am human again, I yelled, "really and truly human, and who are you?"

"The woman who cut me from her ribs called me Leander. Or even Désiré, which can be translated as 'the one who longs,' 'the longing one,' or also 'the desired,'" I heard him say. Not a trace of a French accent in his voice, only a purred "r." I could only see feathers. I whirled them through the basement room in such a way that the best snow flurry would have paled in comparison.

"And what is my desired doing when he doesn't pick feathers from his locks?"

"Désiré would like to become a harlequin," he said. High-pitched voice. He said, "Désirrré." The purring drummed through my ribs like the bass resonance of rock music. He also inquired about my profession.

"Former female troubadour," I replied. "When crazes are solicitously carried to the grave, the beautiful corpse smells of murder. High time to leave the funeral ceremony."

»›Trobadora passé‹ – versteh ich nicht«, sagte Désiré. »Überhaupt nichts versteh ich und noch weniger. Aber so viel schon, daß ich begreif: Ohne deine Flügel kann ich kein Harlekin werden. Und die sind hin.«

»Wieso hin? Ich liebe dich doch.«

»Ja«, sagte er.

»Was heißt hier ›ja‹: Beatriz liebt dich!«

»Naja«, sagte er.

»Was heißt hier ›naja‹: Beatriz de Dia weißt du überhaupt, wer das ist?«

»Nein«, sagte er, »nur ...«

»Nur! – Bist du etwa schon mal von einer Trobdora geliebt und besungen worden?«

»Neinnein«, sagte er, »aber ohne Flügel ...«

»Wer eine richtige Trobadora liebt, kriegt welche.«

»Selber«, fragte er und legte sich Fetzen meines sirenischen Federkleids auf die Arme. Die weißen Ärmel brachten seine schmalen Schultern und Hüften und die brünette Haut effektvoll zur Geltung. »Richtig selber und angewachsen oder bloß mehr so gedacht?«

»Ja«, antwortete ich.

Er grub seine Hosen aus dem Wirrwarr und den Spiegel hervor, besah sich und stolzierte eine Weile mit dem Federschmuck auf den Aktenordnern herum. Dann erkundigte er sich, was er außer Fliegen noch lernen müsse, um Harlekin zu werden.

»Das Fürchten«, sagte ich.

»Und«, fragte er zerstreut, das heißt konzentriert, auf den Spiegel nämlich, in den hinein er Blicke probierte.

»Und Tanzen natürlich«, sagte ich. »Mit dem Leben und mit dem Tod.«

»Und«, fragte er weiter.

»Und glaub bloß nicht, daß du als Harlekin erwünschter bist als ich, sobald du einer bist. Auch wenn dir die Rippenschneiderin den Namen Désiré gegeben hat. Eine geniale Ketzerin. Doch wer anders kann wissen: Wird der Ernst so groß, daß die Schmerztränen versiegen, ist höchste Zeit, Tränen zu lachen. Harlekin sein ist folglich auch kein Spaß. Falls du also eine Gefährtin passenden Alters suchen solltest: Ich bin achthundertvierundfünfzig Jahre alt und schätze dich auf Mitte dreißig.«

"'Former female troubadour'—I don't get it," said Désiré. "Anyway, I don't understand a thing and even less. But yet this much I understand: without your wings I am unable to become a harlequin. And they are ripped to shreds."

"Why 'ripped to shreds?' I really love you."

"Yes," he said.

"What do you mean, 'yes'? Beatrice loves you!"

"Oh well," he said.

"What do you mean, 'oh well': Beatrice de Dia, do you have any idea who that is?"

"No," he said, "it's only . . ."

"Only!—have you ever been loved and celebrated in song by a female troubadour?"

"Noooo," he said. "But without wings . . ."

"If you love a real female troubadour, you'll get them."

"I?" he asked and draped the shreds of my siren's plumage over his arms. The white sleeves dramatically accentuated his narrow shoulders and hips and bronzed skin.

"Literally myself and adhered, or only figuratively?"

"Yes," I replied.

He fished his pants out of the clutter and pulled out the mirror, admired himself and strutted around with the plumage on top of the files and folders. Then he inquired what else he had to learn to become a harlequin, besides flying.

"How to be afraid," I said.

"And?" he asked absentmindedly, meaning focused on the mirror into which he kept casting trial glances.

"And dancing of course," I said. "With life and with death."

"And?" he kept asking.

"And don't you believe for a minute that, as a harlequin, you will be more. Even if the rib cutter has given you the name Désiré. A brilliant heretic. But who else is able to understand: When earnestness grows so large that the tears of pain run dry, it is high time to laugh tears. Hence, being a harlequin is no joke either. So, in case you are looking for a female companion in the right age bracket: I am eight hundred and fifty-four years old, and I'm guessing you are in your mid-thirties."

IRIS KLOCKMANN

Iris Klockmann was born in 1961 in Lübeck, a town in northern Germany, where she resides with her family to this day. She completed training as a physician's assistant and worked as such for several years. Although she has been passionate about writing for a long time, she has managed only recently to earn a living as a freelance writer.[1]

In 2007 she published her first novel for young adults, *Ana und das Tor nach Looanaru* (*Ana and the Gate to Looanaru*). In the story, a young Irish girl is sent on a quest to recover three sacred stones—love, truth, and wisdom—required to open the gates separating the magical worlds from the real. Reviews of that first novel were optimistic, attesting to the author's skill in creating nuanced characters set within a gripping plot.

Also around 2007, Klockmann teamed up with fellow writer Peter Hoeft to write and publish under several pseudonyms. Their successful collaboration resulted first in the publication of a historical novel entitled *Die Frau aus Nazareth* (*The Woman from Nazareth*, 2009), written under the pen name Jonah Martin. Then, under the pen name Gerit Bertram, Klockmann and her co-author published another historical novel, *Die Goldspinnerin* (*The Gold Spinstress*, 2010), set in the fourteenth century in Klockmann's hometown of Lübeck.

---

[1] "I have always wanted to write, but have only been able to realize my dream a few years ago." Author's translation. Eva Maria Nielsen, "Autoreninterview—Jonah Martin: Gespräch mit dem Autorenteam von "Die Frau aus Nazareth," Suite 101.de, last modified August 23, 2009, accessed August 20, 2011, http://www.suite101.de/content/autoreninterview-jonah-martin-a60548.

Their next collaborative piece, soon to be published, is another historical novel, *Das Gold der Lagune* (*The Gold of the Laguna*). Klockmann and her co-author are in the process of writing a fourth historical novel, this time set in medieval Nuremberg. They recently signed a contract for a fifth book that will use the medieval town of Regensburg as the backdrop.

Reviews of Klockmann's and Hoeft's historical prose have been favorable, acknowledging the authors' "solid research of historical details, a good balance between an authentic historical background and a fast-moving plot, and a dynamic style that does not drag out or exhaust itself."[2] Klockmann and her partner were asked if they could envision writing anything other than fantasy or historical novels and they agreed that the idea of writing a thriller is appealing.[3]

Besides working with Peter Hoeft, Klockmann has published short stories in various online collaborative authors' forums, most notably Quo Vadis and Autorenforum.de. Her membership in Autorenforum.de, conceived in 2009 as a website run by authors to offer short story writers an opportunity to discuss and showcase their work, resulted in the creation of several short narratives. Every year, the forum invites submissions on a particular theme and a jury selects the stories to be published.[4] Until recently, Klockmann worked on the website as an administrator and co-publisher.

Klockmann was asked in a recent interview published in the Autorenforum.de newsletter *Tempest*[5] about what had motivat-

---

[2]Stefanie Schulte, "Suchergebnisse für Gerit Bertram," Steffis Bücherkiste, accessed August 2011, http://www.steffis-buecherkiste.de/?s=Gerit+bertram.

[3]Ramona and Thomas Roth-Berghofer. "Ich war schon immer eine Leseratte: Interview mit Gerit Bertram," The Tempest 12-11 (November 20, 2010), accessed August 13, 2011, http://www.autorenforum.de/component/content/article/61-jahrgang-2010/848-ausgabe-12-11-20-november-2010

[4]"K wie. . . ." WortKuss Verlag, accessed August 10, 2011, "K wie...." WortKuss Verlag, accessed August 10, 2011, http://www.wortkuss-verlag.de/autoren-und-mehr/k-wie.

[5]Ramona and Thomas Roth-Berghofer. "Ich war schon immer eine Leseratte: Interview mit Gerit Bertram," The Tempest 12-11 (November 20, 2010), accessed August 13, 2011, http://www.autorenforum.de/component/content/article/61-jahrgang-2010/848-ausgabe-12-11-20-november-2010.

ed her to take up writing, and replied that since early childhood she had been a bookworm and enjoyed reading. Later she began imagining stories and consequently dreamed of writing them down one day. As a mother she ran out of goodnight stories for her daughters, and so started inventing her own tales. Her children begged her to write them down so that they would be able to read them over and over.

"Der Bote" ("The Messenger") appeared in a recent themed collection from the Autorenforum.de site entitled *Nachtfalter und andere Kreaturen der Dunkelheit* (*Moths and Other Creatures of the Dark*, 2009). Klockmann recalls: "That year, the theme was: '. . . and the world stood still.' I considered what would happen if the world literally stood still, for a few seconds or minutes. And then, suddenly, it occurred to me how wonderful it would be if one could offer comfort and hope to people in misery. I imaged that I was an airborne creature with the ability to give dreams . . ."[6] That is how she came up with the idea of a story about a moth with magical qualities.

In a beautiful mountainous region in war-torn Afghanistan, a "messenger" with magical powers bestows deep and soothing dreams. Every night, the creature calms anguished minds to provide them with a brief respite from the dreadful actuality of war. Written in the present tense, "The Messenger" is rich in symbolism and imagery, and lends itself well to being read aloud, illustrating the author's keen sense of rhythm and flow.

---

[6]M. Charlotte Wolf, translated from unpublished private correspondence with Iris Klockmann, August 21, 2011.

IRIS KLOCKMANN

Der Bote

Die Nacht ist mein Freund. Wenn sie ihren Schleier über die Welt senkt, die Welt verhüllt, und nur der Zauber der Sterne noch zarte Lichtpunkte wirft, erwache ich. Zaghaft öffne ich die Flügel und spüre, wie der Wind mich streichelnd berührt. Es ist, als ob jeder Hauch, jedes leise Rauschen der Bäume mir Kraft einhaucht. Bis ich wieder ganz bin. Weit strecke ich die Flügel aus und erhebe mich von dem Ast, auf dem ich beinahe unsichtbar in meinem Versteck ausgeharrt habe.

Von meiner Art gibt es viele. Wir sind Boten, schenken den Menschen das, was sie am meisten ersehnen, wenn sie sich zur Ruhe begeben und die Augen schließen: Träume. Während ich zwischen dem dichten Blätterdach hindurchfliege, den sachten Frühlingswind als Wegweiser, lausche ich auf die zahlreichen Rufe, die mal flüsternd und dann wieder kraftvoll, mit der Luft zu mir getragen werden. Mit dem Aufwind lasse ich mich treiben, überwinde das Gebirge, auf dessen Gipfeln noch Schnee liegt. Weiter unten im Tal befindet sich mein Ziel, der Ruf wird lauter, als ich mich langsam teifer gleiten lasse. Einen Moment verharre ich, horche. Hinter Hecken und dornigen Büschen stehen einige alte Häuser, eins der Fenster ist geöffnet. Von dort scheint der Ruf gekommen zu sein. Lautlos schlüpfe ich hinein. Auf dem Steinboden sehe ich ihn liegen. Die Augen des kleinen Jungen flattern, als habe er mich gehört. Die Decke wird höher gezogen. Ob ihm kalt ist? Ein Seufzen erreicht mich. Er zuckt im Schlaf. Ich spüre, wie Furcht seine Seele mit eisernem Griff umklammert und ihn selbst jetzt begleitet. Die Bilder, die ich empfange, erschüttern mich. Vorsichtig

IRIS KLOCKMANN

The Messenger

The night is my friend. When she drops her veil over the world and covers it up so only the magic of the stars still casts faint dots of light, I wake. Tentatively, I open my wings and feel how the wind touches me, caressing me. It is as if every whiff, every soft rustle of the trees, were breathing strength into me. Until I am whole again. I stretch my wings far apart and lift myself off the branch I have been holding on to in my hideout, almost invisible.

There are many of my kind. We are messengers, giving humans that what they desire most when they retire for the night and close their eyes: dreams. As I fly through the thick canopy with the soft spring breeze pointing the way, I listen to the numerous calls carried to me by the air, sometimes in a whisper and other times powerfully. I let myself drift in the ascending air current, float over the mountains on whose peaks there is still snow. My target is lower down in the valley. The call becomes louder as I slowly glide down. I pause for a moment, listening. Behind hedges and thorny brushes there are a couple of old houses, and one of the windows is open. The call seems to have come from there. I slip in without a sound. I see him lying on the stone floor. The little boy's eyes flutter as if he had heard me. He pulls the cover up higher. I wonder if he is cold. A sigh reaches me. He is twitching in his sleep. I sense how fear clutches his soul with an iron grip, accompanying him even

159

setze ich mich auf seinen Haarschopf. Wenigstens in dieser Nacht
will ich ihm Vergessen schenken. Schlafen soll er, wie es einem
unschuldigen Kind zusteht. Mit jedem neuen Flügelschlag löse ich
die Fesseln seines Geistes, mache ihn frei. Seine Züge entspannen
sich, werden weich und rosig. Tief und gleichmäßig ist nun sein
Atem, ein Lächeln umspielt seinen Mund.

Manche Geschöpfe behaupten, wir gehören dem Bösen. Weil
wir Illusionen lebendig werden lassen, weil wir ihnen Träume geben und die innigsten Wünsche wahr werden lassen; gestohlenes
Glück, das am nächsten Morgen mit dem ersten Lidschlag wie
eine Seifenblase zerplatzt. Gefährlich sei es, denn was geschieht,
wenn sie erwachen und das, was sie sehen, zu schmerzlich ist,
um es ertragen zu können? Doch wiederum, woher nehmen die
Menschen Mut and Kraft für den nächsten Tag, wenn ihre Her-
zen keine Freude mehr empfinden und selbst die Nächte von
Grauen sprechen? Ist es nicht ein Akt der Gnade, den wir in den
dunkelsten Stunden verschenken?

Unweit des Jungen vernehme ich einen weiteren Ruf. Ich ver-
lasse den Raum, schwebe hinaus und lasse mich von der Stimme
leiten. Einen Moment verstummen alle Geräusche. Etwas geschieht. Da. Ein Donnern und Tosen. Der Boden wird erschüttert von dem Heranrollen dieses riesigen Gefährts. Näher, immer näher rückt es vor. Jede einzelne meiner Federn vibriert
unter dem Lärm. Es schmerzt. Doch kann ich innehalten, mich
davonmachen und die Menschen mit ihren Dämonen allein lassen? Also husche ich weiter durch die von tiefen Tönen erfüllte
Dunkelheit. Ich höre nichts. Es ist so laut. Mir ist, als schreie die
Erde unter mir auf. Aber dann – ganz schwach nur – ist da ein
Wimmern. Mein Weg führt mich an eine Feuerstelle. Reglose
Gestalten kauern um schwache Glut, eingehüllt in fadenschei-
nige Decken. Eine Frau, deren Haut fahl im Schein des Feuers
wirkt, presst einen kleinen Körper an sich. Könnte das Entset-
zen auf ihrem Gesicht sich in die Kraft des Windes verwandeln,
wäre es ein Sturm, des über das Tal hinwegfegte. Sie hält sich die
Ohren zu. Wo ist ihr Haus oder die Hütte, in der sie mit ihrer
Familie Zuflucht nehmen kann? Ich schwirre um sie herum, zaghaft, um der Flamme nicht zu nahe zu kommen.

now. The images I receive shock me. Cautiously, I sit down on his hair. I will give him oblivion, at least for tonight. I want him to sleep like an innocent child is entitled to sleep. With every new flap of my wings, I release the chains of his mind, liberate him. His features relax, become soft and rosy. His breathing is deep and even, a smile caresses his lips.

Some creatures say that we belong to the realm of evil because we make illusions come alive, because we give them dreams and make their innermost wishes come true, stolen happiness which will burst like a soap bubble with the first opening of their eyelids the morning after. That it would be dangerous because what happens when they wake up and what they see is too painful to bear? But then again, where does the courage and power come from that is needed by humans to get through the coming day if their hearts do not feel joy any longer, and if even the nights speak of horror? Isn't what we give away in the darkest hours an act of grace?

Not far from the boy I hear another call. I leave the room, float outside, and let myself be guided by the voice. For a moment, all sounds are silent. Then something happens. There. A roaring and thundering. The ground shakes with the rolling of a huge advancing vehicle. Closer and closer it comes. Each and every one of my feathers is vibrating with the noise. It hurts. But can I stop, make off, and leave the humans alone with their demons? So I hurry on through the darkness filled with deep sounds. I don't hear anything. It is so loud. It's as if the earth were crying out beneath me. But then—very faint—there is a whimper. My path leads to a fireplace. Motionless figures are crouching down around the faint embers, covered in threadbare blankets. A woman, whose skin appears sallow in the glow of the fire, is pressing a small body to herself. If the horror in her face could be transformed into the power of the wind, it would become a storm sweeping across the valley. She is covering her ears. Where is her house or the shed where she can find refuge with her family? I whir around her cautiously to avoid getting too close to the flames.

Keine Zeit für Träume, kein Raum für Hoffnung. Hastig und von einem Schluchzen begleitet, rüttelt die Frau an den stillen Leibern. »Wir müssen hier weg! Schnell!«
Ein markerschütternder Knall. Schreie. Rauch ist plötzlich überall, versperrt mir die Sicht und verklebt mein Gefieder. Ein letzter Blick zurück.

Möge das *Große Eine* bei ihnen sein und über sie wachen.

Denn es herrscht Krieg.

Krieg in Afghanistan.

No time for dreams, no room for hope. Hastily and accompanied by sobs, the woman shakes the still bodies. "We have to leave here! Quickly!"

A bloodcurdling explosion. Cries. Suddenly, smoke is everywhere, barring my view and gumming up my plumage. One last glance backwards.

May the *Great One* be with them and watch over them. Because war is being waged.

War in Afghanistan.

HENRY BIENEK

At thirty-eight years old, Henry Bienek is the youngest author represented in this anthology. Presently, he lives in Darmstadt, Hessia, working as a bookkeeper for a real estate company. Besides writing and an interest in music, he loves movies and is an avid reader. His literary taste is varied and ranges from comics, graphic novels, "Heftromane,"[1] and books of all kinds to weekly publications such as the German news magazine *Der Spiegel*. He travels frequently as a member of three different choirs, in which he sings bass.

In addition, Bienek is passionate about online role-playing games, primarily those like Dungeons and Dragons. His preferred genres, in writing as well as in reading, are mystery, fantasy, and horror. Bienek describes his main literary interest as exploring new approaches to and facets of common themes and everyday topics in his stories. He finds inspiration by reading the news about current events and other people's everyday lives, which he then uses as a basis for his stories.[2]

After some attempts at creative writing when he was ten years old, he began to write short stories and poems at age fifteen. To date, he has completed about forty stories, many of which can be found in print and online anthologies.

---

[1]"Heftromane" are the German equivalent of pulp fiction, a genre characterized by the use of stereotypes and simple stylistic devices. See also, Heinz J. Galle, *Groschenhefte. Die Geschichte der deutschen Trivialliteratur*, (Frankfurt am Main and Berlin: Ullstein, 1988).

[2]Andrea Wild, "Interviews with Henry Bienek, 2007 & 2008," Thesaurus Librorum, accessed August 27, 2011, http://thesaurus-librorum.de/?tag=bienek.

In 2002, after a writing hiatus lasting several years, Bienek submitted the story "Alle Menschen sind gleich" ("All Men Are Equal") to the online writing forum Kurzgeschichten.de (Short Stories.de). This story illustrates his fascination with everyday situations that turn into something horrific, literally overnight. Waking up one morning next to his girlfriend, the hero suddenly notices that she no longer has any skin. Shocked, he starts screaming when the skinless creature begins to stir and move and talk. In this story, it is the "not knowing why" something happens and how it happened that makes the situation horrifying.[3]

Three months after publishing that story, Bienek was contacted by Ernst Wurdack, owner of Wurdack-Verlag (Wurdack Publishers), who was looking for submissions to a horror story collection to be titled *Pandaimonion*. Wurdack had liked the story and wanted to include it in the first volume. This renewed Bienek's passion for writing and inspired him to collaborate with other small publishers as well as participate in other online writing forums besides Wurdack-Verlag and Kurzgeschichten.de.

In 2007 and 2008, Bienek recorded an audio version of his stories at Thesaurus Librorum, a podcast site specializing in recordings of classical and contemporary stories, including mystery, horror, poetry, and fairy tales. The horror stories "Samaels Weg" ("Samael's Path," 2007) and "Moderne Schnitzeljagd" ("Modern Scavenger Hunt," 2007), the mystery story "Für Daddy" ("For Daddy," 2007), and the fantasy tale "Der Fluch der Legenden" ("The Curse of Legends," 2008), all confirm that Bienek writes well in each of these genres.

Since 2008 he has published text versions of his stories and also served as a peer reviewer with the multi-faceted authors' forum Edition Geschichtenweber (Story Weavers' Edition), where writers can "test-drive" stories they plan to publish and also receive peer feedback for already published stories.

In 2009, Bienek and his fellow authors decided to compile an anthology dedicated to publisher Ernst Wurdack for the ten-

---

[3]M. Charlotte Wolf, translated from unpublished private correspondence with Henry Bienek, August 27, 2011.

year anniversary of the publishing house. The stories feature a common hero, a fictional version of Ernst Wurdack, who finds himself chasing from one adventure to another, each one more fantastic and surreal than the next. The stories comprise a ring of connected tales in which the hero repeatedly tries to escape back into flesh and blood existence. The stories are linked into plots and storylines of tales previously published by the real-life Wurdack.

Bienek's contribution was "Der Empfang" ("The Reception"), the first of Wurdack's involuntary adventures that appear in the anthology *Das ist unser Ernst!* (*This is our Ernst!,* 2009). Wurdack receives an invitation issued by the mysterious Baron von Draag, a man unknown to him. Puzzled but curious, he accepts and finds an apparently deserted building. But when he is ushered into the building by a butler so standoffish that he even refuses a tip, Wurdack finds a spacious and luxuriously furnished reception hall.

After Wurdack is introduced to a group of illustrious dignitaries and socialites who all seem strangely familiar to him, he is unknowingly catapulted into an otherworldly quest, starting with him onboard a schooner about to be captured by a corsair in the middle of the ocean.

HENRY BIENEK

Der Empfang

Die ausgedruckte Wegbeschreibung auf seinem Beifahrersitz hatte ihn zu einem Hotel geführt, das sich gott- und scheinbar auch gästeverlassen in einer schmalen Seitengasse versteckte und so aussah, als sei es eher zum Abriss denn zur Benutzung freigegeben. Weit und breit gab es weder eine Parkplatzbeschilderung noch sonst irgendeinen Hinweis, sodass Ernst seinen Wagen schließlich zwischen zwei Autos klemmte, die mitten auf der Straße standen. *Ich hoffe, das tun sie nachher auch noch*, dachte er und nahm sich vor, schnellstmöglich jemanden nach einem richtigen Parkplatz zu fragen, damit sein Auto nicht irgendwann mutterseelenallein mitten auf der Straße stand. Wenn er denn jemals jemanden finden sollte.

Er zückte die Einladung, die auf marmoriertes Büttenpapier mit Wasserzeichen gedruckt war und zu einem Treffen der ›Theoretiker Schriftstellerischer Neutralität & Rhetorischer Erzählung‹ einlud. Wer immer die auch sein mochten.

Natürlich hatte Ernst sich geehrt gefühlt, sich allerdings auch vorsichtig in seinem Umfeld erkundigt, was es denn mit diesen Leuten auf sich hatte. Man konnte ja nie wissen . . .

Erschreckenderweise war der Name jedem, den er gefragt hatte, ein Begriff gewesen, auch wenn sich letztendlich alle Befragten ausgesprochen diplomatisch davor gedrückt hatten, Informationen über diese Gruppe preiszugeben.

Es sei eine Ehre, eingeladen zu werden.

Man könne sich glücklich schätzen, wenn man ihre Aufmerksamkeit geweckt habe.

168

HENRY BIENEK

The Reception

The printout of the driving directions on the passenger seat had led him to a hotel which, apparently God- and guest-forsaken, hid away on a small side street and looked as if it were approved for demolition rather than for use.

There wasn't a sign for a parking lot nor anything else to be found so Ernst finally squeezed his vehicle in between two cars that were parked in the middle of the street.

'I hope they'll be there afterwards,' he thought, and made a mental note to ask somebody about a real parking lot so that, eventually, his car would not have to sit all alone in the middle of the street. If he should ever find someone.

He pulled out the invitation printed on marbled, hand-made paper, complete with watermark, which invited him to a meeting of the "Literary theorists of neutrality and rhetorical narrative." Whoever that might be.

Obviously, Ernst had been honored, but he needed to carefully gather information from his surroundings as to what these people were about. You never know . . .

Frighteningly, everybody whom he asked had known the name, had known the concept well, even though, ultimately, all of those he asked had, quite diplomatically, avoided divulging any information about the group.

It would be an honor to be invited.

He should be lucky to have called their attention to him.

Es würde ein Abend werden, den man garantiert nicht vergessen werde.

Während Ernst sich unbehaglich dem schäbigen Etwas von Hotel zuwandte, dessen Fenster blickdicht mit schweren Vorhängen abgedunkelt waren, wie er beim Näherkommen erkannte, fragte er sich argwöhnisch, wie das Wort *unvergessen* gemeint sein könnte.

Als nach Betätigen des Klopfers die schwere Eichentür aufschwang, schien sich dem Verleger eine andere Welt zu öffnen, und für einen kurzen Moment musste er einen Blick auf die Straße werfen, um sich zu vergewissern, dass dies immer noch dieselbe düstere Ecke war wie zuvor.

Vor ihm stand ein livrierter Butler, der ihn lächelnd und nickend in den Vorraum bat, von dem aus man eine Garderobe aus edlem, glattpoliertem Holz erreichte. Alles war peinlichst auf Sauberkeit getrimmt. Aus Richtung der Vorhänge, die weiter in das Gebäude führten, erklang stimmungsvolle Musik und das Klirren von Gläsern.

Nachdem er der Garderobiere seinen Mantel gegeben hatte, wandte sich Ernst dem Vorhang zu. Vergessen waren Zweifel und Argwohn. Jetzt war er gespannt, was ihn hier erwarten mochte. Doch der Butler hielt ihn mit einem leicht echauffierten Räuspern zurück.

»Wenn ich bitten darf . . . ?«, begann er und streckte verlangend seine Hand aus.

Das fängt ja gut an, dachte Ernst und zückte seine Börse. *Jetzt schon Trinkgeld loswerden, und dabei hab ich noch nicht mal was zu essen bekommen.*

Der Butler starrte ihn allerdings nur indigniert an und räusperte sich erneut, als Ernst ihm einen Geldschein hinhielt. Diesen betrachtete der Livrierte von beiden Seiten, ohne ihn allerdings entgegenzunehmen. Schließlich gefror seine Miene gänzlich und unter dem schmalen Strich seiner Lippen presste er ein missgestimmtes »Ich meinte eigentlich Ihre Einladung, mein Herr« hervor.

Blitzschnell verschwand der Schein in der Börse, die Börse in der Hosentasche und Ernst zauberte stattdessen leicht errötet das Billet hervor, das der Andere – nun wieder ganz Profession – mit einem Diener entgegennahm.

It would be an unforgettable evening.

While Ernst turned, somewhat uncomfortably, toward the shabby excuse for a hotel whose windows were blackened out with heavy curtains, which he noticed approaching, he asked himself suspiciously just how the word "unforgettable" was meant.

When, after he knocked, the heavy oak door swung open, it seemed to the publisher as if another world had opened up and for a brief moment he had to glance at the street in order to make sure that this was still the same dark corner as before.

Before him stood a butler in livery who, with a smile and a nod, asked him to enter the vestibule from where he was able to proceed to a coatroom furnished with expensive, well-polished wood. Everything appeared to be scrupulously clean. From the direction of the curtains that led deeper into the building, he heard fun-filled music and the clink of glasses.

After he had handed over his coat to the coatroom attendant, Ernst turned to the curtain. Forgotten were his doubts and suspicions. Now he was curious to see what awaited him. However, the butler held him back with a slight, exaggerated clearing of his throat.

"If I may ask . . . ?" he began, and stretched out his hand demandingly.

"Well, this is a great start!" Ernst thought and pulled out his wallet. "Starting with the tips already, and I haven't even gotten a bite to eat yet."

However, the butler only stared at him indignantly and cleared his throat again when Ernst presented him with a banknote. The liveried man regarded it from both sides, without actually accepting it. Finally, his expression froze and, from behind the small line of his lips, he pushed out, ill-humoredly, "I was actually referring to your invitation, sir."

As quick as a flash, the banknote disappeared into the wallet, the wallet into the pant pockets, and instead, Ernst produced the card, slightly blushing, which the other, acting again very professionally, accepted with a bow.

»Herr Ernst Wurdack . . . Ich freue mich, Sie in unserem Hause willkommen zu heißen.«

Er schnippte mit den Fingern und die Garderobiere griff zielsicher unter ihren Tresen und reichte dem Butler ein Buch, das dieser wiederum an Ernst weiterreichte.

Ernst sah auf den Titel und wurde blass. Das Gesicht auf dem Titelbild kam ihm bekannt vor. Und dann erst der Titel selbst. Das war ja mal ein Begrüßungsgeschenk. Wann und vor allem wie hatten sie das hinbekommen?

Die Stimme des Butlers unterbrach seinen Gedankengang.

»Sie werden bereits erwartet und jeder ist gespannt auf Ihren Vortrag über die neueste Veröffentlichung Ihres Hauses.«

»Wirklich? Welche ist denn gemeint? Ich hatte in letzter Zeit drei Bände, die dicht aufeinanderfolgten . . .«

Das Gesicht des Butlers schien für eine Sekunde zu gefrieren, nur um sich im nächsten Moment in ein verschmitztes Lächeln und wieder gewonnene Contenance aufzulösen.

»Nein, nein Herr Wurdack. Dieses Mal legen Sie mich nicht herein. Das mit dem Geldschein hatte ich ja tatsächlich noch für bare Münze genommen, aber Ihr eigenes Werk zu verleugnen . . . Ich muss schon sagen, Ihr Humor ist etwas . . . eigen.«

Dienstbeflissen schob er den Vorhang zur Seite und Ernst Wurdack hindurch, der – einem aufkeimenden Verdacht folgend – mit einem Auge auf den Einband schielte und tatsächlich seinen Verlagsnamen darauf gedruckt fand.

Das kann nicht euer Ernst sein.

Noch während er ungläubig auf den Einband starrte – nach dem Entdecken dieser Ungeheuerlichkeit hatte sich flugs auch sein zweites Auge auf den Schriftzug ›Wurdack Verlag‹ eingependelt – schob ihm jemand ein Tablett mit gefüllten Champagnerflöten unter die Nase. Ein Bier wäre ihm lieber gewesen.

»Bedienen Sie sich«, näselte eine leicht herablassende Stimme, und reflexartig griff sich Ernst ein Glas, um es nach dem ersten Schock herunterzustürzen. Doch bevor er es an die Lippen führen konnte, bemerkte er, dass er der ungewollte Zielpunkt allgemeiner Aufmerksamkeit war – und kurz davorstand, einen wahrscheinlich unverzeihlichen Affront zu begehen. Genauso

"Mr. Ernst Wurdack . . . I am pleased to welcome you to our establishment."

He snipped his fingers and the cloakroom attendant, un-erringly, reached under the counter and handed the butler a book which the latter passed on to Ernst.

Ernst looked at the tile and paled. The face on the cover image looked familiar. And the title itself, even more so. That was quite a welcome present. When, and even more importantly, how had they managed that?

The butler's voice interrupted his train of thought.

"We've been expecting you, and everybody is curious to hear your lecture on the latest publication from your publishing house."

"Really? Which one are you talking about? I recently published three volumes in close succession . . ."

The expression on the butler's face seemed to freeze for a second, only to dissolve into an impish smile the next moment and recover its usual countenance.

"No, no, Mr. Wurdack. You are not fooling me this time. The episode with the banknote I might have taken at face value, but to deny your own work . . I'll have to say, your sense of humor is somewhat . . . strange."

Assiduously, he pushed the curtain aside and Ernst Wurdack through it who, following a burgeoning suspicion, peered at the book's cover and indeed found the name of his publishing house printed on it.

"You can't be serious."

Still staring at the cover with disbelief—after discovering this monstrosity, he had quickly examined the lettering "Wurdack Publishing" more closely—someone pushed a tray with filled champagne flutes under his nose. He would have preferred a beer.

"Self service," a slightly dismissive voice said with a twang and, out of reflex, Ernst grabbed a glass to gulp down after the first shock had ebbed away. However, before he was able to lift it to his lips, he noticed that he was the involuntary target of everyone's attention—and was about to commit a probably unforgivable affront. He

gut hätte er dem Butler an der Tür auch noch seine ganze Geldbörse anbieten können.

Schnell warf er einen Blick in die Runde, in der Hoffnung, ein vertrautes Gesicht zu sehen und eine Chance zu erhalten, die gespannte Situation ein bisschen aufzulockern. Doch leider sah er sich in dieser Hinsicht getäuscht.

Nicht ein Bekannter war unter den Anwesenden zu erkennen und die Person, die jetzt mit strahlendem Lächein auf Ernst zutrat, schien entweder krank oder drogensüchtig zu sein. Das blasse Gesicht stand jedoch im Gegensatz zu dem festen Händedruck, mit dem seine rechte Hand gequetscht wurde.

»Lieber Herr Wurdack«, dröhnte die Stimme des Mannes durch den Saal, »es ist uns eine Ehre, endlich den Mann kennenzulernen, der so viel für uns getan hat. Doch wie unhöflich von mir. Ich darf mich erst einmal vorstellen. Mein Name ist Baron von Draag. Das dort hinten ist meine Familie . . .« Er zeigte in eine Ecke, wo sich eine ganze Reihe blasser Gestalten aufhielt, die sich höflich verbeugten und ihn mit glitzernden Augen beinahe durchbohrten.

Baron von Draag stellte ihm seine Tochter Belliasa vor, welche allerdings nur ein kurzes Lächeln für ihn übrig hatte, das im Gegensatz zu dem ihres Vaters nicht einmal annähernd ihre Augen erreichte. Die restlichen Familienmitglieder gaben sich ähnlich zurückhaltend, wenn auch nicht ganz so kalt.

Und damit begann der Vorstellungsreigen erst.

Die meisten Namen hatte Ernst schon wieder vergessen, kaum dass er sie gehört hatte. Aber ein paar der Gestalten hatte er sich dann doch merken können.

Da war zum einen Scholain Yadaraf, der äußerst unvollkommen seinem Namen entsprach. Hinter dem Namen hätte Ernst wahrscheinlich eher einen kleingewachsenen israelischen Philosophen erwartet, nicht aber diesen großen Kerl mit schulterlangem, blondem Haar und stahlblauen Augen, dessen Schulterklopfer ihn fast aus dem neuen Anzug gefegt hätte.

Zum anderen waren da Fräulein Ninge und Herr Cherecs, die nicht verschiedener hätten sein können. Herr Cherecs war ein Baum von einem Mann, stämmig und mit so breiten Schultern, dass er allein jeden Türrahmen ausfüllen konnte. Er passte gerade so in seinen Anzug, wirkte darin allerdings wie ein Luft-

might have just as well offered the butler at the door his entire wallet.

Quickly, he glanced around him, hoping to find a familiar face and get a chance to ease the tension of the situation to some extent. However, he seemed to be out of luck.

Not a single acquaintance was to be found among those present, and the person who was presently approaching Ernst with a radiant smile appeared to be either mentally ill or a drug addict. The pale face, however, contradicted the firm handshake in which his right hand was crushed.

"Dear Mr. Wurdack," the man's voice flooded through the hall, "we are honored to finally get to know the man who has done so much for us. But, how impolite of me! First of all, let me introduce myself. I am Baron von Draag. Over there in the back is my family . . ." He pointed to a corner where there lingered a great many pale figures, who politely bowed and nearly pierced him with their glittering eyes.

Baron von Draag then introduced his daughter Belliasa, who only had a brief smile for him which, in contrast to her father's, did not even reach her eyes. The rest of the family behaved similarly reserved, even if not as cold.

And thus the round of introductions began.

Ernst forgot most names as soon as he had heard them. However, he was able to remember a few of them.

On the one hand, there was Scholain Yadaraf, who matched his name only in the most imperfect way. Given his name, Ernst probably would have expected a dwarfish Israeli philosopher, not a tall guy with shoulder length, blond hair and steel blue eyes, who almost knocked him out of his suit when clapping his shoulders.

On the other hand, there were Miss Ninge and Mr. Cherecs, who could not have been more dissimilar. Mr. Cherecs was a tree of a man, stocky and with shoulders so broad he could have filled the door frame all by himself. He barely fit in his suit and looked like a balloon ready to pop. But

ballon, der kurz vorm Platzen stand. Vielleicht konnte das aber auch mit seinem Körperhaarbewuchs erklärt werden, der aus dem Kragen und den Ärmeln des Anzugs ragte.

Im Gegensatz dazu stand Fräulein Ninge, die klein und grazil Herrn Cherecs gerade bis zum Brustkorb reichte und mit ihrer Bubikopffrisur um das schmale Gesicht fast wie ein Junge aussah, der ein Kleid trug.

Waren die beiden Gestalten an sich schon auffällig genug, so waren die Blicke, die die beiden sich zuwarfen, noch seltsamer. Jeder beobachtete den anderen und schien nur darauf zu warten, dass der- bzw. diejenige etwas Falsches sagte oder tat. Dabei behandelten sie Ernst gleichzeitig sehr höflich und jovial, was einem Kunststück gleichkam, bei der Art, wie sich die beiden beäugten.

Mittlerweile hatte Ernst während all der Vorstellungen schon das eine oder andere Glas Champagner angereicht bekommen, das er jedes Mal brav und artig – um nicht zu sagen stoisch – geleert hatte, obwohl ihm ja ein Glas Bier lieber gewesen wäre. Inzwischen schwirrte ihm jedenfalls schon der Kopf vor lauter Alkohol.

Letztendlich war er dann aber doch noch mit seinem Gastgeber, denn als genau das hatte sich Baron von Draag unterdessen zu erkennen gegeben, am Büfett gelandet und dort stehen gelassen worden.

»Essen Sie sich erst einmal satt, aber übertreiben Sie es nicht. Schließlich erwarten wir alle Ihre Rede über das neueste Werk Ihres Hauses«, war das Letzte, was er von ihm zu hören bekommen hatte. Und diese Drohung klebte nun in seinen Gehirnwindungen wie das verdammte Buch in seiner Hand.

Ernst hatte wirklich Hunger und darüber hinaus begannen seine neuen Schuhe vom langen Stehen unangenehm zu drücken. Er hätte sie vorher wohl besser einlaufen sollen.

Doch er konnte sich nicht mit etwas Essbarem an einen ruhigen Platz setzen, solange er nicht wusste, was es mit diesem verdammten Buch auf sich hatte, das ihn bis zum heutigen Tag vollkommen unbekannt gewesen war.

Wenn er es überflog, würde ihm das wohl reichen. Er war ja schließlich nicht auf den Mund gefallen, auch wenn ihn die Anwesenheit so vieler unbekannter, aber anscheinend wohl geson-

that also could have been due to the body hair peering out from his collar and the sleeves of his suit.

By contrast, Miss Ninge, petite and delicate, just reaching Mr. Cherecs's chest and, with her pixie hair cut and small face, almost liked like a boy wearing a dress.

By themselves, the two figures appeared strange enough, but the looks they gave each other were even stranger. Each one of them watched the other closely and seemed to wait for something he or she said or did wrong. At the same time, they treated Ernst with a great deal of politeness and joviality which was quite a feat, given the way the two eyed each other.

Meanwhile, Ernst had been offered quite a few glasses of champagne, which he had emptied meekly and dutifully—not to say stoically—although he would have preferred a beer. By now, his head was buzzing from all the alcohol.

He ultimately ended up at the buffet with his host, because that was exactly what Baron von Draag had in the meantime turned out to be, and been abandoned there.

"For starters, eat until you are full, but don't overdo it. After all, we all expect to hear your speech about the latest work from your publishing house," was the last thing he had heard the baron say. And this threat stuck to his cerebral pathways like the darned book in his hand.

Ernst was really hungry and, on top of that, his new shoes had begun to pinch uncomfortably from standing so long. It would have been a good idea to have broken them in before.

Yet, he was unable to sit down with something to eat in a quiet spot until he knew what this blasted book was all about, which had been entirely unknown to him until that very same day.

If he simply skimmed through it, that might be sufficient. After all, he was never at a loss for words, even if the presence of so many unfamiliar, yet somehow well-mean-

nener Menschen ein wenig auf die Zunge schlug. Jetzt wusste er wieder, warum er dergleichen Veranstaltungen aus dem Weg ging. Er würde einige Köpfe geraderücken und ein paar Freundschaften aufkündigen müssen, wenn er das hier irgendwie überstanden hatte . . .

Ernst suchte sich eine halbwegs ruhige Ecke neben einem der verhängten Saalfenster und begann im Buch zu stöbern. Die Inhaltsangabe brachte ihn nur zum Teil weiter. Beinahe alle Autoren hatten schon etwas für den Wurdack Verlag geschrieben, aber diese Geschichten hatte er garantiert noch nie gelesen. Doch die eine oder andere klang schon vom Titel her vielversprechend.

Er beschloss, bei der ersten Geschichte anzufangen, denn dieser Autor sagte ihm momentan am wenigsten. Er würde sie also wahrscheinlich komplett lesen müssen. Er hoffte nur, dass sie gut war. Es stand ja schließlich sein Name auf dem Spiel.

Die Story handelte von Kapitän Nicholas Faraday, der auf der Jagd nach dem Schwarzen Shannon war, einem Piraten, der das Mündel des Vizekönigs von Panama entführt hatte. Glücklicherweise hielt sich der Autor nicht lange mit Plattitüden auf, sondern stieg gleich bei der Jagd ein, und zwar an der Stelle, wo der Leser schon ahnen konnte, dass die Konfrontation unweigerlich bevorstand.

Der Autor machte seine Sache dabei ausgezeichnet. Beide Schiffe befanden sich gerade in einer Nebelbank und niemand an Bord von Farradays Schiff gab einen Laut von sich, um den Gegner nicht auf sich aufmerksam zu machen. Man konnte die bleierne Stille im Nebel spüren, nur unterbrochen von leichten Knarren des Schiffes im Wasser, das sich nicht vermeiden ließ. Ernst konnte die salzige Luft förmlich schmecken . . .

Irritiert runzelte er die Stirn.

Verdammt, er schmeckte sie tatsächlich!

Als er hochsah, um sich von der Realität zu überzeugen, war der Festsaal verschwunden. Stattdessen lag Nebel in der Luft und von rechts schob sich ein gewaltiger Schatten heran . . .

ing people had cramped his style just a bit. Now he remembered why he avoided events like this one. He would straighten out a few heads and end a few friendships once he had gotten through this, one way or another . . .

Ernst chose a reasonably quiet corner next to one of the covered windows in the hall and began to look through the book. The table of contents was only slightly helpful.

Almost all of the authors had created something for the Wurdack Publishing House before, but he had definitely never read any of these stories. However, one or two sounded promising, judging from the titles.

He decided to start with the first story because the author was least familiar to him. That meant that he would probably have to read the entire story. He only hoped it was a good one. At the end of the day, it was his name that was at stake.

The story was about Captain Nicholas Faraday who was chasing after Black Shannon, a pirate who had abducted the Viceroy of Panama's ward. Fortunately, the author did not employ boilerplate statements, but went straight to the chase, in fact straight to the point where the reader was already able to sense that confrontation between the two was close, inevitably so.

The author did an excellent job with this. Both ships were sitting in a thick fog, and nobody onboard Faraday's ship uttered so much as a sound in order to avoid drawing the enemy's attention to them. One could sense the leaden silence in the fog, interrupted only by the slight creaking of the ship in the water, which was inevitable. Ernst was practically able to taste the salty air . . .

Confused, he wrinkled his forehead.

Cripes, he really tasted it!

When he looked around to assure himself of what was real, the banquet hall had disappeared. Instead, fog was in the air and from the right, a giant shadow was approaching . . .

GABRIELE WOHMANN

Gabriele Wohmann, née Guyot, was born May 21, 1932, the third of four children of a Lutheran cleric. She attended a prestigious private college prep school in northern Germany and graduated in 1950. After completing studies in music, philosophy, and German, Romance, and English languages and literature at the prestigious Goethe University in Frankfurt[1], she returned to the private prep school to work as a teacher. In 1953 she married Reiner Wohmann, and the two reside at the artists' colony of Rosenhöhe (Rose Heights) in Darmstadt.

Wohmann has worked as a freelance writer since 1956. Her body of work is prodigious and so far includes sixty short story collections, seventeen novels, ten poetry anthologies, thirty-four radio plays, and numerous essays and autobiographical pieces, as well as TV dramas and plays for live theater. Her biggest success, the "Erziehungsroman" (education novel) *Paulinchen war allein zu Haus* (*Little Pauline Was Home Alone*, 1974), has been published in twenty-six editions to date.

In most of her works, Wohmann focuses on the family and the potential for conflict in private and intimate relationships.

---

[1]The Goethe University Frankfurt was founded in 1914 and became the institutional home of the Frankfurt School, the preeminent twentieth-century school of philosophy and social thought. Famous scholars associated with this school include Theodor Adorno, Max Horkheimer, Jürgen Habermas, Herbert Marcuse, Erich Fromm, Walter Benjamin, Martin Buber, and Norbert Elias. The university is named after a famous native of Frankfurt, poet and writer Johann Wolfgang von Goethe. ("Geschichte der Universität Goethe-Universität," accessed August 23, 2011, http://www.uni-frankfurt. de/ueber/geschichte/index.html).

She has a sharp ear for emotional undertones and a keen eye for what is really going on between people.[2] More than any other German writer, she shines light on the emotional makeup of the German middle class family and its complex and strained relationships, exposing its workings in minute detail. Writing about the significance of day-to-day life in her works, Wohmann says "Basically, all lasting literature deals with the incredible complications of social interaction, where even the tiniest offense can turn into a catastrophic disaster."[3]

Wohmann began to be recognized by her peers from early on. In 1960, she joined the famous Gruppe 47; from 1960 to 1988 she was a member of the PEN Center of the Federal Republic of Germany. She became a member of the Berlin Academy of the Arts in 1965 and a member of the German Academy for Language and Literature in Darmstadt in 1980. In 1983 she was awarded a prestigious poetry lectureship at the University of Augsburg. Two years later, the city of Mainz appointed her as "writer in residence" and then awarded her another poetry lectureship in 1988. Her numerous prizes include the Culture Prize of the State of Hessia (1988), the Konrad-Adenauer-Prize (1992), the Order of Merit of the Federal Republic of Germany - Cross of Merit (1998), and the Order of Merit of the State of Baden-Wurttemberg (2002).

"Glück und Unglück" ("Good Luck and Bad Luck") appeared in *Wann kommt die Liebe (When Will Love Come*, 2010), a collection of eighteen short stories. With a piercing gaze and clear and simple language, Wohmann analyzes the moral abjectness, narrow-mindedness, and ignorance of the characters whose day-to-day lives are filled with agonizing boredom.

The narrator of "Glück und Unglück" is a teenage girl who just moved with her family to a house in the suburbs,

---

[2]Maria Frisé, *Frankfurter Algemeine Zeitung*, December 9, 2003: 36.
[3]"Gabriele Wohmanns 70: Glückwunsch von Wieland Freund, "Die Welt, May 21, 2002.

a step up from the cramped apartment in the city center where they used to live. Gradually, the narrator reveals that her father suffers from a serious illness, and that the woman she and her sister have called "mother" all these years is actually their stepmother, Alma. The alleged selfishness and petty behavior of the stepmother in the face of the father's life-threatening condition is gradually revealed in the sometimes scathing accounts from the teenage chronicler. Quoting frequently from Alma's overheard phone chats with friends and face-to-face conversation with family members, the narrator insinuates that family disharmony originates with her stepmother. Like a flame fanned by evil winds, the teenager's resentment seems to increase every time Alma delivers another one of her "slights." However, it becomes clear that the family is dysfunctional as a whole, and the relationships among the members are strained due to a latent mutual hostility which is never pushed aside, not even by news of the tragedy about to strike.

GABRIELE WOHMANN

Glück und Unglück

Das Einzige, was man ihr vielleicht doch zugutehalten kann, ist ihre Aufregung nach dieser verdammten Diagnose. Und geredet hat sie immer schon zu viel. Das geht also auch in Ordnung. Meine Schwester suchte wieder einmal nach einem gerechten Ausgleich, aber ich wollte an diesem Tag unserer Mutter überhaupt nichts zugutehalten. Wir hockten auf der Veranda herum, und es war dunstig, und ein Nieselregen schwebte in dem kleinen Taxusdickicht.

Sie schadet ihm mit diesem Dauergerede, sagte ich. Sie schaffts immer, sich selbst zum Mittelpunkt zu machen. Es ist aber Paps' Krankheit, nicht ihre.

Gegen zwei oder noch etwas später, als sie endlich eine Art Mittagsimbiss auf den Tisch stellte, Stück für Stück mit Schnauben, Seufzen, bot unsere Mutter sicher zum fünfzigsten mal an diesem Samstag an, nicht zu verreisen. Unser Vater hat wieder nichts Richtiges dazu gesagt, nur irgend so was wie: Lass doch. Seine Nasenspitze war weiß, das fiel auf, obwohl er ein blasses Gesicht hat.

Unsere Mutter sagte, es wäre besser für ihn, wenn sie in seiner Nähe bliebe, aber ich finde, es hat sich nicht nach einem ernstgemeinten Angebot angehört, und unser Vater sah ablehnend aus. Zu ihrer Freundin sagte sie später am Telephon leise, obwohl er gar nicht in der Nähe war, nur meine Schwester und ich nebenan in der Küche mit dem Geschirr zu tun hatten: Vielleicht möchte er ja auch lieber allein sein. Er könnte sich dann gehenlassen. Die Mädchen haben ihre eigenen Pläne, und irgendwann

GABRIELE WOHMANN

Good Luck and Bad Luck

Maybe the only thing that can be said to her credit is her agitation after the damned diagnosis. And she has always talked too much. So that is just as well. My sister was once again seeking to be fair, but I didn't want our mother to deserve praise for anything at all. We sat around on the veranda; it was muggy and tiny droplets floated in the little yew thicket.

She is hurting him with this constant talking, I said. She always manages to become the center of attention. But it's dad's illness, not hers.

Around two or even a bit later, when she finally managed to put some sort of a midday snack on the table, item by item, accompanied by snuffling and sighing, our mother offered, certainly for the fiftieth time this Saturday, not to go on her trip. Our father did not add anything substantial to that, only something like, "It's all right." The tip of his nose was white, which caught one's eye, even though he had a pale face.

Our mother said that it might be better for him if she stayed around, but this did not seem to be a serious offer, and our father appeared dismissive. She later spoke quietly on the phone to her friend, although he was not even around. Only my sister and I were next door in the kitchen, busy with the dishes. "Maybe he would like to be alone. Then he would be able to let himself go. The girls have made their own plans and the house is going

wird das Haus leer sein, und dann kann er den Urschrei aus-
probieren, von dem ich ihm berichtet habe, gestern, gleich nach
der Diagnose. Ich habs gemacht, den Urschrei ausgestoßen, als
meine gute arme Mutter starb.

Sie hat noch mehr geredet, doch dann hat die Freundin sie
unterbrochen, und sie musste zuhören, bis endlich wieder sie
drankam. Bei ihr hätte das mit dem Urschrei funktioniert, die
schlimmste Trauer war sie losgeworden, aber bei unserem Vater
wäre sie da nicht so sicher. Ich glaube nicht dran, hat sie gesagt,
nicht bei ihm, nicht bei seinem Gefühlshaushalt und Innenleben.
Er ist so introvertiert. Weißt du?

Und sie hat unseren Vater *meinen guten armen Friedhelm*
genannt, *gut* und *arm*, als wäre er schon tot wie ihre Mutter,
und dass nomen omen wäre: Friedhelm, dermaßen friedfertig,
obwohl, ich weiß nicht, ob es das wirklich ist, ich meine Frieden. Er kann auch ganz schön stur sein. Nicht alle stillen Wasser
wären tief.

Wenn meine Schwester mich nicht beschwichtigt hätte, wäre
ich nach nebenan gelaufen und grob geworden oder wasweißich.
Unsere Mutter hat gesagt: Diese schreckliche Angelegenheit hat
aber auch ihr Gutes, wenn man so will, denn glaub mir, was du
blitzartig erkennst, das ist: Du liebst ihn. In deinem Fall wärs
dein Herbert, und wir beide haben oft genug unser Problem mit
der Ehe, das heißt: mit unseren Männern, aber durch so einen
Schock und wenns aufs Ganze geht, wirklich um alles oder nichts,
du verstehst schon, dann nimmst du all deinen Groll in Kauf.
Und das ist ja dann wohl die Liebe, oder? Sie hat gesagt, nachdem sie kurz ihrer Freundin das Reden überlassen hatte, wie
gut, dass sie da und dort nicht fest zugesagt hätte. Stell dir vor,
Elsies Party und ich mittendrin, ich in den Klammern meines
Kummers!

Als könnte man bei einer Party nicht absagen, und wenn man
hundertmal versprochen hätte zu kommen!, schimpfte ich. Und
sogar meine Schwester regte sich auf.

Da ist aber immer noch diese Reise, und wenn sie wirklich
drauf verzichten wollte, hätte sie das sofort melden sollen, andere Leute machen das auch, sie stornieren bei weniger großen
Sorgen, sagte sie, und das sei für ihre Verhältnisse eine Menge.

to be empty eventually and then he can try out his primal scream, the one I told him about yesterday, right after he got the diagnosis. I did it, let out the primal scream when my dear, poor mother died."

She went on talking, but then her girlfriend interrupted her and she had to listen until it was her turn to finally talk again. In her case the primal scream had worked, she had been able to get rid of most of the grief, but with our father she was not so sure. "I don't believe it," she said. "Not in his case, not with his emotional state and his inner life. He is such an introvert. You know?"

And she called our father *my dear, poor Friedhelm; dear* and *poor*, as if he were already dead like her mother and his name was an omen. "Friedhelm, it seems so peaceable; although, I don't know if it is really is so, I mean, *peace.* He can be really very stubborn at times. Not all still waters run deep."

If my sister had not calmed me down, I would have gone next door and gotten rude or who knows. Our mother said, "this terrible business also has a good side, if you want to see it that way, because, believe me, what you realize in an instant is that you love him. In your case that would be your Herbert, and, often enough, we both have had our problem with marriage, that is to say, with our husbands, but through a shock like this and when you risk it all, really all or nothing, you know, then you put up with all your resentment and anger. And that is love, isn't it?" she said, after she briefly allowed her friend to talk, saying how fortunate that she had not accepted right then and there. "Can you imagine Elsie's party, and I in the middle of it, with me being in the clutches of my grief!"

As if you couldn't cancel a party, and even if you had promised to show up a hundred times, I raged. And even my sister got upset.

But there is still this trip, and if she really had wanted to forgo it, she should have notified them right away, other people do it that way too, they cancel in the event of much smaller trouble, she said, and in her case that was

Meine Schwester denkt wie ich, aber sie ist ruhiger. Sie will nicht, dass ich mich aufrege. Wenn sie das zu deutlich macht, rege ich mich erst recht auf. Nachmittags kam die Sonne heraus, und das machte es auch nicht besser. Die Bäume und Sträucher blühten rosa, weiß und gelb, und vorgestern hatte unser Vater noch so zufrieden an der Böschung zwischen dem Heidekraut gehäckelt. Überhaupt war es plötzlich gar nicht mehr das Beste für unsere Familie, dass wir vor vier Monaten in das Haus auf dem großen Grundstück am Wald umgezogen sind, vor allem vielleicht nicht für unseren Vater, dem wir all diese Verbesserungen verdankten.

An diesem Samstag war nichts los mit uns, keiner wusste irgendetwas mit sich anzufangen, nichts schien die Sache wert zu sein, niemand konnte sich konzentrieren, bis auf unsere Mutter. Schon wieder telefonierte sie mit jemandem, dem sie wie allen anderen auch diesen blöden Freispruch aufsagte: Ich habe den Kardiologen eindringlich gefragt, und er hat es genauso eindringlich entschieden verneint. Nein, ganz und gar nicht, seelische Komponenten spielen in seinem Fall keine Rolle. Es ist rein mechanisch. Es ist nicht beispielsweise so, dass seine erste Frau in seiner Seele rumspukt, was neulich jemand vermutete, jemand, der uns überhaupt nicht richtig kennt und dem das große Portrait der guten armen Lisbeth auffiel, es hängt im Treppenhaus, und zwar einfach, weil es ein gutes Gemälde ist und nichts weiter. Rein mechanisch, das leuchtet ja auch bei einer Herzklappe ein. Vermutlich ist sie verkalkt und geht deshalb nicht mehr richtig auf und zu. Es ist etwas Maschinenartiges, also mechanisch. Nicht seelisch. Wenn es um Probleme mit dem Organ Herz geht, denken die meisten unwillkürlich an irgendwelche sonstigen *Herzensangelegenheiten*.

Sie wirkte wieder selbstgerecht und wie befreit, von Mitschuld durch sie konnte also, der Spezialist hat es ja selbst gesagt, keine Rede sein. Meine Schwester und ich, wir glaubten trotzdem dran, ob es nun rein mechanisch war bei unserem Vater oder nicht. Schaden musste ihm auch garantiert ihr Herumstolzieren mit dem Handy und ihr ewiges Herumerzählen. Es ist übrigens nicht ihr einziges Handy, sie hat viele an ver-

quite something to say. My sister thinks like I do, but she is calmer. She does not want me to get upset. If she points that out, I get really upset.

In the afternoon the sun came out, but that did not improve things either. The trees and shrubs bloomed pink, white, and yellow, and the day before yesterday our father had worked away so happily with his hoe among the heathers on the slope. Suddenly, it was no longer the best at all for our family that we had moved to the large property on the edge of the forest four months ago, particularly not for our father, to whom we owed this upgrade.

This Saturday we weren't up to much and nobody knew what to do; nothing seemed worth the effort, nobody was able to concentrate, except for our mother. She was on the phone again with someone to whom she recited this stupid acquittal: "I firmly asked the cardiologist and he answered in the negative just as firmly. No, not at all; psychological components don't play a role in this case. It's simply mechanical. It isn't, for example, that his first wife had been haunting his soul, which is what someone insinuated the other day, someone who does not know us really at all and who noticed the big portrait of dear, poor Lisbeth, up on the wall in the staircase simply because it is a good painting and nothing else. Simply mechanical, that makes sense with a cardiac valve. It might be clogged and that is why it does not open and close properly anymore. It is something like a machine, therefore it is mechanical. Not psychological. Where problems with the heart organ are concerned, most people inevitably think of something like affairs of the heart."

She appeared self-righteous again and as if liberated, so there could be no talk about any share in the guilt on her part, even the specialist had said so. My sister and I, we did believe in it, whether it was now simply mechanical in the case of our father or not. Her strutting around with her cell phone and constant bandying about had to be positively harmful to him as well. By the way, that was not her only cell

schiedenen Stellen, damit sie nie nach ihnen suchen muss, es sind ihre Lieblinge. Wir saßen in unserem Souterrainzimmer, es geht über Eck und hat eine Fensterschiebetür, so dass jeder seinen eigenen Raum hat, und wir genießen das. In der alten Wohnung hatten wir selbstverständlich auch jede ein Zimmer für sich, aber das waren bloß Kajüten, sehr schmal und beengt wie alles dort. Vor lauter Ödnis und aus Langeweile, der ganze Tag war nur eine Warterei, aßen wir Farmer-Riegel, ohne wirklichen Appetit, doch immer noch einen, und unsere Mundhöhlen waren schon wie verätzt von dem scharfen süßen Aprikosengeschmack. Das Zimmer hat vier Fenster, jedes Abteil zwei. Der Ausblick der Ostfenster geht auf eine steile Backsteinmauer, die den Wall abstützt und bei uns Kaimauer heißt, weil sie an einen Hafen erinnert. Das Haus hat Hanglage. Im Süden ist das Gelände flacher, aber der Wall immer noch so hoch, dass man nur die Köpfe der Leute sieht, die auf dem Weg zwischen Wall und Kiefernwäldchen entlanggehen. Sie gehen meistens langsam, Blick nach unten, und solang man nur ihr Profil sehen kann, und das ist bis zu unserem breiten Eisenstabtor in der Zufahrt, denkt man, sie wären alle depressiv. Aber sobald sie im zweiten Fenster auftauchen, wo der Wall fast auf die Weghöhe abfällt, erkennt man ihre Hunde, die sie ausführen, und zwar ohne Leine, und deshalb beobachten sie die Hunde, und sie sehen dann wie ganz normale Leute aus, nur wie sehr konzentrierte Leute, die darauf warten, dass ihre Hunde die Verdauung erledigen.

Unsere Mutter ging durchs Haus spazieren, und so kam sie auch des Wegs, als wir dort im Souterrainzimmer herumsaßen, die Tür zur unteren Diele hatten wir nur halb zugemacht, damit wir mitkriegten, was so vorging. Unsere Mutter wandelte natürlich mit ihrem unentbehrlichen Handy umher, das zu ihrem größten Glück endlich wieder einmal piepste. Sie hörte jemandem zu, dann sagte sie: Na schön, er hat keine Verschlimmerung gespürt, er wusste ja, dass er diese Oberbauchschmerzen hatte, weil er herzkrank ist, schön und gut, ohne Diagnose ginge es ihm jetzt so gut wie immer, heute so gut wie gestern, und es war ja nur der routinemäßige Kontrolltermin beim Kardiologen. Heute

phone; she had quite of few of them placed in different places so that she never had to look for them; they are her loves.

We were hanging out in our room in the basement; it is a corner room and has a glass sliding door, so each of us has our own space, and we enjoy that. Naturally, in the old place we each had a room of our own, but they were only like ship cabins, very narrow and cramped, like everything else there. Because of all the bleakness and because we were so bored, we ate granola bars without any real appetite, but yet we still ate another one and the inside of our mouths felt burnt from the acidic, sweet taste of apricots. The room had four windows, each part with two. The view out the east window is toward a steep brick wall which supports the retaining wall; we call it quay wall because it is reminiscent of a harbor. The house is located on a slope. On the south side the terrain is more level, but the wall is still so high that you can only see the heads of the people who walk along the path between the wall and the little pine forest. Usually they walk slowly, looking downwards, and as long as you can only see their profile, which is until they reach our wide iron bar gate in the driveway, you might think they are completely depressed. But as soon as they appear in the second window, where the wall is almost level with the path, you notice they are walking dogs without a leash, which is why they watch their dogs, and then they look like normal people, only like very focused people waiting for their dogs to finish their business.

Our mother was on a walk through the house and so she happened along our way as we were hanging out in the basement room; we had shut the door to the entryway only halfway in order to see what was all going on. Needless to say, our mother was strolling about with her indispensable cell phone which, to her utter delight, had begun to beep again. She listened to somebody and then she said, "Fine, he hasn't noticed anything getting worse and he knew that he had pain in his upper abdomen because of his cardiac condition, well and good; without a diagnosis, he would be as well as usual, today as good as yesterday, and it was only a routine check-

wäre ein Tag wie jeder, *ohne* Diagnose. Aber *mit* Diagnose, und das muss ich mir mitten in meinen Sorgen richtig einpauken, *mit* ist es einfach besser. Denn wenn er so weitergemacht hätte, wäre er wahrscheinlich schon in wenigen Wochen nicht mehr unter uns.

Nicht mehr unter uns! Wie sie das bringt!, sagte ich.

Sie muss immer alles verzwirbeln, sagte meine Schwester. Sie ist auch beim Fernsehen auf jedes Melodram scharf.

Man könnte meinen, sie genießt es, sagte ich, und meine Schwester blickte großäugig und trübsinnig vor sich hin, und ich zischelte: Pass auf, hör dir das an!

Unsere Mutter sagte gerade: Ich hatte heute Morgen mitten im Fitness-Programm einen komischen Zustand. Es war wie eine Pause, die das Leben machte, mein Leben hier in mir drin, irgendwo zwischen Schlüsselbein und Brust, mein Leben legt einen Stillstand ein, und ich war gerade bei der Übung Knieanheben in der Hocke, und zwar zirka zwei bis drei Zentimeter hoch, du musst die unbedingt auch machen, wegen der Bauchmuskulatur . . . also mein Leben machte eine Atempause, und ich musste mich vorbeugen und zusammenkrümmen und dann aufstehen, ich dachte, sonst gehst du ein . . .

Die oder der andere sagte was, und danach klang unsere Mutter beleidigt: Was redest du denn da, du Unschuldsengel! Das sollen Blähungen gewesen sein? O nein, meine Liebe, das war Projektion, frage jede Psycho-Koryphäe, und für die Dauer dieser Pause, die mein Leben machte, hatte *ich* Friedhelms Krankheit. Wäre ja nur allzu schön, wenn du recht hättest. Und dann seufzte sie tief und ist weiterspaziert, und wir waren einer Meinung: Sie hatte wieder ein Beispiel dafür geliefert, dass immer sie der Mittelpunkt sein muss von allem, was passiert.

Wir würden übrigens Alma zu ihr sagen, niemals Mutter, aber an unsere richtige Mutter erinnern wir uns nicht. Nur sind wir beide fest davon überzeugt, dass sie *richtig* gewesen wäre und zu uns gepasst hätte, einfach schon genetisch uns ähnlicher als unser Vater. Von dem haben wir wohl nicht allzu viel geerbt, obwohl, man kennt ihn ja kaum. Sie haben uns erst, als wir zwölf und vierzehn waren, alles gesagt, und da sind wir uns ganz schön reingelegt vorgekommen. Wir haben

up at the cardiologist's. Today would be a day like any other
without a diagnosis. However, *with* a diagnosis, and I have
to remind myself of this in my sorrow, *with* one it is simply
better. For if he had gone on like that, most likely he would
no longer be among us in a few weeks.

No longer among us! How she says that, I said.

She always has to twist things around, my sister said.
Even when she watches TV, she loves all the soap operas.

One would think she enjoys it, I said, and my sister
looked into space, big-eyed and somber, and I whispered:
"Pay attention, listen to that!"

Our mother was just saying, "This morning, while doing
my fitness program, I was in a strange state. It was as if life
took a pause, my life here inside me, somewhere between
my collarbone and my chest, my life stopped and I was just
doing the exercise knee lift squat, approximately one to
two inches high, you absolutely must do that one because
of your abdominal muscles . . . anyway, my life took a
break and I had to bend forward and double over and then
get up, I thought, otherwise I am going to die."

The other man or woman said something and after
that our mother sounded offended. "What are you saying, you angel of innocence! That this was supposed to be
indigestion? Oh no, my dear, that was a projection, ask
every psycho-expert, and for the time my life was paused,
I had Friedhelm's illness. Wouldn't that be nice if you were
right?" And then she sighed deeply and continued her
stroll, and we both agreed: she had just given another example of how she always had to be the center of attention
of everything that was happening.

By the way, we would rather call her Alma, never Mother, but we can't remember our real mother. Only that we
are both convinced that she would have been *right* and
that she would have matched us, or simply resembled us
more genetically than our father. Apparently we have not
inherited too much of him, although we hardly know him.
They only told us the whole story when we were twelve
and fourteen, and we felt like we had been conned. We

uns viel zu lang mit einem schlechten Gewissen gequält, weil wir immer versucht hatten, unsere Mutter zu lieben, und weil das nicht funktioniert hat. Dann wussten wir, warum. Aber es war zu spät. Auch um auf *Alma* statt *Mutter* umzuschalten. Wir probierten das aus, der Alma-Mutter war es nicht recht, und das hätte uns nicht gestört, doch unser Vater schien darunter zu leiden. Gegen fünf saßen wir zu viert am Teetisch, unsere Mutter hatte uns auf die Veranda gerufen. Es war ganz gut, dass sie diese Idee hatte, schon damit nicht alles so lähmend zerfloss, alles an diesem blöden Samstag, und die Sonne war hinter dicker Bewölkung verschwunden, und es hat wieder etwas geregnet, was man aber nur erkannte, wenn man in das Taxusdickicht sah, von dem der nässliche Schleier sich abhob.

Unsere Mutter hat doch tatsächlich mitten in all der Telefoniererei gebacken, und zwar Muffins, ihre schmecken ziemlich anders als die gekauften, viel besser, und sie kriegt sie schön feucht hin, und dass sie an so etwas dachte, fanden wir richtig gut.

Dann aber fing sie wieder mit dem Fehlermachen an und hat diese Geschichte von der *Pause* erzählt, die *ihr Leben machte*, immerhin in Kurzform, und unser Vater sagte, es hätte Luft im Magen sein können, und darauf erwarteten wir natürlich, dass sie wie vorhin bei ihrer Handy-Freundin Dampf ablassen würde, aber sie hat nur *Hoffentlich* und *Schön wärs* geseufzt und dann gesagt: Was soll denn *das?* Ihr Ton war sofort wieder alltagsmäßig und erzürnt und die Frage ihr Kommentar zur Rücksendung einer Muffinhälfte, die vom Teller unseres Vaters auf ihren gerutscht war. Wir wussten natürlich, was das *sollte*, und sie wusste es auch. Unser Vater muss nämlich vor seiner Operation ziemlich viel abnehmen, und sie selber hatte kommandiert: Du stehst von jetzt an unterm FDH-Imperativ, mein Ärmster! So etwas bringt sie glatt, dabei ist sie selbst schuld an seinem Körperumfang. Sie füllt ihn unheimlich ab, als wäre er eine Mastgans, und das wäre bei ihr der Fütterungstrieb, sagt sie, kommt wieder mit ihren Psychologen, und die entdecken die wahre Liebe hinter diesem Trieb, also ist damit auch sie der Mittelpunkt. Sie behauptet: Ich kann

had suffered from a bad conscience for far too long since we always tried to love our mother and hadn't been able to. Then we knew why. But it was too late. Too late for switching to from *Alma* to *Mother,* as well. We tried that; the Alma-Mother did not like it and that would not have bothered us, but our father appeared to be hurt by it.

Around five, the four of us sat at the tea table; our mother had called us to the veranda. It was a good thing she had had this idea, primarily so that everything didn't dissolve into paralysis, everything on this stupid Saturday; the sun had disappeared behind thick clouds and it had rained a bit again, however, you would only notice that when you looked into the yew thicket where the wet fog stood out.

Our mother had actually managed to bake alongside all the calling on the phone, muffins in fact; hers taste quite different from the store bought ones, much better, and she manages to make them nicely moist; we found it nice that she had thought of something like that.

But then she started making mistakes again and told this story about the *pause* that *her life had taken,* albeit in a shortened version, and our father replied that it could have been air in her stomach and naturally, we expected her to vent her anger like she had done earlier to her cell phone friend, but she only sighed, "One can only hope," and "That would be nice," and then she said, "And what is *that* supposed to mean?" Her tone was immediately day-to-day-business-like and angry again, and the question served as her comment to the return of half a muffin, which had slid from our father's plate onto hers. Obviously, we all knew what that was *supposed to mean,* and she knew it too. That is to say, our father has to lose rather a lot of weight before his operation and she herself had decreed, "From now on, you are under my half rations imperative, poor you! She says that so point-blank, even though his size is her fault entirely. She fills him up with enormous amounts of food as if he were a fattened goose; in her case that would be her feeding drive, she says, brings up her psychologists again, and they have discovered true love behind this drive, so she is again the

mich nicht bremsen, wenn es ums Aufpäppeln meiner Lieben geht. Schon ziemlich früh haben wir zwei, meine Schwester und ich, es besser verstanden als unser Vater, uns von ihrer Mast zu distanzieren. Aber unser argloser Vater fällt auf seine Schwächen und auf ihre Verführungen immer wieder rein. Seit er mit dem Arzt gesprochen hat, nicht mehr. Das heißt, er versucht es immerhin, sich zu wehren. Und dann kriegt sie schlechte Laune, sagt zum Beispiel, dass der Arzt übertreibt, erstens, und zweitens die Wissenschaft weiter wäre und der Arzt rückständig, weil man längst vom sogenannten Idealgewicht abgekommen wäre.

Jetzt habe ich extra zur Aufmunterung für uns alle diese Muffins gebacken, tausendmal besser als alle, die wir früher ausprobiert hatten, von McDonald's und sämtlichen Test-Cafés und Bäckereien, beschwerte sich unsere Mutter. Mit der rechten Hand fuhr sie sich vom Nacken her durch ihr schulterlang in Wellen fallendes Haar, was sie oft macht, wenn sie dramatisch ist. Sie hat übrigens schöne Haare, eine Menge davon und dick, und meine Schwester und ich, wir haben ziemlich dünne glatte Haare wie unser Vater, und wir wissen ja mittlerweile, warum wir ihre Prachtmasse nicht erben konnten. (Sie sieht auch sonst nicht übel aus, hat sogar Geschmack bei den Sachen, die sie anzieht, das muss man ihr lassen, wenn es auch nicht unser Geschmack ist.) Und dann rief sie: Übrigens, wer sagt eigentlich mir, dass ich nicht auch gefährlich krank bin? Niemand hat mich untersucht. Mein letzter Check-up liegt ewig lang zurück.

Das war nun wirklich der Höhepunkt. Ich sagte: Du siehst sehr gesund aus, und meine Schwester sagte: Wenn du was Gefährliches hättest, würdest du es merken. An irgendwas würdest du es merken. Und unser Vater dachte wohl, jetzt brauche nicht auch er noch etwas beizusteuern. Ich fand allerdings, und meine Schwester bestimmt auch, er hätte endlich mal ein Machtwort sprechen müssen. Aber so etwas ist von ihm so leicht nicht zu erwarten.

Nicht verübeln sollten wir unserer Mutter, dass sie in die Runde fragte: Und wie bringen wir den Rest des Tages rum? Und den Sonntag? Wir können nicht von jetzt an dauernd

center of attention. She claims, "I can't stop myself when it comes to coddling my loved ones." Rather early on, my sister and I were better at distancing ourselves from her fattening than our father was. However, our unassuming father gives in to his weaknesses and her persuasions, again and again. But not since he has spoken with the doctor. That is to say, at least he is trying to fight back. And then she develops a bad temper, saying things like the doctor is exaggerating, first of all, and second, science has advanced and the doctor is behind because the notion of an ideal weight had been abandoned for a long time.

"So, to cheer us all up, I baked these muffins, a thousand times better than all of those we tried before, from McDonald's and all the test cafés and bakeries," our mother complained. Beginning at the nape of her neck, she ran the fingers of her right hand through her shoulder-length hair that cascades down in waves, which she does a lot when she is being dramatic. By the way, she has beautiful hair, a lot of it and thick, and my sister and I have pretty thin and straight hair like our father, and by now we know why we couldn't inherit her gorgeous mass. (She doesn't look bad at all otherwise, even has taste in the things she wears, one has to give her that, even it if it isn't our taste). And she called out, "Incidentally, who says that I am not dangerously ill either? Nobody has examined me. I haven't had a checkup in ages."

Now, the nerve! I said, "You look very healthy," and my sister said, "If you had something dangerous, you would notice. You would notice somehow." And our father didn't think he had to contribute something on top of that. I thought, however, and I'm sure my sister also did, he should have put his foot down. But you can hardly expect something like that from him.

We shouldn't hold it against our mother that she asked, looking around, "And how are we going to spend the rest of the day? And Sunday? We can't continue letting

den Kopf hängen lassen. Werktags ist alles etwas leichter. Die Wochenenden sind heimtückisch.

Sie hat damit ja nur ausgesprochen, was in uns allen vorging. Trotzdem einigten meine Schwester und ich uns darauf, dass sie ziemlich taktlos war. Weil wir auf der gleichen Wellenlänge senden, meine Schwester und ich, vermute ich, dass auch sie dachte, unser Vater hätte eingreifen sollen. Wir kritisieren ihn nicht gern. Wir haben es nicht gern, eine Schwäche bei ihm zu spüren, und deshalb drücken wir uns davor. Nie kann er es sein, der die Initiative ergreift. Soll die ganze Familie bis zu seiner grässlichen Operation, man wird ihm die Brust in der Mitte aufsägen, so öde herumhängen? Und deshalb, weil sie eigentlich recht hatte, war es halbwegs auch ein bisschen gelogen, als meine Schwester und ich uns hinterher über sie empörten. Unsere Mutter hatte nämlich unserem stummen Vater auf den Kopf zugesagt, und zwar sehr laut und ganz schön grob: Und du, was hört man so von dir? Der uns das alles eingebrockt hat, klar, du kannst nichts dafür, aber vielleicht könntest du dich ja mal zu irgendeiner Idee aufraffen. Oder ist das zu viel verlangt? Und mein Vater hat nervös gelächelt und gezögert und dann gesagt: Heute Abend zum Beispiel gibts *Glück und Ungück*. Haben wir zweimal schon verpasst.

Das ist ein Ratespiel, in dem es um Millionen geht, und man kann von hoch oben nach ganz unten fallen. Und meine Mutter hat, dem Himmel sei Dank, nichts mehr weiter gesagt, nichts Spöttisches, und wie wir daran gedacht, dass er sich nicht aufregen darf.

our heads hang. During the week everything is a bit easier. Weekends are sneaky."

Actually, she only expressed what we were all thinking. Nevertheless, my sister and I agreed that she had been pretty tactless. Since we broadcast on the same wave length, my sister and I, I assume she also thought that our father should have intervened. We don't like to criticize him. We don't like to sense weakness in him and therefore we shirk it. He never takes the initiative. Is the whole family supposed to hang around drearily until his operation, when they will cut open the center of his chest with a saw? And therefore, because she had been right after all, it was sort of a half lie when my sister and I were disgusted with her afterwards. That is to say, our mother had told our silent father straight to his face, and very loud and pretty rude indeed, "And you, what have you got to say? You, who brought this onto us, of course, it's not your fault, but maybe you could pull yourself together and come up with some ideas. Or is that asking too much?" And my father laughed nervously, hesitated, and then said, "Tonight, for example, Good Luck and Bad Luck is on TV. We already missed it twice."

It's a quiz show with millions at stake where you can fall from high up and hit rock bottom. And my mother said, "Thank heavens." Nothing else, nothing derisive, like us considering the fact that he was not supposed to get upset.

MICHAEL INNEBERGER

Born in 1968 in the spa town of Bad Reichenhall in Upper Bavaria, Michael Inneberger grew up nearby in picturesque Marzoll, a few miles from the Austrian border, and went to school in Freilassing and Traunstein. After completing military service in Traunstein, he became a certified electrician specializing in electronics. Presently, he lives with his family in Nußdorf, a charming village in the Chiemgau region. When not writing, Inneberger, a dedicated skier, likes to spend time on the ski slopes of the Bavarian Alps.

Inneberger started writing about ten years ago, trying his hand at children's plays. Noticing that his three-year-old son was fascinated by "Kasperlgeschichten"[1] (Punchinello stories), Inneberger began creating them for his son and for his friends' children. They were a huge success with the younger crowd, so Inneberger was encouraged to keep on writing.

Since 2007 he has been writing poetry and short prose texts, more than a dozen of which have been published in anthologies. His first anthology, *Geschichten aus der Welt—um uns herum*[2] (*Stories from the world—around us*, 2010), comprises eleven

---

[1]Kasperl is a seventeenth-century puppet character from southern Germany and Austria. Kasperletheater ("Punchinello play") has often been equaled with puppet theater. The name Kasper means "keeper of the treasure" in Persian. The first Kasperletheater was staged in Munich in 1858. Like his cousin Punch, Kasperl often uses a "slapstick" to beat the Devil, Witch, and Crocodile. ("Kasperletheater – Die ganze Welt der Spielwaren," accessed August 28, 2011, http://www.weltderspielwaren.de/spielzeug-katalog/kasperletheater.htm.

[2]Michael Inneberger, *Geschichten aus der Welt – um uns herum* (Norderstedt: Books on Demand, 2010).

short stories and poems. Recently, Inneberger completed a sci-fi young adult novel, which is awaiting publication. His latest project is a fantasy novel set in medieval times, also intended for young adults.

Acclaim for his work, mostly received at live prose "jam" sessions, includes both first and second prizes for his story "Klempner Huber" ("Plumber Huber"), a first prize for "Diebestour" ("Thieving Spree"), and second prizes for "Target Donau" ("Target Danube") and "Zugabe" ("Encore"), all in 2010.

Critical responses to Inneberger's texts have been good, acknowledging his skill in tackling difficult topics as a means to inspire contemplation and reflection as well as more humorous subject matter.[3] Inneberger is a member of the "Chiemgauer Autorengruppe" (Chiemgau Authors' Group) and editor-in-chief of the website Autorenwort.de (Authors' Word), the group's online publication.

Fellow writer Anna Dorb has this to say about the stories in his anthology: "Michael Inneberger's stories entertain and at the same time fascinate me. They are little stories that all begin like a new day. One does not know what to anticipate, or what surprises are in store. One moment, they make me smile, and in the next I am gripped with terror, sometimes with devastating force."[4] Another review praises the versatile range of stories presented in the collection,[5] among them the sorrowful, yet somehow comforting "Urlaub auf ewig" ("Eternal Vacation") and the futuristic satire "Klempner Huber" ("Plumber Huber").

"Urlaub für ewig"/"Eternal Vacation"

"Urlaub auf ewig" is a sad parable of what can happen when one makes wrong choices. The hero chooses money over love, a fateful decision that ends in tragedy.

---

[3]Norbert Wehr, the literary critic and editor-in-chief of the literary magazine *Schreibheft: Zeitschrift für Literatur*, opines that Inneberger's stories are "Begabt erzählte Geschichten (told with skill and talent). Author's translation.

[4]Anna Dorb, "Eine sehr interessante und kurzweilige Lektüre," accessed March 2, 2011, http://www.amazon.de/Geschichten-aus-Welt-herum-Kurzgeschichten/dp/3842319495/ref=sr_1_1?ie=UTF8&qid=1314556469&sr=8-1.

[5]"Mit Klempner Huber zum Erfolg," *Traunreuter Anzeiger*, November 23, 2010.

The story opens as Paul Goldhuber, a successful software businessman, takes leave from work to get ready for the annual vacation with his wife Maria, ten years his junior. As Paul goes about preparing for the trip, the reader learns bit by bit that things have not been going smoothly in the Goldhuber marriage. Paul's stream of consciousness reveals, through flashbacks and interior monologues, that their love has gone sour. As he worked increasingly longer hours in his pursuit of wealth, Maria felt increasingly neglected. She took a lover her own age, although he was less attractive than Paul, both physically and financially.

Then, after a brutal event beyond anyone's control forces Paul to face that his marriage has been destroyed forever, he resorts to acting out a desperate fantasy, trying to restore their lost happiness.

"Klempner Huber"/"Plumber Huber"

The story exemplifies Inneberger's concern with the loss of individual and cultural identity, presented in a humorous manner as an ordinary craftsman wrestles with the perils of life in a unified Europe in a not too distant future. Plumber Huber, living in a futuristic Chiemgau (a region that evokes more notions of tranquil Bavarian "Gemütlichkeit" than of a restless way of life driven by technological and entrepreneurial innovation) is accidentally summoned to deal with an emergency on a space shuttle sitting on the launch pad—the toilet is plugged. While taking care of the problem by using his traditional low-tech tools in the high-tech environment, he misses the call for take-off and becomes trapped in the space-bound vehicle.

The fate of that lovable yet shrewd craftsman, who might appear somewhat antediluvian to technology enthusiasts, has made Huber hugely popular with all kinds of audiences. As the new motto of Inneberger's public readings, in Bavarian dialect, confirms, "Da Huba is scho längst Kult im Chiemgau!" ("Huber has long since attained cult status in the Chiemgau!").

MICHAEL INNEBERGER

Urlaub für ewig

Die Geschichte, die ich Euch heute erzählen will, ereignete sich vor vielen, vielen Jahren, im Sommer anno 2007, im Chiemgau. Ihr fragt Euch sicher, was ich mit dieser Geschichte zu tun habe, oder warum ich mich noch so genau daran erinnere? Nun ja, eigentlich war ich nicht direkt dabei, als es geschah. Trotzdem: Wer sollte Euch die Ereignisse der damaligen Zeit besser erzählen können als ich?

Um zu beginnen, drehen wir das Datum zurück auf den 03.08.2007 und steigen dort in die Geschehnisse ein:

Der Nachmittag dieses Freitags stellte sich für Paul Goldhuber etwas stressig, aber dennoch aussichtsvoll dar.

Er hatte seine E-mail Post erledigt, und sein Arbeitsplatzrechner meldete: »Windows wird heruntergefahren. Sie können den Computer jetzt ausschalten.«

Mit einem schwarzen Jackett über dem Arm stand er aufbruchbereit im Türrahmen zum Büro seines Geschäftspartners.

»Also dann Ludwig, ich habe das Wichtigste noch erledigt«, machte sich Paul bemerkbar.

Ludwig blickte vom Monitor auf, erhob sich vom Bürostuhl, eilte um den Schreibtisch herum und streckte Paul beide Hände entgegen:

»Paul, ich wünsche dir einen erholsamen Urlaub. Keiner hat ihn sich mehr verdient als du.«

Paul ergriff die Hände von Ludwig und für einen kurzen Moment drückte er sie fest.

»Halt die Ohren steif«, nickte Paul fast melancholisch.

MICHAEL INNEBERGER

Eternal Vacation

The story I am going to tell you happened many, many years ago, in the summer of 2007, in the Chiemgau region.

You are probably asking what I have to do with this story, or why I remember it so clearly?

Well, actually I was not there when it happened. However: who else but I is better able to tell you about the events from then?

To begin, let's turn the date back to March 8, 2007, and step in:

That Friday afternoon turned out to be somewhat stressful, yet still auspicious for Paul Goldhuber.

He had finished going through his e-mail messages and his work computer announced, "Windows is shutting down. You may now turn off the computer."

With his black jacket over his arm and ready to go, he stood in the doorway to his business partner's office.

"All right then, Ludwig, I was able to finish the most important work," Paul said, drawing attention to himself. Ludwig looked up from his monitor, got up from his office chair, hurried around the desk, and extended both hands to Paul:

"Paul, I wish you a restful vacation. Nobody's earned it more than you."

Paul took Ludwig's hands and, for a short moment, squeezed them hard.

"Keep a stiff upper lip," Paul nodded, almost melancholy.

Die Mittagszeit war eine ungewöhnliche Feierabendzeit für Paul. Normalerweise kam er erst sehr spät aus dem Büro.

Eigentlich konnte er sein laufendes Projekt nicht sich selbst oder seinem Geschäftspartner überlassen, da Ludwig gewissermaßen ebenso urlaubsreif war. Dennoch nahm er sich seit Jahren regelmäßig im August eine zweiwöchige Auszeit.

Paul Goldhuber führte zusammen mit seinem Freund Ludwig Korn ein florierendes Softwarehaus.

In den letzten 15 Jahren hatten die beiden das Unternehmen kontinuierlich ausgebaut und neue Geschäftsstrukturen erschlossen. Ihre Klientel erstreckte sich mittlerweile quer durch Europa.

Da sich der Firmensitz in Chieming befand, waren sie relativ zentral angesiedelt und konnten Ihre Kunden mit der firmeneigenen Cessna vom Salzburger Airport aus in wenigen Stunden erreichen.

Paul Goldhuber liebte seinen Job, so sehr er dadurch auch in Anspruch genommen wurde. Er hatte auch eine große Verantwortung für seine mittlerweile 19 Mitarbeiter zu tragen.

Da blieb ihm in den letzten Jahren nur wenig Zeit zur Erholung.

Er wusste, dass vor allem seine Frau unter seiner 70-Stunden-Woche und den wenigen freien Tagen, die er sich gönnte, zu leiden hatte. Trotzdem fühlte er stets ihre positive Haltung ihm gegenüber und zu seiner wichtigen Arbeit. Schließlich musste sie aufgrund der seit Jahren tiefschwarzen Firmenbilanzen nicht mehr arbeiten und konnte sich um das große Anwesen und den Garten am Chiemsee kümmern.

Im Januar hatte er sich zuletzt zwei Tage frei genommen, obwohl er aufgrund der Auftragssituation eigentlich keine Zeit dafür verspürte. Maria hatte ihm da zu seinem Geburtstag einen zweitägigen Wellnessaufenthalt in so einem Nobelhotel in St. Moritz geschenkt. Zu seinem runden Fünfziger hatte er sie schließlich nicht enttäuschen können. Also hatte er bei diesem Wellnessprogramm mitgemacht, obwohl er bisher nicht unbedingt auf der Wellnesswelle mit geschwommen war.

Ganz anders dagegen war der regelmäßige Urlaub im Sommer für ihn. Diese zwei Wochen waren mittlerweile in seine Pro-

It was unusual for Paul to stop working and go home at noon. Normally, he came home very late from the office. Strictly speaking, he couldn't afford to leave his project in progress by itself or with his business partner, since Ludwig was just as ready for a vacation. Nonetheless, for years he had regularly taken two weeks off in August.

Together with his friend Ludwig Korn, Paul Goldhuber operated a booming software business.

During the last fifteen years, both of them had continually expanded their business and opened up new business resources. Their clientele now stretched across Europe. Since their company was situated in Chieming, they were relatively centrally located and were able to reach their clients from the Salzburg airport via their business-owned Cessna in a few hours.

Paul Goldhuber loved his job, even though it kept him very busy. He also carried a lot of responsibility for his now nineteen coworkers.

That had meant little time for rest and relaxation over the last couple of years.

He knew that his wife, in particular, suffered from his seventy-hour work week and the few free days which he allowed himself. All the same, he always sensed her positive attitude toward him and his important work. After all, since the company's balance sheets had been in the black for years, she didn't have to work anymore and was able to take care of the large estate and garden on the Chiemsee.

Last time he took two days off was in January, although he didn't think he would have time for that because of the order situation at work. At that time, Maria had given him a two-day wellness stay in a posh hotel in St. Moritz as a birthday present. After all, he couldn't afford to disappoint her on occasion of his fiftieth birthday. So he participated in the wellness program, although up until then he hadn't participated in the wellness craze.

However, the customary vacation during summer was an entirely different ballgame. By now he had managed to

jektplanungen eingebaut und er konnte die Zeit seit 10 Jahren für sich freimachen.

Zusammen mit Maria fand er in diesen vierzehn Tagen in ihrem gemeinsamen Landhaus in der Toskana Ruhe und Erholung, um danach frisch aufgetankt wieder an die Arbeit zu gehen.

Dieses Jahr blieb ihm nichts anderes übrig, als die Koffer für sich und Maria allein zu packen.

Er wusste in etwa, was für die zwei Wochen notwendig war, holte die beiden Hartschalenkoffer aus dem Keller herauf und legte sie nebeneinander auf ihr Ehebett. Das Bett, indem sie zuletzt intim waren. Wann war das noch gewesen, überlegte er.

Er begann, Marias hübsche Kleider zusammenzulegen und sorgfältig in einen der Koffer zu packen, damit sie nicht zu sehr verknitterten.

Jene Kleider, die sie dann wieder anziehen konnte, wenn sie beide zusammen in ihrem italienischen Lieblingsrestaurant die leckeren Rigatoni und den herrlich mundenden Rotwein aussuchen würden . . .

Er hatte den halben Koffer seiner Frau gepackt, als er vor der Spiegeltüre des massiven Buchenkleiderschrankes in ihrem großen Schlafzimmer stand.

Er unterbrach seine Tätigkeit und blieb stehen, um sein Spiegelbild darin zu betrachten.

Warum hat sie das getan? überlegte er.

Bin ich nicht mehr attraktiv genug? fragte er sich.

Sicher hatte er neben seiner Arbeit wenig Zeit, um sich noch sportlich zu betätigen, das war ihm klar.

Er drehte sich etwas zur Seite, um seinen Bauchansatz einzuschätzen. Es war nicht zu bestreiten, dass dieser in den letzten zwei bis drei Jahren etwas gewachsen war.

Na ja, wenn er so recht überlegte, konnte die Zellteilung seines Bauchgewebes auch schon vor fünf bis sechs Jahren begonnen haben. Er machte die rasende Zeit dafür verantwortlich, dass er sich nicht mehr so genau erinnerte.

Jedoch fand er seinen Überhang nicht schlimmer als den anderer Männer in seinem Alter. Schließlich war er ja bereits fünfzig!

plan his projects around these two weeks and for the last ten years had succeeded in taking time off.

Together with Maria he found peace and relaxation in their cottage in Tuscany during those fourteen days and was able to resume work afterward, recharged and with renewed energy.

This year, he had no other choice but pack his and Maria's suitcases all by himself.

He pretty much knew what they both needed for those two weeks, so he got the two hard shell suitcases from the basement and put them on their marital bed, side by side. The bed in which they had been intimate the last time. He wondered when that had been.

He began to fold Maria's pretty dresses and pack them carefully into one of the suitcases so they would not wrinkle.

Those dresses, which she would then be able to wear again when they mutually decided on the delicious rigatoni and the delicious red wine in their favorite Italian restaurant . . .

He was done packing half of his wife's suitcase when he stood in front of the mirrored door of the massive armoire in their large bedroom.

He interrupted his activity and stood to give his mirror image a searching look.

Why did she do it? he mused.

Am I no longer attractive enough? he asked himself.

Certainly, the fact that he had little time to exercise on top of his occupation was evident to him.

He turned a little to one side to take a look at his waistline. There was no denying that it had grown some in the last two to three years.

Well, if he really thought about it, maybe the cell division of his stomach tissue had even started five to six years ago. He held the racing time responsible for the fact that he could not remember clearly.

Though he didn't think his paunch was worse than that of other men of his age.

After all, he was already fifty!

Da konnte man doch keine Sixpacks eines jungen Zwanzigjährigen mehr erwarten, oder? fragte er sich.

Sein Blick wanderte zu seinen Haaren. Die sind doch noch größtenteils vorhanden, nickte er leicht vor dem Spiegel. Klar konnte er an den Seiten und Schläfen jetzt mehr graue als braune Haare zählen, wenn er es genauer betrachtete. Aber graues Haar macht einen Mann mit fünfzig doch noch interessanter, hatte er mal in einem Film gehört.

Oder war es ein Buch, in dem er das gelesen hatte?

Auf alle Fälle sah er immer gepflegt aus. Das war er schon allein seinen Kunden und seiner Position schuldig, rechtfertigte er sich.

Auch jetzt stand er in einem schwarzgrauen Anzug, tadellos gesellschaftsfähig gekleidet, vor dem Spiegel. In einem seiner vielen Anzüge, die seine Frau doch immer liebevoll und sorgfältig für ihn gebügelt hatte.

Woran lag es also? zermürbten ihn seine Gedanken.

Gut . . ., Maria war zehn Jahre jünger als er. Aber es hatte sie doch nie gestört, und sie hatten sich doch geliebt, glaubte er.

Er liebte sie doch!

Sie sah auch sehr attraktiv aus für eine Frau mit vierzig, konnte er nur bestätigen.

Die letzten Tage in seiner Arbeit hatte er es durch Ablenkung noch verdrängen können, doch jetzt stand Paul allein vor dem Spiegel, und seine Gedanken überwarfen sich.

Der andere war auch erst vierzig.

Also doch das Alter, kam ihm wieder in den Sinn.

Gut, über Aussehen konnte man streiten, aber Paul konnte nicht behaupten, dass der andere attraktiver war als er.

Was war also letztlich der Grund, warum Maria so handelte?

Er suchte nach einer Erklärung.

Dabei nahm er das blaue Abendkleid aus dem Schrank, in dem er sie immer am attraktivsten fand und legte es in den Koffer.

Marias wichtigste Sachen für den Urlaub hatte er zusammengepackt. Jetzt war sein Koffer noch aufzufüllen.

Er versuchte, seine Gedanken zu verdrängen. Morgen würde ihr gemeinsamer Urlaub beginnen, und alles würde wieder gut werden.

One could not expect to see the six-pack abs of a young twenty year old, right? he asked himself.

His gaze continued to his hair. It was still mostly there; he nodded slightly in front of the mirror. He was clearly able to count more gray than brown hair on his temples now, if he looked closely. But gray hair makes a guy in his fifties even more interesting, he had heard in a movie once.

Or had he read it in a book?

In any case, he always looked well-groomed. He owed this simply to all of his clients and his position, he justified.

Even now, standing in front of the mirror in a blackish gray suit, he was socially acceptable and impeccably dressed. In one of the many suits which his wife had always ironed for him, lovingly and carefully.

So what was the reason? he thought, worn down.

All right . . . Maria was ten years younger than he was. But it had never bothered her and, in any case, they had loved each other.

He loved her, after all!

She was very attractive for a woman of forty, of that he was sure.

During the last days of work he had been able to put it out of his mind, but now Paul stood in front of the mirror, alone, and his thoughts were racing.

The other guy was only forty as well.

It crossed his mind that it had to be age, then.

All right, one could argue over looks, but Paul could not claim that the other guy was more attractive than he was.

So, ultimately, what was the reason for Maria's actions?

He looked for an explanation.

While doing so, he took a blue evening gown from the armoire, the one she always looked the most beautiful wearing in his eyes, and put it into the suitcase.

He was done packing Maria's most important things for the vacation. Now he needed to fill his suitcase.

He tried to block out his thoughts. Tomorrow their joint vacation would begin, and everything would be alright again.

Er war sich absolut sicher, dass sie wieder zueinander finden würden.

In der folgenden Nacht schlief er unruhig, aber kurz vor seinem Urlaub hatte er noch nie gut geschlafen.

Samstag, kurz vor Mittag trug er die Koffer durch die Verbindungstür vom Haus in die große Doppelgarage.

Dort stand nur noch der Mercedes, mit dem er nun vorlieb nehmen musste.

Das BMW Cabrio war ja Schrott.

Er stieg ein und betätigte die Fernbedienung, um das Garagentor zu öffnen.

In Grabenstätt fuhr Paul auf die A8 in Richtung Salzburg. Während der ganzen Fahrt hing er tief seinen Gedanken nach, als er zu seinem Erstaunen plötzlich feststellte, in unterbewusster Fahrweise den Airport erreicht zu haben.

Den Wagen stellte er auf dem Dauerparkplatz ab.

Die Cessna stand in den Farben blau / weiß und frisch aufgetankt hinter dem Hangar zum Abflug bereit.

Als routinierter Pilot überprüfte er die Maschine vor jedem Abflug anhand einer Sicherheits-Checkliste.

Unzählige Male war er mittlerweile geflogen und hatte bereits Start- und Landemanöver unter widrigen Wetterbedingungen hinter sich.

Er stand neben der Cessna und blickte zum Himmel. Besseres Wetter als heute konnte er sich gar nicht wünschen. Die Augustsonne meinte es gut. Er würde beste Aussicht von oben haben. Bereits auf der morgendlichen Wetterkarte im Frühstücksfernsehen hatte er bis nach Italien wunderbare Flugvoraussetzungen festgestellt.

Seinen Start hatte er für 14.00 Uhr beantragt. Er hatte also noch genügend Zeit, um die Koffer einzuladen und die Sicherheitsüberprüfungen durchzuführen.

Um 13.50 Uhr setzte er sich auf den Pilotensitz und wartete.

Seit zehn Jahren waren sie zusammen in den Urlaub geflogen.

Seine Gedanken schweiften zurück in die Vergangenheit.

Bisher war Maria immer dabei gewesen.

Sie wusste, dass sie an diesem Tag fliegen würden.

Er hatte ihr ja den Termin gesagt.

He was absolutely sure that they would once more grow to love each other.

The following night he slept fitfully, but he had never been able to sleep well right before a vacation.

On Saturday, shortly before noon, he carried the suitcases from the house through the connecting door into the two-car garage.

Only the Mercedes was left, which was his only choice.

After all, the BMW convertible was totaled.

He got in the car and used the remote to open the garage door.

In Grabenstätt, Paul took the A8 toward Salzburg. Throughout his drive, he was deep in thought when he suddenly, to his surprise, noticed that he had reached the airport subconsciously.

He parked the car in the long-term parking lot.

The Cessna, blue and white and freshly fueled, stood behind the hangar, ready for takeoff.

An experienced pilot, he checked the plane every time before takeoff using a security checklist.

By now, he had been flying numerous times and had even gone through starting and landing maneuvers during adverse weather conditions.

He stood next to the Cessna and looked up into the sky. Really, he couldn't wish for better weather than today. The August sun was a good sign. He would have the best view from up there. Already on the weather forecast during the morning breakfast TV show, he had noticed that the flight conditions were supposed to be magnificent all the way to Italy.

His takeoff had been confirmed for 2:00 pm. That meant he had enough time to load the suitcases and conduct the security checks.

At 1:30 he sat down in the pilot's seat and waited.

For ten years, they had flown together on their vacation.

His thoughts wandered back into the past.

Until now, Maria had always been there.

She knew that they were going to leave on this day.

After all, he had told her the date.

Zu Hause in ihren Küchenkalender hatte sie an diesem Datum rot aufgeschrieben:»Abflug in die Toskana.«

Er wartete. Sie hatte ja noch zehn Minuten Zeit.

Sie würde bestimmt kommen.

So wie jedes Jahr würden sie zusammen in den Süden fliegen.

Sie würden in ihr Haus in der Toskana einziehen und dort wieder die schönsten Tage eines jeden Jahres zusammen verbringen. In diesen zwei Wochen hätten sie wieder Zeit füreinander finden können. Zeit, die ihnen sonst im Berufsalltag gefehlt hatte.

Er war sich sicher, dass sie kommen würde.

Wie könnte es sonst anders sein?

Sie hatten nicht immer viel Zeit füreinander gehabt, das war ihm bewusst.

Aber sie würde zu ihm zurückkommen und alles würde wieder gut werden.

Der andere hatte ihr doch nicht viel zu bieten. Nein.

Er hatte nicht mal ein eigenes Haus. Er lebte nur in einer Mietwohnung eines Mehrfamilienhauses.

Außerdem war sein Astra bestimmt schon zehn Jahre alt.

Maria war Besseres gewöhnt, dachte er sich.

Und sie liebte doch das Haus in der Toskana genauso wie er.

Er sah auf seine Schweizer Designarmbanduhr, die er von Maria zum 46. Geburtstag bekommen hatte. Oder war es doch der 47. Geburtstag?

14.00 Uhr.

Sie würde kommen. Er wusste es.

Aus dem Cockpitfenster hielt er in alle Richtungen nach ihr Ausschau.

Einige Minuten später hörte er jemanden die Cessna betreten.

Er blickte sich um und Maria war da.

»Ich wusste, dass du es dir überlegen würdest«, sagte er erfreut.

Er verschloss die Flugzeugtüre und setzte sich wieder auf den Pilotensitz. Er beobachtete Maria, wie sie neben ihm Platz nahm.

Er startete die Cessna.

Langsam rollte er damit vom Stellplatz zur Startbahn.

Über das Funkgerät bat er um Starterlaubnis.

At home, on her kitchen calendar, she had written down on the date in red: "Departure to Tuscany."

He waited. She still had ten minutes, in any case.

She would definitely come.

Just like every year, they would fly south together.

They would move into their house in Tuscany and again spend the most beautiful days of the year there together. During these two weeks, they would be able to find time again for each other. Time that was otherwise lacking in their daily work routine.

He was sure she would come.

How could it be any different?

They hadn't always had a lot of time for each other, he realized. But she would come back to him and everything would be all right again.

The other guy didn't have much to offer her, after all. Definitely not.

He didn't even have his own house. He lived in a rented apartment in a multi-family home.

And, moreover, his Astra was at least ten years old.

Maria was used to better things, he thought.

And she loved the house in Tuscany just like he did.

He looked at his Swiss designer watch, which he had gotten from Maria on occasion of his fourty-sixth birthday. Or maybe it was his fourty-seventh birthday?

2:00.

She would come. He knew it.

From the cockpit window, he looked around for her in every direction.

A few minutes late, he heard someone enter the Cessna.

He turned around, and there was Maria.

"I knew you would consider it," he said, pleased.

He locked the door of the plane and sat down in the pilot's seat again. He watched Maria sit down next to him.

He started the Cessna.

Slowly, he rolled the plane from the parking site to the runway.

Er erhielt das »Ready for take-off.«

Das Flugzeug rollte an, und immer schneller sausten die Positionslichter der Startbahn an ihm vorbei.

Er zog die Nase der Cessna hoch, und diese schwang sich mühelos in die Luft.

Es war immer ein herrliches Gefühl für ihn gewesen, den Bodenkontakt zu verlieren.

Das war echte Freiheit!

Freiheit, um die er die Vögel immer beneidet hatte.

Der Himmel kam ihm tiefblau entgegen.

Er blickte zu Maria hinüber. Sie sah heute wunderschön aus.

So wunderschön wollte er sie am liebsten immer in Erinnerung behalten.

Er wusste jetzt, dass er sie immer lieben würde.

Er würde ihr vergeben.

Wenn sie bei ihm blieb, würde er vergessen, dass sie sich mit dem anderen getroffen hatte.

Er versuchte es, als eine kleine Schwäche ihrerseits abzutun.

Ein Fehltritt, der passieren kann.

Er lächelte sie an. Sie erwiderte sein Lächeln, wie nur himmlische Engel es vermochten zu lächeln.

Die Cessna verließ den Luftraum über der Stadt, und Paul steuerte in Richtung Chiemsee.

Maria hatte es doch immer so geliebt in den letzten Jahren, bevor sie in Richtung Alpen abdrehten, einen Rundflug über dem Chiemsee zu genießen.

Das Schloss Herrenchiemsee, die Fraueninsel, die vielen kleinen Segelboote, das silberne Glitzern des Wassers . . .

Maria fand es immer fantastisch, das alles von oben zu sehen.

Paul war so glücklich, dass sie sich für ihn entschieden hatte.

Sie waren doch schon jahrelang verheiratet und würden für immer zusammengehören.

Nichts konnte sie trennen. Auch keine Affäre!

Sie würden immer alles zusammen überstehen. Komme, was wolle! Jeder Sturm geht irgendwann vorüber.

Sie hatte das BMW Cabrio für ihren Flirtausflug benutzt.

He received the "Ready for takeoff."

The plane started rolling, and the lights of the runway raced by him faster and faster.

He pulled the nose of the Cessna up and it effortlessly took to the sky.

Losing contact with the ground had always been a wonderful sensation for him.

That was true freedom!

Freedom, that he had always envied birds for having.

Deeply blue, the sky met him.

He looked over at Maria. She looked gorgeous today.

He wanted to always remember her as being that gorgeous.

Now he knew that he would always love her.

He would forgive her.

If she stayed with him, he would put it out of his mind that she had been with the other guy.

He tried to shrug it off as a little weakness on her part. A lapse, which can happen.

He smiled at her. She smiled back at him in a way only heavenly angels are able to smile.

The Cessna left the airspace above the town, and Paul began to steer toward the Chiemsee.

After all, over the last couple of years Maria had so enjoyed an aerial flight tour over the Chiemsee before they turned away toward the Alps.

Herrenchiemsee Castle, the Ladies' Island, the many little sailboats, the silvery glitter of the water . . .

Maria always thought it fantastic to see all of this from above.

Paul was so happy she had chosen him.

After all, they had been married for years and would belong together forever.

Nothing could separate them. Not even an affair!

Together, they would weather everything, always. Come what may! Every storm blows over, eventually.

She had used the BMW convertible for her flirty excursions.

Paul hatte dieses Fahrzeug geliebt. Ein Auto war nur ein Gebrauchsgegenstand und ersetzbar.
Er trauerte dem Wagen nicht hinterher. Schuld?
Vermutlich war Maria von ihrem Mitfahrer abgelenkt gewesen.
Wen interessierte das noch?
Maria und er würden jetzt Zeit füreinander haben.
Paul flog die Cessna in Richtung Kampenwand. In unmittelbarer Bergnähe ließ Paul das Flugzeugruder los, um nach Marias Hand zu greifen ...
Sie lächelte ihn an. Das war ein unglaublich schöner Anblick.
Er wollte dieses Lächeln für immer einfrieren.
Paul war überwältigt von der massiven Rauheit der Bergwand, die auf ihn zukam. Schroffe Felsen, die unbezwingbar erschienen. Eine Schönheit, wie sie nur die Natur erschaffen kann.
Zum Greifen nah vor seiner Maschine.
Er und Maria würden jetzt Zeit füreinander haben. Sie würden wieder zueinander finden, war er sich sicher.
Paul war glücklich in diesem Augenblick.
Sie würden jetzt zusammen Urlaub machen, Urlaub für ewig ...!
In den Chiemgauer Tageszeitungen erschienen im Abstand von einem Monat die folgenden beiden Todesanzeigen:

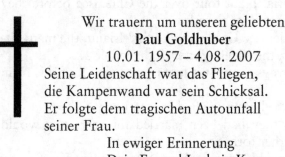

Wir trauern um unseren geliebten
Paul Goldhuber
10.01. 1957 – 4.08. 2007
Seine Leidenschaft war das Fliegen,
die Kampenwand war sein Schicksal.
Er folgte dem tragischen Autounfall
seiner Frau.
In ewiger Erinnerung
Dein Freund Ludwig Korn

Paul had loved that vehicle. But an automobile was only a commodity and replaceable.

He didn't mourn the car. Who was guilty?

Presumably, Maria had been distracted by her passenger. Yet, who still wanted to know?

Maria and he would now have time for each other.

Paul steered the Cessna toward the face of the Kampen peak. In immediate proximity to the mountain, Paul let go of the controls to reach for Maria's hand . . .

She smiled at him. That was an incredibly beautiful sight. He wanted to freeze this smile forever.

Paul was taken in by the massive ruggedness of the mountain's face, which came right at him. Jagged cliffs that seemed indomitable. A beauty only nature can create.

Within reach of his plane.

He and Maria would now have time for each other. They would grow to love each other again, he was certain.

At that very moment, Paul was happy.

Now they would go on vacation, an eternal vacation . . . !

In the Chiemgau daily papers, within a month of each other, the following two obituaries were published:

We mourn our deeply beloved

Paul Goldhuber

January 10, 1957 - August 4, 2007

Flying was his passion,

The Kampen peak was his fate.

His death followed his wife's tragic car accident.
You will always be remembered.

Your friend, Ludwig Korn

> ✝ Wir trauern um unsere geliebte
> **Maria Goldhuber**
> 18.02.1967 – 09.07.2007
> Ein tragischer Autounfall ließ sie
> zu früh von uns gehen.
> In tiefer Trauer
> Paul Goldhuber

P.S.:
Jetzt werdet ihr Euch sicher noch fragen, wer ich bin und warum ich diese Geschichte so genau kenne?

Aber das könnt ihr herausfinden, wenn ihr euren »Urlaub für ewig« plant . . .

We mourn our deeply beloved

Maria Goldhuber

February 18, 1967 – July 9, 2007

Ripped away from us much too early by a

tragic car accident.

Deeply in mourning, Paul Goldhuber

P.S:
You are probably asking yourself who I am and why I know this story so well.

You will find that out when you plan your own "eternal vacation . . ."

MICHAEL INNEBERGER

Klempner Huber

Der Huber spürte ein Vibrieren in seiner Arbeitshose. Er holte sein V-Phone aus der Tasche und betrachtete kurz das Holodisplay. Ein digitales Hologramm von einem Kopf rotierte um sich selbst und signalisierte ihm dadurch einen Bildanruf. Mit seinem Finger quittierte er auf das Display, den Videoanruf entgegenzunehmen.

»A so a Mist, jetza geht des Ding scho wieda ned gscheid. Wia soll der Fingerabdruckscanner a bloß mit dreckige Finga gehen? I kon mir ja ned ständig die Pratzen bei da Arbeit waschen«, murrte der Huber und versuchte durch Aneinanderreiben von Zeigefinger und Daumen seine schwarzen Finger einigermaßen sauber zu bekommen.

»A Graffe erfinden's oiwei. So was taugt ned für an Handwerker«, pulverte er ärgerlich auf sein Pocketoffice der Marke Chiemseebiber.

»Huber. Solaroperator und Inhouse Health Technics«, meldete er sich, so gut es ging auswendig gelernt, nachdem das Gerät letztlich doch seine Fingerrillen als Passworteingabe akzeptiert hatte und schaute dabei in die 3D-WideHD Linse seines Gerätes.

Diese geschwollene Berufstitulierung kam etwas holprig mit bairischem Dialekt über seine Lippen.

So richtig konnte er sich mit diesen europäisch eingeführten Berufsbezeichnungen nicht anfreunden.

Vor dreißig Jahren hatten es seine Berufsvettern noch einfacher, behauptete er immer am Stammtisch. Da konnte man noch »Gas, Wasser, Scheiße« dazu sagen witzelte er gerne un-

222

MICHAEL INNEBERGER

Plumber Huber

Huber felt his workpants vibrate. He took the V-phone from his pocket and briefly regarded the holographic display. The digital hologram of a head rotated around in circles, thus signaling a video call to him. He pressed his finger on the display to accept the video call.

"Cripes, what a pity, now this thing isn't working right again. Just how is the fingerprint scanner supposed to work with such dirty fingers? Anyhow, I don't have time to rinse my paw all the time while I'm working," Huber grumbled, and tried to get his blackened fingers at least somewhat clean by rubbing his index finger and thumb together.

"They're always inventing such junk. No good for a workman," he said, as he punched away angrily on his pocket office, a "Chiemsee Beaver."

Recalling what he had tried to learn by heart as much as possible and after the device had finally accepted his fingerprint as password, he looked into the 3-D wide-HD lens of his phone and announced, "Huber. Solar Operator and In-house Health Technician."

This exaggerated job title crossed his lips, somewhat clumsily, in a Bavarian dialect.

In reality, he hadn't been able to come to terms with these job titles, which had been implemented across Europe.

Thirty years ago, his predecessors in the profession had had it much simpler, he claimed at get-togethers over beers with his friends. Back then you were still able to call it "gas,

ter seinen Stammtischkollegen beim Dorfwirt. Aber Gas war
vor fünf Jahren bereits durch umweltfreundliche Alternati-
ven abgelöst worden. Und Dorfwirt durfte der Huber ja auch
nicht mehr sagen. Der Dorfwirt war ja jetzt der Tenancier
Auberge de la Gestion. Der Huber konnte das sowieso nicht
aussprechen.

Die EU setzte damals, nach der ersten Staaten-Verringerung
aufgrund einiger Pleiteländer, auf noch mehr Integration und
Vereinheitlichung der übrig gebliebenen Mitgliedsländer. So
ziemlich alles wurde europäisiert. Also wurde aus der Toiletten-
Reinigungsfrau die Chemical Cleaning Toilet Headleader. Und
aus ihm, dem Handwerks-Sanitär Meister wurde der Inhouse
Health Technics Master. Klar, das war einfacher. So konnte man
aus ganz Europa einen Sanitär-Meister zu sich bestellen, da diese überall einen einheitlichen Namen im Telefonbuch führten.
Seither jedoch hatte die Huber-Firma noch keinen Videoruf aus
Frankreich oder England erhalten.

Dem Huber war natürlich damals völlig einleuchtend gewesen, dass das Ganze ein sorgfältig durchdachter und genial ge-
planter Coup einiger einflussreicher Europaratsmitglieder war,
um der zu dieser Zeit müden Wirtschaft neue Impulse zu geben.
Tatsächlich klappte das hervorragend. Firmen, Handwerksbe-
triebe, Geschäfte, Software, so ziemlich alles musste durch die
Besitzer, Inhaber, Programmierer, Ämter und so weiter und so
fort, geändert werden. Firmenschilder, Geschäftspapiere, Werbung an Firmenfahrzeugen, Internetseiten, Branchenverzeich-
nisse, Telefonlisten, einfach alles wurde erneuert und an einheit-
liche Strukturen angepasst.

Querbeet profitierten alle Branchen von den milliarden-
schweren Investitionen und millionenfachen Aufträgen, euro-
paweit.

Da die Aufträge und Ausschreibungen tatsächlich nur inner-
halb des europäischen Wirtschaftsraumes beauftragt werden
durften, drehte sich die Konjunkturspirale in Europa schwindel-
erregend nach oben. Der Huber drehte sich darin mit und profi-
tierte davon genauso, wie sämtliche weitere Betriebe im
Chiemgau. Die Arbeitslosigkeit sank damals auf den tiefsten
Stand der bairischen Geschichte.

water, crap," he liked to joke with his fellow workers at the village inn. Yet, five years ago gas had already been replaced by environmentally friendly alternatives. And Huber wasn't allowed to say village innkeeper anymore either. For now, the village innkeeper was the Tenancier Auberge de la Gestion. Huber was unable to pronounce that anyway.

In those days, after the first member state reduction due to a few bankrupt nations, the EU had focused on even more integration and standardization of the remaining member states. Pretty much everything had been Europeanized. Thus, the toilet cleaning lady had become a Chemical Cleaning Toilet Head Leader. And he, the master plumbing craftsman, had become an In-house Health Technics Master. Sure, that was simpler. That way, you could call a master plumber from all over Europe because they were called the same in all phone directories. Since then, however, the Huber Company had yet to receive any video calls from France or the UK.

It was crystal clear to Huber even then that all of this had been a carefully thought out and ingeniously planned coup of some influential European council members in order to give new impulses to the, at the time, sluggish economy. And indeed, it had worked perfectly. Companies, craft enterprises, businesses, software, pretty much everything had to be changed by the proprietors, owners, programmers, agencies, etc., etc. Company signs, business papers, advertisements on business vehicles, internet pages, classified and phone directories, absolutely everything had to be remade and adapted to standardized structures. Across the board, all trades and sectors profited from billion dollar investments and contracts that ran into the millions, all across Europe.

Since contracts and calls for bids were only allowed to be within the boundaries of the European economic region, the economic boom in Europe had spiraled upwards at a dizzying tempo. Huber spiraled along with it and profited just as much as all businesses in the Chiemgau region had. Then, unemployment had sunk to its lowest level in the history of Bavaria.

Alle konnten zufrieden sein, auch der Huber.

Trotzdem verlor der Huber etwas, mit dem er aufgewachsen war.

Etwas an das er sich gewohnt hatte.

Etwas das seit Generationen in Bayern bestanden hatte.

Ein großes Stück Tradition und Brauchtum brach einfach weg.

Er verlor dadurch seine Vergangenheit.

Nein, nicht nur seine Vergangenheit, sondern auch die seiner Väter.

Für den Huber waren die Erneuerungen Geschenk und Fluch zugleich.

Es entstand Wachstum und Wohlstand in Bayern.

Hartz IV war ein Begriff, der nur noch in nostalgischen Re-Prints alter Tageszeitungen zu finden war.

Vor der Umstellung herrschte euphorische Aufbruchstimmung. Ein Neuaufbau sondergleichen entwickelte sich im Bayernland. Angesteckt, wie durch einen Virus wurden in diesem Zuge die Privathäuser einer Renovierungswelle nie da gewesenen Ausmaßes unterzogen.

Die Bayern verdienten und investierten.

Die Bayern investierten und renovierten.

Die Bayern renovierten und erneuerten.

Die Bayern erneuerten ihr Land.

Es wurde erfunden und entwickelt, was das Zeug hielt.

Nie gab es so viele Patentanmeldungen wie in dieser Zeit.

Die Leute waren verrückt nach den Erfindungen. Es wurden Standards gesetzt, die als Statussymbol angesehen wurden. Jeder musste alles besitzen, da der Nachbar ja auch alles hatte.

Die Bayern verbesserten ihre Standards, erneuerten ihre Lebensweise und ihre Sprache gleich mit.

Jeder war nach der Umstellung gezwungen, sich den Erneuerungen anzupassen. Sowohl in ihrer Sprache als auch in ihrem Tagesablauf fanden sich die Bayern gefordert, mit den Änderungen Schritt zu halten und sich umzugewöhnen.

Everybody could be satisfied, even Huber.

Nevertheless, Huber had lost something with which he had grown up.

Something that he had gotten used to.

Something that had existed in Bavaria for generations.

A large part of tradition and customs simply vanished.

Because of that, he had lost his past.

Not, not only *his* past, but also that of his ancestors.

For Huber, the innovations were both a blessing and a curse.

In Bavaria, economic expansion and prosperity followed.

The concept of Hartz[1] was only to be found in nostalgic reprints of old daily newspapers.

Before the transition, there was an initial euphoric atmosphere of change. In the Bavarian state, a reconstruction beyond comparison ensued. As if infected by a virus, residential dwellings underwent a wave of renovation never seen before in this course.

The Bavarians earned money and invested.

The Bavarians invested and renovated.

The Bavarians renovated and rebuilt.

The Bavarians rebuilt their state.

They invented and developed for what it was worth.

People were crazy for inventions. Standards were set that were regarded as status symbols. Everybody had to own everything, since the neighbors also had everything.

The Bavarians improved their standard of living, their way of living, and their language in the same breath.

After the transition, everybody was forced to adapt to the innovations. In their language as well as in their daily routines, the Bavarians found themselves challenged to keep up with the changes and adjust.

---

[1]Hartz = welfare benefits. The Hartz concept is a set of recommendations that resulted from a commission on reforms to the German labor market in 2002. Named after the head of the commission, Peter Hartz, it went on to become part of the German government's Agenda 2010 series of reforms, known as Hartz I - Hartz IV. The reforms of Hartz I - III took place between January 1, 2003, and 2004; Hartz IV began on January 1, 2005.

Dem Huber ist das, wie wir gemerkt haben, bis heute noch nicht gelungen. Er hat seine ursprünglichen bairischen Sprachgewohnheiten größtenteils beibehalten und die neuen Einflüsse nur auf das notwendigste, arbeitstechnische an sich heran gelassen. Es war für den Huber nicht einfach zu sehen, wie sein geliebtes Bayernland langsam in einem Einheitsbrei zusammengemischt wurde.

Um noch mal auf die Tageszeitungen zurückzukommen: in Papierform benutzte diese seit Jahren niemand mehr. Zeitungen waren, wie alles andere digitalisiert. Die News, wie sie allgemein nur noch bezeichnet wurden, kamen als digitales Abo ins Haus. Wenn man Zeit hatte, las man die Berichte auf dem Multimediaschirm, gemütlich im Wohnzimmer. Oder man ließ sie sich ganz einfach vom HausRobo vorlesen. Die neusten Modelle konnten mit ihren Besitzern sogar Diskussionsrunden über die aktuellen Themen führen.

Briefkästen an den Hauswänden waren mittlerweile auch ein Relikt. Aktuelle Werbeaktionen und Sonderangebote von örtlichen Firmen konnten durch USB-Supporter, in die sich die Briefträger änderten, zugestellt werden. Ein USB-Supporter ging von Haus zu Haus und lud seine Daten in den Haus-USB-Port, der sich unter jeder Namensklingel befand. Jedem Bürger stand es natürlich frei, Werbung zu akzeptieren. Hatte er die Software seines Ports auf werbefrei gestellt, konnten die Supporter keine Werbung übertragen. Auch Reklame nur bestimmter Firmen zuzulassen war möglich. So konnte jemand, der gerade seinen Garten umgestalten wollte, natürlich Werbung und Angebote von Gartencentern zulassen. In diesem Sinn konnten den Bürger, je nach Bedürfnis alle Firmen erreichen oder nur bestimmte Branchen.

Die Betriebe hatten die Möglichkeiten in den Verteilzentren, die für die Verbreitung zuständig waren, ihre Werbung einzuspeisen, oder in Auftrag zu geben. Bezahlt wurde nach so genannter Zustellmenge, die nach Übermittlung errechnet wurde. Selbst Briefe und Rechnungen wurden nur noch über USB-Post verteilt. Um zu verhindern, dass unberechtigte Empfänger die

As we have seen, Huber has not yet succeeded in doing that. For the most part, he had managed to keep his original Bavarian language habits and allowed the new influences to touch him only when absolutely necessary, and only as far as his work was concerned.

It was not easy for Huber to watch how his beloved state of Bavaria slowly succumbed to cultural uniformity.

To refer back to newspapers: for years, they had not been used in paper format.

Newspapers, like everything else, were digital. The News, as they were now called as a whole, came as a digital subscription. When there was time, one read the reports on the media screen, perhaps while sitting comfortably in the living room. Or, even simpler, one could have them read to by the House Robo. The latest models were even able to hold discussions about current topics with their owners.

By now, home mailboxes had become relics of the past as well.

Current ad campaigns and sales announcements from local businesses were delivered via USB supporters, which had replaced the postal carriers. A USB supporter went from house to house and uploaded the data into each house's USB port, which was located beneath the electric bell. Naturally, every resident was free to accept advertisements. Once a resident switched the software of his port to ad free, the supporters were unable to transmit ads. Also, it was possible to only accept ads from certain businesses. That way, someone who wanted to have a garden landscaped was able to accept ads and offers from garden centers. In this way, residents could be reached by all businesses as needed or only by certain branches.

The companies were able to upload their ads to or place orders via the distribution centers responsible for circulation. Payment was made based on the volume of delivered ads, which were calculated after transmission. Even letters and bills were only distributed via USB-mail. To prevent

Post zugestellt bekamen, konnten die Dokumente natürlich nur über einen Hauscode geöffnet werden.

Und so kam es schließlich dazu, dass eine USB-Werbung des Herrn Huber auf dem Büromonitor eines hochmodernen Traunsteiner Unternehmen landete.

»Space Travel Company, Traunstein«, lächelte ihm das dreidimensionale Bild eines etwa fünfunddreißigjährigen Mannes auf dem Display seines V-Phone entgegen. Der Huber kannte die Space Company. Ein findiger Multimilliardär hatte die Idee gehabt, vor den Toren der Stadt eine Touristen-Raumfahrt zu gründen.

Gut, die Flüge waren nicht bezahlbar, zumindest nicht für den Huber. Nebenbei aber entwickelte es sich zu einem Touristenmagnet, da an der Aussichtsplattform viele Schaulustige die Abflüge beobachteten.

Trotzdem kamen sie, die Reichen und Prominenten, um das »angesagteste Abenteuer zwischen Jangtsekiang und Mississippi« zu erleben, so ein Werbeslogan der Company.

»Grüß Gott Hr. Huber. Hier spricht Kleiber, der Public Office Manager. Sie wurden uns als kompetenter Master empfohlen. Unser Space Ship die Hochberg 1 hat ein Problem mit der chemischen Bordtoilette. Leider ist unser Company Mitarbeiter, der ansonsten diese Technik repariert, erkrankt. Könnten Sie sich vorstellen uns hierbei zu helfen? Das Schiff soll in einer Stunde zum Mond fliegen und die fünf Fluggäste schlüpfen bereits in ihre Raumanzüge«, nickte Herr Kleiber, als ob er bereits die Zustimmung von Hr. Huber hätte.

»Na ja, Klo is Klo«, sagte der Huber knapp und zuckte mit den Schultern.

»Prächtig, dann beeilen Sie sich. Ich erwarte Sie an der Türe zum Terminal Check-In«, wirkte der Hr. Kleiber sichtlich erleichtert. Sein Holo-Bild wirbelte wie in einem Wasserstrudel umher, wurde immer kleiner und verschwand schließlich als Punkt.

Der Huber packte seine Werkzeugtasche in den Elektrotransporter und aktivierte die Bluetoothverbindung vom V-Phone zum Bordcomputer. Er teilte seinem V-Phone die Adresse in langsam

unauthorized recipients from receiving mail, documents could only be opened using a house code.

And thus it happened that a USB-ad by Mr. Huber landed on the office monitor of an ultra-modern Traunstein business.

"Space Travel Company, Traunstein," smiled the three-dimensional picture of an approximately thirty-five-year-old man from the display of his V-phone. Huber knew the space company. A resourceful multi-millionaire had had the idea to found a tourist space center right outside the gates of the city.

Well, the flights weren't affordable, at least not for Huber. However, along the way it had turned into a tourist magnet since many curious onlookers watched the take-offs from the observation deck.

All the same, the rich and the prominent came to take part in "the hottest adventure between the Yangtze Kiang and the Mississippi," according to a company slogan.

"Hello, Mr. Huber. Kleiber, Public Office Manager, speaking. You were recommended to us as a competent master plumber. Our space ship, the Hochberg 1, has problems with the chemical toilet. Unfortunately, our company employee, who is usually in charge of repairs for this system, has fallen ill. Would you consider helping us out with this problem? The ship is supposed to leave for the moon in an hour, and the five passengers are already slipping into their space suits," nodded Mr. Kleiber, as if he had already received Mr. Huber's consent.

"Oh well, a can is a can," Huber said curtly, and shrugged his shoulders.

"Perfect, then hurry up. I will be waiting for you at the door to the terminal check-in," Kleiber said, visibly relieved. His holographic image swirled round and round as if in a whirlpool, then became smaller and smaller, and finally disappeared in a dot.

Huber packed his tool bag into the electric-powered transporter and subsequently activated the Blue Tooth connection between the V-phone and the board computer. He

ausgesprochenen Worten mit, da es schon öfter Probleme mit seinem bairischen Dialekt gab. Der Elektrotransporter setzte sich automatisch in Gang. Das V-Phone navigierte ihn durch den Traunsteiner Elektro-Verkehr, ohne dass ein manuelles Eingreifen durch den Huber notwendig wurde, zur Space Company. Street View sei Dank! Aufgrund der Autopiloten in den Fahrzeugen rollte der Verkehr seit ein paar Jahren fast unfallfrei über die Straßen.

Als nur noch Elektrofahrzeuge in Traunstein unterwegs waren, merkte der Huber erst, wie leise eine Stadt sein konnte.

Die Abgase verschwanden aus den Städten und Umweltplaketten gehörten schnell der Vergangenheit an.

Die Innenstädte erfuhren eine Renaissance an Lebensqualität und Ruhe. Pflanzen und Blumen trugen ihren Beitrag zu einem harmonischen Stadtbild.

Ohne Geräuschfaktor war eine erholsame Nachtruhe, selbst in den Innenstädten, wieder mit geöffneten Fenstern möglich.

Der Huber konnte sich gar nicht mehr vorstellen, wie es die Menschen so lange Zeit mit den lauten, stinkenden Knatterkisten zusammen ertragen hatten und diese nicht bereits viel eher abschafften.

Der Huber stellte sein Fahrzeug auf dem großen Parkplatz am Hochberg ab und holte seine Tasche aus dem Kofferraum. Er ging zum Haupteingang. Wie versprochen erwartete ihn Hr. Kleiber dort bereits.

Der Huber beugte sich nach unten, um den Hr. Kleiber die Hand zu schütteln, die dieser ihm entgegenreichte:

»Servus, i bin da Huba.«

»Kleiber. Gut, dass Sie so schnell einspringen konnten. Folgen Sie mir.«

Ein Genfutter-Gnom überlegte der Huber. Als sich etwa 2020 das genmanipulierte Saatgut fast selbstständig durch Vermehrung über das Land verbreitete und die Bayern die vermischten Ernten einbrachten, kamen ein paar Jahre später die ersten Gen-Gnome zur Welt. Es gibt ein paar hundert davon hier in Traunstein. Der Huber ließ sich sein Bedauern nicht anmerken und folgte dem kleinen Mann, der fast im Laufschritt vor ihm her trabte. Er scheint es eilig zu haben, überlegte der

recorded the address into his V-phone, speaking slowly, since on there had been problems before with his Bavarian dialect. The electric-powered transporter started automatically. The V-phone navigated them through the electric-powered Traunstein traffic all the way to the space company, without requiring manual intervention on Huber's part. Thank God for "street view!" Because of the autopilot installed in the vehicles, street traffic moved virtually without accidents.

Once there were only electric-powered vehicles in Traunstein, Huber began to realize how quiet a city could be.

Exhaust fumes disappeared from the cities and "environmentally friendly" vehicle certificates soon became a thing of the past.

The inner cities had experienced a renaissance in quality of life and peace. Plants and flowers also contributed to a harmonious cityscape. Without the constant noise, it was possible to experience a quiet night with the windows open, even in the inner cities.

Huber couldn't even imagine anymore how people had managed live with the stinking and rumbling clunkers, and why they hadn't done away with them much sooner.

Huber parked his vehicle in the big parking lot at the Hochberg and fetched his bag from the trunk. He went to the main entrance. As promised, Mr. Kleiber was already waiting for him there.

Huber bent down in order to shake Mr. Kleiber's hand, stretched out toward him:

"Hi there, I'm Huber."

"Kleiber. Great that you were able to fill in so quickly. Follow me."

A genetically engineered food individual, mused Huber. Around 2020, genetically manipulated seeds had spread across the state by means of natural proliferation.

Bavarians harvested the mixed crop, and a few years later the first genetically modified little people had been born. A few hundred of those lived in Traunstein. Huber did not allow his regrets to show and followed the little man who trotted in front of him, his feet moving almost twice as

Huber, hatte jedoch keine Mühe ihm mit seiner Werkzeugtasche zu folgen.

Was Hr. Huber an dieser Stelle nicht wusste und ihm später zum Verhängnis wurde, war die hektische Aufregung des kleinen Hr. Kleiber. Dieser vergaß schlichtweg den Hr. Huber als Handwerker im Raumschiff an der Flugleitstelle anzumelden.

Im Abflughangar angekommen präsentierte der kleine Hr. Kleiber völlig außer Atem und immer wieder zwischendurch tief Luft holend:

»Das . . . das ist unser Baby. Die Hochberg 1. Die Vollendung . . . alles . . . alles . . . technischen Know How. Ein Meilenstein bayerischer Entwicklungsgeschichte.«

Der Huber betrachtete das stromlinienförmige, schwarze Raumschiff der Größe eines E-LKW.

»Bärig. Da legst di nieda«, nickte er anerkennungsvoll.

Hr. Kleiber war weiterhin in treibender Hektik. Mit einem Handgriff öffnete er die seitliche Druckschleuse, die sich mit einem lauten pneumatischen Schmatzen auftat und nach unten klappte.

Der kleine Hr. Kleiber stieg problemlos durch die Luke ins Innere. Der Huber folgte ihm hinterher, stieß jedoch aufgrund seiner Größe, mit einem lauten »Boing«, mit der Stirn an den oberen Lukenrahmen.

»Ze fix«, fluchte er und rieb sich mit der Handfläche seine obere Gesichtshälfte.

»Hier müssen Sie den Kopf einziehen«, empfahl ihm Hr. Kleiber, ohne sich umzusehen.

»Danke, i hob grad getestet, was passiert, wenn i des ned mach«, brummelte der Huber zwecks dieser zu späten Warnung zurück.

»Hier im Inneren gibt es zehn komfortable Schalensitze, die sich elektronisch in Schlafliegen umwandeln lassen. Jeder Sitz hat genügend Beinabstand und sein eigenes Panoramafenster ins Weltall.«

Was Hr. Kleiber mit Panoramafenster bezeichnete, registrierte der Huber jedoch nur als kleines Bullauge.

»Jeder Sitz hat seine Multimediakonsole und Sie können ihre Bilder und Videos aus dem Schiff gleich an ihre Video-Community-Kontakte per Moon-Mail versenden. Hinten finden Sie

fast. He appears to be in a hurry, Huber thought, but had no trouble following him with his tool bag.

What Huber did not notice at the time, and what later was to be his downfall, was the hectic excitement of little Mr. Kleiber. The latter simply forgot to register Huber as a mechanic boarding the space ship with the control tower.

Upon arriving at the departure hangar, Mr. Kleiber announced, completely out of breath and intermittently taking deep breaths, again and again:

"This . . . this is our baby. The Hochberg 1. The perfection of . . . all . . . all . . . technical know-how. A milestone in the history of Bavarian development.

Huber regarded the streamlined, black space ship the size of an electric-powered semi truck.

"Swell. I'll be darned," he nodded appreciatively.

Mr. Kleiber was still pressing forward in a hurry. With one hand movement, he opened the hydraulic lock on the side, which opened with a loud pneumatic thud and then folded down. Little Mr. Kleiber went inside through the hatch without any problems. Huber followed him but, because of his height, hit his forehead on the top of the hatch ceiling with a loud bang.

"Hot damn," he cursed and rubbed the upper half of his face with his palm.

"You have to duck here," recommended Mr. Kleiber, without turning around.

"Thanks, but I just found out what happens if I don't," muttered Huber, in repsonse to the belated warning.

"The interior has ten comfortable, ergonomic seats that can be electronically turned into loungers for sleeping. Each seat has lots of leg room and its own panorama window facing into space."

What Mr. Kleiber termed panorama window, however, Huber only saw as a small bull's eye window.

"Each seat has a multimedia console, and you can instantly send pictures and videos from the ship to your video community contacts via Moon Mail. In the rear you will find

unsere Weltallbar zum gemütlichen Verweilen. Buchen Sie einen Flug bei uns und ihre Freunde werden sie beneiden«, beschrieb der Hr. Kleiber voller Leidenschaft die Innenausstattung.

»Ja schee und wo is jetza nachad des Scheißheisl da herinnen?«, fragte der Huber völlig interesselos an dem modernen Schnickschnack.

»Ach ja, das hätte ich jetzt in der Aufregung beinahe vergessen«, prustete der kleine Mann lachend heraus.

»Folgen Sie mir.«

Der kleine Hr. Kleiber trabte wieder.

Hinten um die Weltallbar herum.

Der Huber fast schon genauso hinterdrein.

»Links durch die Türe haben wir die Bordtoilette und hinter der rechten Türe finden Sie die Duschkabine«, deutete der kleinwüchsige Mann mit dem kurzen Arm.

»Was darin läuft sieht aus wie Wasser, sind aber in Wirklichkeit chemische Partikel, die wieder abgesaugt, gereinigt und mehrmals verwendet werden.«

»Die Toilette ist verstopft«, sagte Hr. Kleiber ganz schlicht und banal.

»Des ham ma glei«, schwang der Huber sein rechtes Bein über den Kopf von Hr. Kleiber und stieg einfach über den kleinen verdutzten Mann hinweg in die Bordtoilette.

»Ich lasse Sie hier mal alleine arbeiten. Ich habe noch dringende Sachen zu erledigen«, stellte Hr. Kleiber mit einem Blick auf die Zeitanzeige seines Armbandmonitors fest.

»Wenn Sie fertig sind, schicken sie mir einen Videoruf. Dann hole ich sie wieder ab«, fügte Hr. Kleiber hinzu, schloss die Bordtoilettentüre und trabte wie gewohnt davon.

Hr. Huber öffnete seine Werkzeugtasche und holte seinen altmodischen, roten Klostopfer heraus und machte sich an seinen Auftrag.

»Ois volla Hightech und trotzdem Probleme mit a verstopften Schüssel«, murmelte der Huber.

Während der Huber so vor sich hinarbeitete, begann es in der Bordtoilette zu dröhnen und vibrieren.

»De ham ned bloß Probleme mitana Verstopfung. Do schepperts woanders a no«, sagte Hr. Huber zu sich während alles um ihn wackelte.

our space bar for comfortable lounging. When you book a flight with us, all your friends will envy you," Mr. Kleiber passionately described the interior design and equipment.

"Yeah, great, and where do I find the crapper here?" Huber asked, completely uninterested in the modern gadgets.

"Oh, yes, I almost forgot about it in all the excitement," the little man burst out laughing. "Follow me."

The little Mr. Kleiber trotted on.

Around the space bar in the back.

Huber followed behind him, virtually in the same fashion.

"Through the door to the left you will find the onboard toilet, and behind the right door you will find a shower," the short-statured man pointed with his short arm.

"What you see running in there looks like water, but in reality those are chemical particles that are being suction cleaned and recycled for repeated use."

"The toilet is clogged," Mr. Kleiber bluntly stated.

"We'll soon be finished," Huber replied; then he simply swung his right leg over Mr. Kleiber's head and climbed over the diminutive, puzzled man straight into the onboard bathroom.

"I'll leave you alone to work. I have to take care of some urgent business," Mr. Kleiber stated, looking at the time display on his armband monitor.

"When you are done, send me a video phone call. Then I'll pick you up from here," Mr. Kleiber added, and closed the bathroom door, trotting away in his usual manner.

Mr. Huber opened his tool bag, pulled out his old-fashioned, red toilet plunger, and began to work on his project.

"Everything chock full of high tech, and still problems with a plugged bowl," Huber muttered.

While Huber worked away in this fashion, it began to buzz and vibrate inside the bathroom.

"They don't only have problems with the plumbing. There's also clanking going on elsewhere," Mr. Huber said to himself while everything around him shook. Regardless, he continued with his work.

Nichtsdestotrotz setzte er seine Arbeit fort.

Der Fachmann, Verzeihung Master Huber, schaffte es natürlich die Angelegenheit wieder aus der Welt, bzw. aus dem Klo zu bringen.

»So des wär erledigt«, freute er sich und verließ die Bordtoilette.

»Öha«, rutschte ihm heraus, als er die Passagiere bereits in ihren Raumanzügen auf den Sitzen warten sah.

»An guadn Flug wünsch i«, nickte ihnen Hr. Huber zu und wollte den Griff für die Seitenschleuse betätigen, da diese schon jemand geschlossen hatte.

»Halt! Was machen Sie da?« brüllte jemand.

Erschrocken fuhr Hr. Huber herum.

Der Bordpilot beugte sich in seinem Pilotensitz nach hinten und blickte ihn fragend an.

»Aussteign, wenn's recht is.«

»Aber das können Sie nicht«, erwiderte der Pilot.

»Koa Problem, i woas wie des geht. Bleim's ruhig sitzen«, winkte der Huber ab.

»Ich meine damit, Sie können nicht aufmachen, weil wir uns bereits auf einer Höhe von sechzig Kilometer befinden. Wenn Sie jetzt aufmachen, dann fliegen wir alle zur Luke hinaus.«

»Machans koane Witz Herr Pilot«, sagte der Huber. In diesem Moment bemerkte er wie seine Werkzeugtasche nach oben schwebte. Alsdann begann er langsam selbst den Kontakt zum Boden zu verlieren. Vergebens versuchte er, etwas zum Einhalten zu finden, als er auch schon quer durch das Schiffsinnere seiner Tasche hinterher schwebte.

»Halt's mi fest«, rief er verzweifelt, als er über den Köpfen der Weltraumtouristen in der Schwerelosigkeit hing. Mit seinen Armen wedelte er wie ein Vogel, da er Angst hatte abzustürzen.

»Meine Damen und Herren, wir befinden uns nun in der Schwerelosigkeit. Sie können sich jetzt von ihren Sitzen abschnallen und ihre ersten Flugversuche unternehmen. Bitte beachten Sie, sich nicht von den Bordwänden mit ihren Füßen abzustoßen, um Luftzusammenstöße zu vermeiden. Die Space Travel Company wünscht ihnen eine angenehme Schwerelosigkeit«, lautete die Durchsage des Bordpiloten.

Needless to say, the expert, pardon, master plumber, Huber, managed to get rid of the problem or rather, the matter in the toilet.

"So, there. All done," he said, pleased, and left the bathroom.

"Whoa," he let slip out, when he saw the passengers already waiting in their seats, dressed in their space suits.

"I wish you a good journey," Huber nodded to them and went to disengage the hydraulic side lock, since it seemed to have been locked already.

"Stop! What do you think you're doing?" someone shouted.

Startled, Mr. Huber jerked around.

The pilot turned around in his seat and looked at him questioningly.

"Getting out, if you don't mind."

"But you can't do that," the pilot replied.

"No problem. I know how it works. Just stay in your seat," Huber waved aside his reply.

"I mean, you can't open the door now because we are thirty-seven miles up in the air. If you open the door now, we'll all fly out the hatch."

"Don't joke around with me, Mr. Pilot," Huber said. At this very instant, he noticed that his tool box had begun to float upward. In a similar fashion, he gradually started losing contact with the ground too. Unsuccessfully, he struggled to find something to hold on to, and then he was following his bag that floated through the inside of the ship.

"Hold me down," he shouted in despair, suspended weightless above the heads of the space tourists. He waved his arms like a bird because he was afraid to crash to the floor.

"Ladies and gentlemen, we have just reached zero gravity. Please feel free to unfasten your seatbelts and get ready to undertake your first attempts at flying.

Please do not push off the walls of the cabin with your feet in order to avoid midair collisions. The Space Travel Company wishes you a pleasant zero gravity experience," the pilot announced.

»Des hob i selba a g'merkt«, erwiderte der Huber, sichtlich mit Stabilisierungsversuchen seines, um die eigene Achse drehenden Körpers bemüht.

Der rote Klostopfer kam vorbei geflogen und Herr Huber fing ihn mit der ausgestreckten Hand ein. Mit einer grazilen Bewegung stieß er sich sanft, mit seinem rechten Fuß von einer Wand ab.

Den Sauger nach vorne gerichtet, schwebte er quer durch das Schiff und floppte sich an einer glatten Wandstelle fest.

»Grüß Gott, Huber – Gas, Wasser, Scheiße«, stellte er sich den Umherfliegenden vor.

Autorenwort:
Unsere Zukunft im Hightech Standort Bayern.

Tradition und Fortschritt, sowohl in der Sprache als auch in der Technik.

Heiter beschauliche Gedanken über den Chiemgau in einer vielleicht gar nicht allzu fernen Zeit, in einer noch immer bestehenden Europäischen Union.

Ich glaube, George Lucas hätte die Geschichte so begonnen:

>»Es war einmal
>vor langer Zeit,
>in einer weit, weit
>entfernten
>Europäischen Union
>in der Galaxis . . .«

"I noticed that myself," Huber replied, obviously busy stabilizing his body, as it was spinning around in circles.

The red toilet plunger flew by and Huber reached for it and caught it with his outstretched hand. In a well-designed movement, he softly pushed off the wall using his right foot.

Aiming the plunger in front of him, he floated across the ship and sucked onto a smooth part of the wall.

"Good day, Huber—gas, water, crap," he introduced himself to those floating around.

Author's note:
Our future in the high-tech industry location of Bavaria.

Tradition and progress, both in language as well as in technology.

Cheerfully contemplative thoughts about the Chiemgau region

In a time maybe not too far away,

In a still existing European Union.

I think George Lucas would have started the story as follows:

"A long time ago
In the European Union
In a galaxy
Far, far away . . ."

Dr. M. Charlotte Wolf was born and raised in Germany, and has lived in the United States for almost twenty years. Her studies in those countries have resulted in a Ph.D. in Interdisciplinary Studies (Literature, Women's Studies, Instructional Technology), and an M.A. in German. She also completed course work in American/English Studies, Linguistics, and Philosophy. Dr. Wolf's professional experience includes public school administration, teaching, and coaching. In addition, she has worked as a freelance translator and editor for twenty-five years. In her free time she likes writing poetry, cooking, practicing yoga and meditation, watching movies (foreign, film noir), hiking, and reading sci-fi and mysteries.

A CATALOG OF SELECTED
DOVER BOOKS
IN ALL FIELDS OF INTEREST

A CATALOG OF SELECTED DOVER
BOOKS IN ALL FIELDS OF INTEREST

100 BEST-LOVED POEMS, Edited by Philip Smith. "The Passionate Shepherd to His Love," "Shall I compare thee to a summer's day?" "Death, be not proud," "The Raven," "The Road Not Taken," plus works by Blake, Wordsworth, Byron, Shelley, Keats, many others. 96pp. 5³⁄₁₆ x 8¼. 0-486-28553-7

100 SMALL HOUSES OF THE THIRTIES, Brown-Blodgett Company. Exterior photographs and floor plans for 100 charming structures. Illustrations of models accompanied by descriptions of interiors, color schemes, closet space, and other amenities. 200 illustrations. 112pp. 8⅜ x 11. 0-486-44131-8

1000 TURN-OF-THE-CENTURY HOUSES: With Illustrations and Floor Plans, Herbert C. Chivers. Reproduced from a rare edition, this showcase of homes ranges from cottages and bungalows to sprawling mansions. Each house is meticulously illustrated and accompanied by complete floor plans. 256pp. 9⅜ x 12¼. 0-486-45596-3

101 GREAT AMERICAN POEMS, Edited by The American Poetry & Literacy Project. Rich treasury of verse from the 19th and 20th centuries includes works by Edgar Allan Poe, Robert Frost, Walt Whitman, Langston Hughes, Emily Dickinson, T. S. Eliot, other notables. 96pp. 5³⁄₁₆ x 8¼. 0-486-40158-8

101 GREAT SAMURAI PRINTS, Utagawa Kuniyoshi. Kuniyoshi was a master of the warrior woodblock print — and these 18th-century illustrations represent the pinnacle of his craft. Full-color portraits of renowned Japanese samurais pulse with movement, passion, and remarkably fine detail. 112pp. 8⅜ x 11. 0-486-46523-3

ABC OF BALLET, Janet Grosser. Clearly worded, abundantly illustrated little guide defines basic ballet-related terms: arabesque, battement, pas de chat, relevé, sissonne, many others. Pronunciation guide included. Excellent primer. 48pp. 4³⁄₁₆ x 5¾. 0-486-40871-X

ACCESSORIES OF DRESS: An Illustrated Encyclopedia, Katherine Lester and Bess Viola Oerke. Illustrations of hats, veils, wigs, cravats, shawls, shoes, gloves, and other accessories enhance an engaging commentary that reveals the humor and charm of the many-sided story of accessorized apparel. 644 figures and 59 plates. 608pp. 6⅛ x 9¼. 0-486-43378-1

ADVENTURES OF HUCKLEBERRY FINN, Mark Twain. Join Huck and Jim as their boyhood adventures along the Mississippi River lead them into a world of excitement, danger, and self-discovery. Humorous narrative, lyrical descriptions of the Mississippi valley, and memorable characters. 224pp. 5³⁄₁₆ x 8¼. 0-486-28061-6

ALICE STARMORE'S BOOK OF FAIR ISLE KNITTING, Alice Starmore. A noted designer from the region of Scotland's Fair Isle explores the history and techniques of this distinctive, stranded-color knitting style and provides copious illustrated instructions for 14 original knitwear designs. 208pp. 8⅜ x 10⅞. 0-486-47218-3

Browse over 9,000 books at www.doverpublications.com

CATALOG OF DOVER BOOKS

ALICE'S ADVENTURES IN WONDERLAND, Lewis Carroll. Beloved classic about a little girl lost in a topsy-turvy land and her encounters with the White Rabbit, March Hare, Mad Hatter, Cheshire Cat, and other delightfully improbable characters. 42 illustrations by Sir John Tenniel. 96pp. 5³⁄₁₆ x 8¼.　　0-486-27543-4

AMERICA'S LIGHTHOUSES: An Illustrated History, Francis Ross Holland. Profusely illustrated fact-filled survey of American lighthouses since 1716. Over 200 stations — East, Gulf, and West coasts, Great Lakes, Hawaii, Alaska, Puerto Rico, the Virgin Islands, and the Mississippi and St. Lawrence Rivers. 240pp. 8 x 10¾.
0-486-25576-X

AN ENCYCLOPEDIA OF THE VIOLIN, Alberto Bachmann. Translated by Frederick H. Martens. Introduction by Eugene Ysaye. First published in 1925, this renowned reference remains unsurpassed as a source of essential information, from construction and evolution to repertoire and technique. Includes a glossary and 73 illustrations. 496pp. 6⅛ x 9¼.　　0-486-46618-3

ANIMALS: 1,419 Copyright-Free Illustrations of Mammals, Birds, Fish, Insects, etc., Selected by Jim Harter. Selected for its visual impact and ease of use, this outstanding collection of wood engravings presents over 1,000 species of animals in extremely lifelike poses. Includes mammals, birds, reptiles, amphibians, fish, insects, and other invertebrates. 284pp. 9 x 12.　　0-486-23766-4

THE ANNALS, Tacitus. Translated by Alfred John Church and William Jackson Brodribb. This vital chronicle of Imperial Rome, written by the era's great historian, spans A.D. 14-68 and paints incisive psychological portraits of major figures, from Tiberius to Nero. 416pp. 5³⁄₁₆ x 8¼.　　0-486-45236-0

ANTIGONE, Sophocles. Filled with passionate speeches and sensitive probing of moral and philosophical issues, this powerful and often-performed Greek drama reveals the grim fate that befalls the children of Oedipus. Footnotes. 64pp. 5³⁄₁₆ x 8 ¼.　　0-486-27804-2

ART DECO DECORATIVE PATTERNS IN FULL COLOR, Christian Stoll. Reprinted from a rare 1910 portfolio, 160 sensuous and exotic images depict a breathtaking array of florals, geometrics, and abstracts — all elegant in their stark simplicity. 64pp. 8⅜ x 11.　　0-486-44862-2

THE ARTHUR RACKHAM TREASURY: 86 Full-Color Illustrations, Arthur Rackham. Selected and Edited by Jeff A. Menges. A stunning treasury of 86 full-page plates span the famed English artist's career, from *Rip Van Winkle* (1905) to masterworks such as *Undine, A Midsummer Night's Dream,* and *Wind in the Willows* (1939). 96pp. 8⅜ x 11.
0-486-44685-9

THE AUTHENTIC GILBERT & SULLIVAN SONGBOOK, W. S. Gilbert and A. S. Sullivan. The most comprehensive collection available, this songbook includes selections from every one of Gilbert and Sullivan's light operas. Ninety-two numbers are presented uncut and unedited, and in their original keys. 410pp. 9 x 12.
0-486-23482-7

THE AWAKENING, Kate Chopin. First published in 1899, this controversial novel of a New Orleans wife's search for love outside a stifling marriage shocked readers. Today, it remains a first-rate narrative with superb characterization. New introductory Note. 128pp. 5³⁄₁₆ x 8¼.　　0-486-27786-0

BASIC DRAWING, Louis Priscilla. Beginning with perspective, this commonsense manual progresses to the figure in movement, light and shade, anatomy, drapery, composition, trees and landscape, and outdoor sketching. Black-and-white illustrations throughout. 128pp. 8⅜ x 11.　　0-486-45815-6

THE BATTLES THAT CHANGED HISTORY, Fletcher Pratt. Historian profiles 16 crucial conflicts, ancient to modern, that changed the course of Western civilization. Gripping accounts of battles led by Alexander the Great, Joan of Arc, Ulysses S. Grant, other commanders. 27 maps. 352pp. 5⅜ x 8½.   0-486-41129-X

BEETHOVEN'S LETTERS, Ludwig van Beethoven. Edited by Dr. A. C. Kalischer. Features 457 letters to fellow musicians, friends, greats, patrons, and literary men. Reveals musical thoughts, quirks of personality, insights, and daily events. Includes 15 plates. 410pp. 5⅜ x 8½.   0-486-22769-3

BERNICE BOBS HER HAIR AND OTHER STORIES, F. Scott Fitzgerald. This brilliant anthology includes 6 of Fitzgerald's most popular stories: "The Diamond as Big as the Ritz," the title tale, "The Offshore Pirate," "The Ice Palace," "The Jelly Bean," and "May Day." 176pp. 5⅜ x 8½.   0-486-47049-0

BESLER'S BOOK OF FLOWERS AND PLANTS: 73 Full-Color Plates from Hortus Eystettensis, 1613, Basilius Besler. Here is a selection of magnificent plates from the *Hortus Eystettensis,* which vividly illustrated and identified the plants, flowers, and trees that thrived in the legendary German garden at Eichstätt. 80pp. 8⅜ x 11.   0-486-46005-3

THE BOOK OF KELLS, Edited by Blanche Cirker. Painstakingly reproduced from a rare facsimile edition, this volume contains full-page decorations, portraits, illustrations, plus a sampling of textual leaves with exquisite calligraphy and ornamentation. 32 full-color illustrations. 32pp. 9⅜ x 12¼.   0-486-24345-1

THE BOOK OF THE CROSSBOW: With an Additional Section on Catapults and Other Siege Engines, Ralph Payne-Gallwey. Fascinating study traces history and use of crossbow as military and sporting weapon, from Middle Ages to modern times. Also covers related weapons: balistas, catapults, Turkish bows, more. Over 240 illustrations. 400pp. 7¼ x 10⅛.   0-486-28720-3

THE BUNGALOW BOOK: Floor Plans and Photos of 112 Houses, 1910, Henry L. Wilson. Here are 112 of the most popular and economic blueprints of the early 20th century — plus an illustration or photograph of each completed house. A wonderful time capsule that still offers a wealth of valuable insights. 160pp. 8⅜ x 11.   0-486-45104-6

THE CALL OF THE WILD, Jack London. A classic novel of adventure, drawn from London's own experiences as a Klondike adventurer, relating the story of a heroic dog caught in the brutal life of the Alaska Gold Rush. Note. 64pp. 5³⁄₁₆ x 8¼.   0-486-26472-6

CANDIDE, Voltaire. Edited by Francois-Marie Arouet. One of the world's great satires since its first publication in 1759. Witty, caustic skewering of romance, science, philosophy, religion, government — nearly all human ideals and institutions. 112pp. 5³⁄₁₆ x 8¼.   0-486-26689-3

CELEBRATED IN THEIR TIME: Photographic Portraits from the George Grantham Bain Collection, Edited by Amy Pastan. With an Introduction by Michael Carlebach. Remarkable portrait gallery features 112 rare images of Albert Einstein, Charlie Chaplin, the Wright Brothers, Henry Ford, and other luminaries from the worlds of politics, art, entertainment, and industry. 128pp. 8⅜ x 11.   0-486-46754-6

CHARIOTS FOR APOLLO: The NASA History of Manned Lunar Spacecraft to 1969, Courtney G. Brooks, James M. Grimwood, and Loyd S. Swenson, Jr. This illustrated history by a trio of experts is the definitive reference on the Apollo spacecraft and lunar modules. It traces the vehicles' design, development, and operation in space. More than 100 photographs and illustrations. 576pp. 6¾ x 9¼. 0-486-46756-2

A CHRISTMAS CAROL, Charles Dickens. This engrossing tale relates Ebenezer Scrooge's ghostly journeys through Christmases past, present, and future and his ultimate transformation from a harsh and grasping old miser to a charitable and compassionate human being. 80pp. 5³⁄₁₆ x 8¼. 0-486-26865-9

COMMON SENSE, Thomas Paine. First published in January of 1776, this highly influential landmark document clearly and persuasively argued for American separation from Great Britain and paved the way for the Declaration of Independence. 64pp. 5³⁄₁₆ x 8¼. 0-486-29602-4

THE COMPLETE SHORT STORIES OF OSCAR WILDE, Oscar Wilde. Complete texts of "The Happy Prince and Other Tales," "A House of Pomegranates," "Lord Arthur Savile's Crime and Other Stories," "Poems in Prose," and "The Portrait of Mr. W. H." 208pp. 5³⁄₁₆ x 8¼. 0-486-45216-6

COMPLETE SONNETS, William Shakespeare. Over 150 exquisite poems deal with love, friendship, the tyranny of time, beauty's evanescence, death, and other themes in language of remarkable power, precision, and beauty. Glossary of archaic terms. 80pp. 5³⁄₁₆ x 8¼. 0-486-26686-9

THE COUNT OF MONTE CRISTO: Abridged Edition, Alexandre Dumas. Falsely accused of treason, Edmond Dantès is imprisoned in the bleak Chateau d'If. After a hair-raising escape, he launches an elaborate plot to extract a bitter revenge against those who betrayed him. 448pp. 5³⁄₁₆ x 8¼. 0-486-45643-9

CRAFTSMAN BUNGALOWS: Designs from the Pacific Northwest, Yoho & Merritt. This reprint of a rare catalog, showcasing the charming simplicity and cozy style of Craftsman bungalows, is filled with photos of completed homes, plus floor plans and estimated costs. An indispensable resource for architects, historians, and illustrators. 112pp. 10 x 7. 0-486-46875-5

CRAFTSMAN BUNGALOWS: 59 Homes from "The Craftsman," Edited by Gustav Stickley. Best and most attractive designs from Arts and Crafts Movement publication — 1903–1916 — includes sketches, photographs of homes, floor plans, descriptive text. 128pp. 8¼ x 11. 0-486-25829-7

CRIME AND PUNISHMENT, Fyodor Dostoyevsky. Translated by Constance Garnett. Supreme masterpiece tells the story of Raskolnikov, a student tormented by his own thoughts after he murders an old woman. Overwhelmed by guilt and terror, he confesses and goes to prison. 480pp. 5³⁄₁₆ x 8¼. 0-486-41587-2

THE DECLARATION OF INDEPENDENCE AND OTHER GREAT DOCUMENTS OF AMERICAN HISTORY: 1775-1865, Edited by John Grafton. Thirteen compelling and influential documents: Henry's "Give Me Liberty or Give Me Death," Declaration of Independence, The Constitution, Washington's First Inaugural Address, The Monroe Doctrine, The Emancipation Proclamation, Gettysburg Address, more. 64pp. 5³⁄₁₆ x 8¼. 0-486-41124-9

THE DESERT AND THE SOWN: Travels in Palestine and Syria, Gertrude Bell. "The female Lawrence of Arabia," Gertrude Bell wrote captivating, perceptive accounts of her travels in the Middle East. This intriguing narrative, accompanied by 160 photos, traces her 1905 sojourn in Lebanon, Syria, and Palestine. 368pp. 5⅜ x 8½. 0-486-46876-3

A DOLL'S HOUSE, Henrik Ibsen. Ibsen's best-known play displays his genius for realistic prose drama. An expression of women's rights, the play climaxes when the central character, Nora, rejects a smothering marriage and life in "a doll's house." 80pp. 5³⁄₁₆ x 8¼. 0-486-27062-9

DOOMED SHIPS: Great Ocean Liner Disasters, William H. Miller, Jr. Nearly 200 photographs, many from private collections, highlight tales of some of the vessels whose pleasure cruises ended in catastrophe: the *Morro Castle, Normandie, Andrea Doria, Europa,* and many others. 128pp. 8⅜ x 11¼.   0-486-45366-9

THE DORÉ BIBLE ILLUSTRATIONS, Gustave Doré. Detailed plates from the Bible: the Creation scenes, Adam and Eve, horrifying visions of the Flood, the battle sequences with their monumental crowds, depictions of the life of Jesus, 241 plates in all. 241pp. 9 x 12.   0-486-23004-X

DRAWING DRAPERY FROM HEAD TO TOE, Cliff Young. Expert guidance on how to draw shirts, pants, skirts, gloves, hats, and coats on the human figure, including folds in relation to the body, pull and crush, action folds, creases, more. Over 200 drawings. 48pp. 8¼ x 11.   0-486-45591-2

DUBLINERS, James Joyce. A fine and accessible introduction to the work of one of the 20th century's most influential writers, this collection features 15 tales, including a masterpiece of the short-story genre, "The Dead." 160pp. 5³⁄₁₆ x 8¼.

0-486-26870-5

EASY-TO-MAKE POP-UPS, Joan Irvine. Illustrated by Barbara Reid. Dozens of wonderful ideas for three-dimensional paper fun — from holiday greeting cards with moving parts to a pop-up menagerie. Easy-to-follow, illustrated instructions for more than 30 projects. 299 black-and-white illustrations. 96pp. 8⅜ x 11.

0-486-44622-0

EASY-TO-MAKE STORYBOOK DOLLS: A "Novel" Approach to Cloth Dollmaking, Sherralyn St. Clair. Favorite fictional characters come alive in this unique beginner's dollmaking guide. Includes patterns for Pollyanna, Dorothy from *The Wonderful Wizard of Oz,* Mary of *The Secret Garden,* plus easy-to-follow instructions, 263 black-and-white illustrations, and an 8-page color insert. 112pp. 8¼ x 11.   0-486-47360-0

EINSTEIN'S ESSAYS IN SCIENCE, Albert Einstein. Speeches and essays in accessible, everyday language profile influential physicists such as Niels Bohr and Isaac Newton. They also explore areas of physics to which the author made major contributions. 128pp. 5 x 8.   0-486-47011-3

EL DORADO: Further Adventures of the Scarlet Pimpernel, Baroness Orczy. A popular sequel to *The Scarlet Pimpernel,* this suspenseful story recounts the Pimpernel's attempts to rescue the Dauphin from imprisonment during the French Revolution. An irresistible blend of intrigue, period detail, and vibrant characterizations. 352pp. 5³⁄₁₆ x 8¼.   0-486-44026-5

ELEGANT SMALL HOMES OF THE TWENTIES: 99 Designs from a Competition, Chicago Tribune. Nearly 100 designs for five- and six-room houses feature New England and Southern colonials, Normandy cottages, stately Italianate dwellings, and other fascinating snapshots of American domestic architecture of the 1920s. 112pp. 9 x 12.   0-486-46910-7

THE ELEMENTS OF STYLE: The Original Edition, William Strunk, Jr. This is the book that generations of writers have relied upon for timeless advice on grammar, diction, syntax, and other essentials. In concise terms, it identifies the principal requirements of proper style and common errors. 64pp. 5⅜ x 8½.   0-486-44798-7

THE ELUSIVE PIMPERNEL, Baroness Orczy. Robespierre's revolutionaries find their wicked schemes thwarted by the heroic Pimpernel — Sir Percival Blakeney. In this thrilling sequel, Chauvelin devises a plot to eliminate the Pimpernel and his wife. 272pp. 5³⁄₁₆ x 8¼.   0-486-45464-9

AN ENCYCLOPEDIA OF BATTLES: Accounts of Over 1,560 Battles from 1479 B.C. to the Present, David Eggenberger. Essential details of every major battle in recorded history from the first battle of Megiddo in 1479 B.C. to Grenada in 1984. List of battle maps. 99 illustrations. 544pp. 6½ x 9¼. 0-486-24913-1

ENCYCLOPEDIA OF EMBROIDERY STITCHES, INCLUDING CREWEL, Marion Nichols. Precise explanations and instructions, clearly illustrated, on how to work chain, back, cross, knotted, woven stitches, and many more — 178 in all, including Cable Outline, Whipped Satin, and Eyelet Buttonhole. Over 1400 illustrations. 219pp. 8⅜ x 11¼. 0-486-22929-7

ENTER JEEVES: 15 Early Stories, P. G. Wodehouse. Splendid collection contains first 8 stories featuring Bertie Wooster, the deliciously dim aristocrat and Jeeves, his brainy, imperturbable manservant. Also, the complete Reggie Pepper (Bertie's prototype) series. 288pp. 5⅜ x 8½. 0-486-29717-9

ERIC SLOANE'S AMERICA: Paintings in Oil, Michael Wigley. With a Foreword by Mimi Sloane. Eric Sloane's evocative oils of America's landscape and material culture shimmer with immense historical and nostalgic appeal. This original hardcover collection gathers nearly a hundred of his finest paintings, with subjects ranging from New England to the American Southwest. 128pp. 10⅝ x 9. 0-486-46525-X

ETHAN FROME, Edith Wharton. Classic story of wasted lives, set against a bleak New England background. Superbly delineated characters in a hauntingly grim tale of thwarted love. Considered by many to be Wharton's masterpiece. 96pp. 5³⁄₁₆ x 8 ¼. 0-486-26690-7

THE EVERLASTING MAN, G. K. Chesterton. Chesterton's view of Christianity — as a blend of philosophy and mythology, satisfying intellect and spirit — applies to his brilliant book, which appeals to readers' heads as well as their hearts. 288pp. 5⅜ x 8½. 0-486-46036-3

THE FIELD AND FOREST HANDY BOOK, Daniel Beard. Written by a co-founder of the Boy Scouts, this appealing guide offers illustrated instructions for building kites, birdhouses, boats, igloos, and other fun projects, plus numerous helpful tips for campers. 448pp. 5³⁄₁₆ x 8¼. 0-486-46191-2

FINDING YOUR WAY WITHOUT MAP OR COMPASS, Harold Gatty. Useful, instructive manual shows would-be explorers, hikers, bikers, scouts, sailors, and survivalists how to find their way outdoors by observing animals, weather patterns, shifting sands, and other elements of nature. 288pp. 5⅜ x 8½. 0-486-40613-X

FIRST FRENCH READER: A Beginner's Dual-Language Book, Edited and Translated by Stanley Appelbaum. This anthology introduces 50 legendary writers — Voltaire, Balzac, Baudelaire, Proust, more — through passages from *The Red and the Black, Les Misérables, Madame Bovary,* and other classics. Original French text plus English translation on facing pages. 240pp. 5⅜ x 8½. 0-486-46178-5

FIRST GERMAN READER: A Beginner's Dual-Language Book, Edited by Harry Steinhauer. Specially chosen for their power to evoke German life and culture, these short, simple readings include poems, stories, essays, and anecdotes by Goethe, Hesse, Heine, Schiller, and others. 224pp. 5⅜ x 8½. 0-486-46179-3

FIRST SPANISH READER: A Beginner's Dual-Language Book, Angel Flores. Delightful stories, other material based on works of Don Juan Manuel, Luis Taboada, Ricardo Palma, other noted writers. Complete faithful English translations on facing pages. Exercises. 176pp. 5⅜ x 8½. 0-486-25810-6

FIVE ACRES AND INDEPENDENCE, Maurice G. Kains. Great back-to-the-land classic explains basics of self-sufficient farming. The one book to get. 95 illustrations. 397pp. 5⅜ x 8½. 0-486-20974-1

FLAGG'S SMALL HOUSES: Their Economic Design and Construction, 1922, Ernest Flagg. Although most famous for his skyscrapers, Flagg was also a proponent of the well-designed single-family dwelling. His classic treatise features innovations that save space, materials, and cost. 526 illustrations. 160pp. 9⅜ x 12¼.
0-486-45197-6

FLATLAND: A Romance of Many Dimensions, Edwin A. Abbott. Classic of science (and mathematical) fiction — charmingly illustrated by the author — describes the adventures of A. Square, a resident of Flatland, in Spaceland (three dimensions), Lineland (one dimension), and Pointland (no dimensions). 96pp. 5³⁄₁₆ x 8¼.
0-486-27263-X

FRANKENSTEIN, Mary Shelley. The story of Victor Frankenstein's monstrous creation and the havoc it caused has enthralled generations of readers and inspired countless writers of horror and suspense. With the author's own 1831 introduction. 176pp. 5³⁄₁₆ x 8¼. 0-486-28211-2

THE GARGOYLE BOOK: 572 Examples from Gothic Architecture, Lester Burbank Bridaham. Dispelling the conventional wisdom that French Gothic architectural flourishes were born of despair or gloom, Bridaham reveals the whimsical nature of these creations and the ingenious artisans who made them. 572 illustrations. 224pp. 8⅜ x 11. 0-486-44754-5

THE GIFT OF THE MAGI AND OTHER SHORT STORIES, O. Henry. Sixteen captivating stories by one of America's most popular storytellers. Included are such classics as "The Gift of the Magi," "The Last Leaf," and "The Ransom of Red Chief." Publisher's Note. 96pp. 5³⁄₁₆ x 8¼. 0-486-27061-0

THE GOETHE TREASURY: Selected Prose and Poetry, Johann Wolfgang von Goethe. Edited, Selected, and with an Introduction by Thomas Mann. In addition to his lyric poetry, Goethe wrote travel sketches, autobiographical studies, essays, letters, and proverbs in rhyme and prose. This collection presents outstanding examples from each genre. 368pp. 5⅜ x 8½. 0-486-44780-4

GREAT EXPECTATIONS, Charles Dickens. Orphaned Pip is apprenticed to the dirty work of the forge but dreams of becoming a gentleman — and one day finds himself in possession of "great expectations." Dickens' finest novel. 400pp. 5³⁄₁₆ x 8¼.
0-486-41586-4

GREAT WRITERS ON THE ART OF FICTION: From Mark Twain to Joyce Carol Oates, Edited by James Daley. An indispensable source of advice and inspiration, this anthology features essays by Henry James, Kate Chopin, Willa Cather, Sinclair Lewis, Jack London, Raymond Chandler, Raymond Carver, Eudora Welty, and Kurt Vonnegut, Jr. 192pp. 5⅜ x 8½. 0-486-45128-3

HAMLET, William Shakespeare. The quintessential Shakespearean tragedy, whose highly charged confrontations and anguished soliloquies probe depths of human feeling rarely sounded in any art. Reprinted from an authoritative British edition complete with illuminating footnotes. 128pp. 5³⁄₁₆ x 8¼. 0-486-27278-8

THE HAUNTED HOUSE, Charles Dickens. A Yuletide gathering in an eerie country retreat provides the backdrop for Dickens and his friends — including Elizabeth Gaskell and Wilkie Collins — who take turns spinning supernatural yarns. 144pp. 5⅜ x 8½. 0-486-46309-5